Study Guide
Chapters 12-27
Stephen C. Schaefer

Third Edition
ACCOUNTING

Charles T. Horngren
Stanford University

Walter T. Harrison, Jr.
Baylor University

Michael A. Robinson
Baylor University

PRENTICE HALL, Englewood Cliffs, New Jersey 07632

Production manager: Amy Hinton
Acquisitions editor: Robert Dewey
Associate editor: Diane deCastro
Manufacturing buyer: Ken Clinton

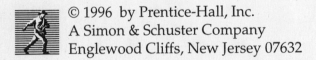

© 1996 by Prentice-Hall, Inc.
A Simon & Schuster Company
Englewood Cliffs, New Jersey 07632

Printed in the United States of America

10 9 8 7 6 5 4 3 2

ISBN 0-13-306234-1

Prentice-Hall International (UK) Limited, *London*
Prentice-Hall of Australia Pty. Limited, *Sydney*
Prentice-Hall Canada Inc., *Toronto*
Prentice-Hall Hispanoamericana, S.A., *Mexico*
Prentice-Hall of India Private Limited, *New Delhi*
Prentice-Hall of Japan, Inc., *Tokyo*
Simon & Schuster Asia Pte. Ltd., *Singapore*
Editora Prentice-Hall do Brasil, Ltda., *Rio de Janeiro*

Contents

Preface   iv

Acknowledgments   iv

Chapter 12   The Foundation for Generally Accepted Accounting Principles   287

Chapter 13   Accounting for Partnerships   306

Chapter 14   Corporate Organization, Paid-in Capital, and the Balance Sheet   336

Chapter 15   Retained Earnings, Dividends, Treasury Stock,
              and the Income Statement   358

Chapter 16   Long-Term Liabilities   381

Chapter 17   Investments and Accounting for International Operations   407

Chapter 18   Statement of Cash Flows   433

Chapter 19   Financial Statement Analysis for Decision Making   454

Chapter 20   Introduction to Management Accounting:
              Manufacturing Accounting and Job Order Costing   479

Chapter 21   Process Costing   499

Chapter 22   Cost-Volume-Profit Analysis and the Contribution Margin
              Approach to Decision Making   525

Chapter 23   Cost Behavior Analysis   549

Chapter 24   The Master Budget and Responsibility Accounting   577

Chapter 25   Flexible Budgets and Standard Costs   597

Chapter 26   Strategy, Cost Management, and Continuous Improvement   623

Chapter 27   Special Business Decisions and Capital Budgeting   645

Preface

This Study Guide will assist you in mastering ACCOUNTING, Third Edition, by Charles T. Horngren, Walter T. Harrison, Jr., and Michael A. Robinson. The 13 chapters in the first volume of this Study Guide correspond to the first 13 chapters in the textbook. Each chapter of this Study Guide contains three sections: Chapter Review, Test Yourself, and Demonstration Problems.

Chapter Review. The Chapter Review parallels the chapter in your textbook. It is organized by learning objective and provides a concise summary of the major elements in each objective. Emphasis is given to new terms and concepts, particularly in the earlier chapters, where it is essential for the student to be conversant with accounting terminology. A Chapter Overview links each chapter to previous or subsequent topics.

Test Yourself. The Test Yourself section is divided into five parts: matching, multiple choice, completion, exercises, and critical thinking. Answers are provided at the back of the chapter for each section, along with explanations, when appropriate. The five sections provide a comprehensive review of the material in each chapter. You should use them after you have read each chapter thoroughly to determine which topics you understand and those requiring further study.

Demonstration Problems. Two demonstrations problems are provided for each chapter. These problems attempt to incorporate as many of the topics in the chapter as possible. For some chapters, the first demonstration problem must be completed before the second one is attempted. For those chapters, complete the first one, check your answers, make any necessary corrections, then go on to the second problem. The solutions to the demonstration problems provide explanations as well.

THIS STUDY GUIDE IS NOT A SUBSTITUTE FOR YOUR TEXTBOOK. It is designed as an additional support tool to assist you in succeeding in your accounting course.

Comments about the Study Guide are encouraged and should be sent to me in care of the publisher.

Stephen C. Schaefer
Contra Costa College

Acknowledgments

Thanks to Loc Huynh, a former student and graduate of the Haas School of Business at the University of California-Berkeley, for his invaluable assistance in the preparation of this Study Guide. Loc did all the word processing, and his comments and suggestions were always thought-provoking and worthwhile. Thanks to current and former students, who are a constant source of inspiration and challenge. Thanks also to the following people who contributed to the accuracy of the Study Guide:

Stanley Chu
Borough of Manhattan Community College

Jeffrey A. Kirk
The Clorox Company

Hugo Vega
Contra Costa College

Chapter 12

The Foundation
for Generally Accepted
Accounting Principles

 ## Chapter Overview

Generally accepted accounting principles (GAAP) have been referred to throughout the past 11 chapters. We have seen how GAAP impacts on the recording process (Chapters 2 and 3), financial statements (Chapters 3 and 4), internal control (Chapter 7), and valuing ending inventory (Chapter 9), to cite just a few examples. In this chapter you are given the opportunity to begin integrating these generally accepted principles. The specific learning objectives for this chapter are:

1. Identify the basic objective of financial reporting
2. Identify and apply the underlying concepts of accounting
3. Identify and apply the principles of accounting
4. Allocate revenue to the appropriate period by four methods
5. Report information that satisfies the disclosure principle
6. Apply the materiality constraint and the conservatism constraint to accounting

Chapter Review

OBJECTIVE 1

Identify the basic objective of financial reporting.

Generally accepted accounting principles (GAAP) are primarily influenced by the **Financial Accounting Standards Board** (FASB) and its predecessor organization, the **Accounting Principles Board** (APB). However, the **Securities and Exchange Commission** (SEC) has ultimate authority to establish accounting principles for publicly held companies.

The FASB has been developing a **Conceptual Framework** to define the nature and function of financial accounting. The basic objective of financial reporting is to provide information that is useful for investment and lending decisions. Information should be relevant, reliable, and comparable. Relevant information is useful. Reliable information is unbiased and free from significant error. Comparable information can be compared from period to period.

OBJECTIVE 2

Identify and apply the underlying concepts of accounting.

The **entity concept** provides that the transactions of the organization be accounted for separately from the transactions of other organizations and persons, including the owner(s) of the entity.

The **going-concern concept** is an assumption that the business will continue to operate in the future. This concept enables accountants to assume that a business will continue long enough to recover the cost of its assets.

The **time-period concept** provides that financial information be reported at regular intervals so that decision makers can compare business operations over time to assess the success or failure of the business. This concept is the basis for accruals and adjusting entries prepared at the end of an accounting period.

The **stable-monetary-unit concept** assumes that the value of the monetary unit never changes. Accountants ignore the effects of inflation and make no accounting adjustments related to changes in the purchasing power of the dollar. Many parties believe that inflation adjustments should be made to accounting information. FASB encourages large companies to supply inflation-adjusted data in financial reports.

OBJECTIVE 3

Identify and apply the principles of accounting.

The **reliability principle** states that accounting information should be free from significant error and bias. The information should also be verifiable by people outside the business.

The **comparability principle** states that 1) accounting information should be comparable from business to business and 2) accounting information for a single business should be comparable from period to period. For a single business, comparability (also called consistency) is enhanced by using the same accounting methods from period to period. A single business may change its accounting methods provided that it discloses the change, the reasons for the change, and the effect of the change on income.

The **cost principle** states that transactions are to be recorded at cost. When assets are purchased, they are recorded at cost, and the accounting records of the asset are maintained at cost. The actual cost of an asset or service is considered to be verifiable, objective evidence of value.

OBJECTIVE 4
Allocate
revenue to the
appropriate
period by four
methods.

The **revenue principle** tells the accountant when to record revenue and how much revenue to record. Generally, revenue is recorded when it is earned and not before. Three conditions must be met before revenue is recorded:

1. The seller has done everything necessary to expect to collect from the buyer.
2. The amount of revenues can be objectively measured.
3. Collectibility is reasonably assured.

Generally, these conditions are met when the seller delivers the goods or renders services to the buyer. However, this may not always be an appropriate standard to use. Four methods serve as guides in applying the revenue principle:

1. With the **sales method,** revenue is recorded when a sale occurs. This method is used with most sales of goods and services. For a cash sale, Cash is debited and Sales Revenue is credited. For a credit sale, Accounts Receivable is debited and Sales Revenue is credited.

2. With the **collection method,** the seller records revenue only when cash is received. The collection method is used when the receipt of cash is uncertain. Professionals such as doctors and attorneys frequently use the collection method.

3. The **installment method** is used for installment sales when collection is doubtful. Gross profit (Sales Revenue minus Cost of Goods Sold) is recorded as cash is collected. The gross profit percentage is equal to:

$$\text{Gross profit percentage} = \frac{\text{Gross profit}}{\text{Total installment sale}}$$

For each cash receipt, the gross profit is computed by multiplying the cash receipt times the gross profit percentage. The Cost of Goods Sold expense is recognized when cash is received:

$$\text{Cost of goods sold} = (1 - \text{Gross profit percentage}) \times \text{Cash}$$

4. The **percentage-of-completion method** is frequently used by construction firms for projects that extend over several years. This method recognizes revenue as work is performed. The percentage of completion is usually computed by dividing costs incurred during the year by total estimated project cost:

$$\text{Percentage of completion this year} = \frac{\text{Cost incurred this year}}{\text{Total estimated project cost}}$$

Revenue for the year is equal to the percentage of completion times total revenue:

$$\text{Revenue this year} = \text{Percentage of completion} \times \text{Total project revenues}$$

Income for the year is equal to revenue for the year minus cost for the year. Note, as with the DDB method of depreciation, the final year is merely a balancing year.

The **matching principle**, in conjunction with the revenue principle, governs income recognition. Recall that expenses are matched against revenues.

OBJECTIVE 5
Report
information that
satisfies the
disclosure
principle.

The **disclosure principle** requires that a company's financial statements report enough information for users to make knowledgeable decisions about the company. In order to satisfy the disclosure principle, companies add to the **financial statements notes** that disclose significant accounting policies, probable losses, and accounting changes.

Significant accounting policies include the revenue-recognition method, inventory method, and depreciation method used. Typically, these are summarized in the first note to the financial statements. **Probable losses** are losses that are likely to occur and have amounts that can be estimated. **Accounting changes** are changes in accounting principles and significant changes in accounting estimates.

In addition, notes to the financial statements should disclose **subsequent events** and information regarding **business segments**.

Subsequent events occur after the financial statement date but before the financial statements are issued and affect the interpretation of the financial statements.

Business segments are the separate product lines and industries within a diversified company.

The market value for financial instruments (such as receivables, investments, etc.) may be different than the carrying value reported on the balance sheet.

OBJECTIVE 6
Apply the materiality constraint and the conservatism constraint to accounting.

The **materiality concept** requires accountants to accurately account for significant items and transactions. Information is significant (or material) if it is likely to cause a statement user to change a decision because of that information. The accounting treatment for a $3 pencil sharpener is not likely to affect any decisions; the pencil sharpener is immaterial. However, failing to record a $1 million liability would affect the decisions of many users. Thus, the $1 million is material.

The definition of materiality varies from company to company. A large corporation such as General Motors might consider $10,000 to be immaterial, while the neighborhood grocery store would consider $10,000 to be very material.

The **conservatism concept** requires that income and assets be reported at their lowest reasonable amounts. This does not mean that assets or income should be deliberately understated. It does mean that when different values can be assigned to a transaction, the less optimistic value should be used. The lower-of-cost-or-market method (LCM) for valuing assets is a clear example of conservatism.

Carefully review the exhibits in your text for examples of GAAP.

Test Yourself

All the self-testing materials in this chapter focus on information and procedures that your instructor is likely to test in quizzes and examinations.

I. Matching *Match each numbered term with its lettered definition.*

1. disclosure principle
2. change in accounting principle
3. change in accounting estimate
4. comparability principle
5. completed-contract method
6. going-concern concept
7. stable-monetary-unit concept
8. reliability principle
9. sales method
10. cost principle
11. collection method
12. installment method
13. materiality concept
14. subsequent events
15. time-period concept

A. holds that a company's financial statements should report enough information for outsiders to make knowledgeable decisions about the company

B. a change that occurs in the normal course of business as a company alters earlier expectations

C. a change in accounting method such as from the LIFO method to the FIFO method for inventories or a switch from the SYD depreciation method to the SL method

D. accountants' assumption that the business will continue operating for the foreseeable future

E. accountants' basis for ignoring the effect of inflation and making no adjustments for the changing value of the dollar

F. events that occur after the end of a company's accounting period but before publication of its financial statements and which may affect the interpretation of the information in those statements

G. ensures that accounting information is reported at regular intervals

H. method of applying the revenue principle, in which gross profit is recorded as cash is collected

I. method of applying the revenue principle in which revenue is recorded at the point of sale

J. method of applying the revenue principle, used by construction companies, in which all revenue earned on the project is recorded in the period when the project is completed

K. method of applying the revenue principle used when receipt of cash is uncertain, in which the seller waits until cash is received to record the sale

L. requires that accounting information be free from material errors and bias

M. specifies that accounting information must be comparable from business to business and that a single business's financial statements must be comparable from one period to the next

N. states that assets and services are recorded at their purchase cost and that the accounting record of the asset continues to be based on cost rather than current market value

O. states that a company must perform strictly proper accounting only for items and transactions that are significant to the business's financial statements

 ## II. Multiple Choice *Circle the best answer.*

1. The FASB stated that in order to be useful in decision making, information should be all of the following except:
    A. conservative
    B. relevant
    C. reliable
    D. comparable

2. Reporting accounting information at regular intervals is called for by the:
    A. entity concept
    B. yearly concept
    C. time-period concept
    D. going-concern concept

3. The concept that underlies the use of accruals is the:
    A. entity concept
    B. time-period concept
    C. going-concern concept
    D. stable-monetary-unit concept

4. The concept that is the basis for ignoring inflation in financial reporting is the:
    A. entity concept
    B. time-period concept
    C. going-concern concept
    D. stable-monetary-unit concept

5. The underlying basis for the cost principle is the:
    A. matching principle
    B. relevance principle
    C. reliability principle
    D. comparability principle

6.   Which type of business is most likely to use the collection method to record revenues?
      A.   building contractor
      B.   grocery store
      C.   department store
      D.   physician

7.   Which type of business is most likely to use the percentage-of-completion method to record revenues?
      A.   physician
      B.   grocery store
      C.   department store
      D.   a maritime contractor specializing in building oil tankers

8.   Amortization of the cost of a franchise is justified by the:
      A.   disclosure principle
      B.   comparability principle
      C.   expense recognition principle
      D.   matching principle

9.   A company bought equipment and thought it would have an 8-year life. After 2 years, the company decided that the equipment would be useful for only 3 more years. This is an example of a:
      A.   contingency
      B.   recording error
      C.   change in accounting estimate
      D.   change in accounting principle

10.   Which of the following subsequent events is most likely to be disclosed in the financial statements?
      A.   plant closure because of a labor strike
      B.   death of the controller of the company
      C.   adoption of a new pension plan requiring a substantial increase in cash outlays
      D.   introduction of a new product line

III. Completion *Complete each of the following statements.*

1. _____ is to provide information that is useful in making investment and lending decisions.

2. Assets are reported on the balance sheet at their _____ .

3. Information that is free of material error and bias is said to be _____ .

4. A summary of the firms significant accounting policies can be found in the

   _____ .

5. Accounting principles are currently formulated by the _____

   _____ .

6. The _____ has the ultimate responsibility for establishing accounting rules for publicly held companies.

7. GAAP stands for _____ .

8. Lower of cost or market (LCM) is an example of _____ .

9. Reporting the market value for financial instruments is an example of

   _____ .

10. The gross profit percentage is used with the _____ method of revenue recognition.

IV. Exercises

1. Fun Time Construction Co. builds amusement parks. One contract calls for the construction of a theme park for $200,000,000. The total cost is estimated at $150,000,000 over the three years it will take to complete the park ($30,000,000 in the first year, $37,500,000 in the second year, and $82,500,000 in the third year).

   A. Compute the construction income for Years 1, 2, and 3 using the completed-contract method.

B. Compute the construction income for Years 1, 2, and 3 using the percentage-of-completion method.

Year	Cost for Year	Total Project Cost	% of Project Completion for Year	Total Project Revenue	Revenue for Year	Cost for Year	Construction Income for Year
1							
2							
3							

2. E-Z Pay Manufacturing Co. sold equipment for $800,000. The equipment cost $200,000. In year 1, it received a $200,000 down payment. Annual installments of $100,000, $200,000, and $300,000 were received in years 2 through 4.

A. Compute the gross profit from the sale for years 1 through 4 using the sales method.

B. Compute the gross profit from the sale for years 1 through 4 using the installment method.

3. For each of the following situations, indicate the amount of revenue to report for the current year ended December 31, 19X4 and for the next year, 19X5.

A. On September 1, collected one year's rent of $3,600 in advance on an apartment leased to a small business.

B. October 31, loaned $60,000 at 12% on a 2-year note.

C. Sold concert tickets, collecting $325,000 in advance. At December 31, $280,000 of the concert tickets had been used or expired. The remainder are for concerts to be performed in 19X5.

4. Identify the amount at which each of the following assets should be reported in the financial statements of Lee Company. Cite the principle or concept that is most applicable to each answer.

A. Lee purchased machinery for $8,000 less a $160 cash discount. Lee paid shipping charges of $125 and installation charges of $250. After using the equipment for nine months, Lee paid $250 to have it cleaned.

B. Lee purchased land and an office building for $475,000 and paid $5,000 to have the land surveyed, $22,500 for landscaping. Lee is offering the land and office building for sale at $800,000 and has received a $610,000 offer.

C. Inventory has a cost of $61,000, but its current market value is $68,000.

V. Critical Thinking

The stable-monetary-unit concept assumes that the value of the monetary unit (in our case, the dollar) never changes. This allows accountants to ignore any effects of inflation. Your text indicates that FASB encourages large companies to provide inflation-adjusted information in their financial reports. Assume you own a company located in a country where inflation has been rapid and persistent. For purposes of this question, let's assume inflation at 100% a month! How might you "adjust" your financial statements given that historical cost is now irrelevant?

_____

_____

_____

_____

 ## VI. Demonstration Problems

Demonstration Problem # 1

Chapter 12 of the text discusses the following principles and concepts:

Entity concept	Comparability principle	Matching principle
Going-concern concept	Reliability principle	Disclosure principle
Time-period concept	Cost principle	Conservatism concept
Materiality concept	Revenue principle	

Indicate which of the above concepts or principles is being violated in each of these eleven situations:

1. A restaurateur mixes personal banking and other accounting records with those of the restaurant business.

2. A successful computer retailing business suffers its first operating loss in 10 years. The business is still in strong condition financially and the owners have no plans to cease operating. Nevertheless, the firm's accountant has prepared the financial statements of the business on the assumption that the business might close and liquidate at any time.

3. Instead of making adjusting entries for accrued revenues and expenses, the accountant records these types of transactions whenever revenue is actually received or expenses are paid.

4. Two weeks before the close of a company's business year, an industrial accident resulted in the death of several employees and the possible discharge of toxic environmental waste into an ocean bay. Since no lawsuits had yet been filed by potential claimants, the company decided not to mention the accident in its annual reports.

5. The owner of land purchased for $200,000 has received several offers to buy it for $800,000. Based on this, the owner has revalued the land on his books at $800,000.

6. A mechanical stapler costing $7 is depreciated over its expected economic life of 10 years.

7. Gilpin Mine, Inc., a distributor of precious gems, has had three treasurers in the past 5 years. Each treasurer adopted a different inventory valuation and/or depreciation method.

8. A residential contractor signs a contract to build a four-bedroom home for $225,000. The builder records the entire amount as revenue at the time the agreement is signed.

9. A realtor paid for office equipment in cash, not by check, and has misplaced the receipt. The realtor thinks the equipment cost approximately $600, and enters $600 in the accounting records.

10. North State Petroleum signed a 36-month lease and initiated a very extensive oil pumping program. Approximately 10,000 barrels of crude oil are being removed daily. The company has the right to pump as much oil as it can for the duration of the lease. Because the ultimate profitability of the venture cannot be determined until the lease has expired, the company has decided not to issue financial statements until that time.

11. In an effort to show net income in a more favorable manner, a firm has intentionally capitalized repair expenditures that would ordinarily be expensed, and has suspended the use of the lower-of-cost or market rule in anticipation of an expected sales increase.

Demonstration Problem #2

On January 6, 19X1, Quality Construction Corporation signed a contract with a real estate entrepreneur to develop a 100-acre site into a residential subdivision consisting of 200 homes, each on 1/2 acre lots. The total value of the contract was $30,000,000, with cash payments distributed as follows:

Upon signing	$ 1 million
Quarterly payments during 19X1 of $1 million each	4 million
Quarterly payments during 19X2 of $4 million each	16 million
Quarterly payments during 19X3 of $2.25 million each	9 million
Total	$30 million

Quality is charging the entrepreneur $150,000 per residence and estimates its cost to develop each site and build the house at $120,000. Title to all 200 homes will not transfer until the project is complete. Actual construction costs incurred by Quality Construction Corporation were as follows:

19X1	$ 5.1 million
19X2	13.4 million
19X3	6.2 million

Required

Prepare schedules showing revenues, costs, and net income for 19X1, 19X2, and 19X3 using the collection method, the completed contract method, and the percentage of completion method.

Collection Method

	Collections	Costs	Income
19X1			
19X2			
19X3			
Totals			

Completed Contract Method

	Revenues	Costs	Income
19X1			
19X2			
19X3			
Totals			

Percentage of Completion Method

	Actual Costs	Total Estimated Costs	% Annual Completion	Total Revenue	Annual Revenue	Annual Income
19X1						
19X2						
19X3						
Totals						

Solutions

I. Matching

1. A 2. C 3. B 4. M 5. J 6. D 7. E 8. L
9. I 10. N 11. K 12. H 13. O 14. F 15. G

II. Multiple Choice

1.   A   The FASB believes information should be relevant, reliable, and comparable. Conservatism is an accounting concept.

2.   C   The entity concept draws a sharp accounting boundary around the organization. The going-concern concept presumes that the business entity will continue to exist absent evidence to the contrary. The "yearly concept" has no meaning.

3.   B   In order to record revenues in the correct time period and to correctly match expenses with those revenues, accruals are often necessary.

4.   D   The stable-monetary-unit concept has wide practical acceptance; however, it is limited in that it ignores the changing purchasing power of currency.

5.   C   Cost is a reliable value for assets and services because cost is supported by completed transactions between parties with opposing interests.

6.   D   The collection method of recording revenues should be used only if receipt of cash is uncertain. Of the organizations listed, only the physician falls into that category.

7.   D   The percentage-of-completion method is appropriate when a contract requires a number of years to complete and the total expenses can be reasonably estimated.

8.   D   Matching means to identify and measure all expenses incurred during the period and to "match" them against the revenue earned during that period Since a franchise is deemed to benefit the period in which revenue is earned as a result of the franchise, expensing a portion of its cost through amortization is also appropriate.

9.	C	A change in accounting principle is a change in accounting method. A change in accounting estimate occurs in the normal course of business as the company alters earlier expectations.

10.	C	Choices A, B, and D are nonaccounting matters and are not disclosed in the footnotes unless they are necessary to properly interpret the financial statements. Also, financial impacts arising from these choices are not easily determined. Choice C is an accounting matter that will have bearing on future results.

III. Completion

1.	primary objective of financial reporting
2.	historical cost
3.	reliable
4.	in the footnotes to the financial statements (usually the first footnote)
5.	Financial Accounting Standards Board (FASB)
6.	Securities and Exchange Commission (SEC)
7.	Generally Accepted Accounting Principles
8.	conservatism
9.	disclosure principle
10.	installment

IV. Exercises

1.

A.

Construction income will be $-0- for years 1 and 2. In year 3, construction income will be:

Revenue – Expenses = Construction income

$200,000,000 – 150,000,000 = \underline{\$50,000,000}$

B.

Year	Cost for Year		Total Project Cost		% of Project Completion for Year		Total Project Revenue		Revenue for Year		Cost for Year		Construction Income for Year
1	30	÷	150	=	20%	x	200	=	40	–	30	=	10
2	37.5	÷	150	=	25%	x	200	=	50	–	37.5	=	12.5
3	82.5	÷	150	=	45%	x	200	=	110	–	82.5	=	27.5
	150						200						50

2.

A.

Year	Revenue	–	Expense	=	Gross Profit
1	800,000		200,000		600,000
2	-0-		-0-		-0-
3	-0-		-0-		-0-
4	-0-		-0-		-0-

B.

Installment sale – Cost of equipment sold = Gross profit

800,000 – 200,000 = 600,000

Gross profit percentage = Gross profit ÷ Installment sale = 600,000 ÷ 800,000 = 75%

Year	Collection	x	GP %	=	Gross Profit
1	$200,000	x	75%	=	$150,000
2	100,000	x	75%	=	75,000
3	200,000	x	75%	=	150,000
4	300,000	x	75%	=	225,000
	$800,000				$600,000

3.

A. $3,600 / 12 months = $300 per month
 19X4   4 months at $300 per month = $1,200
 19X5   8 months at $300 per month = $2,400

B. 19X4   Interest for 2 months (November and December)
            $60,000 x .12 x 2/12 = $1,200
 19X5   Interest for 12 months
            $60,000 x .12 x 12/12 = $7,200

C. 19X4 $280,000
 19X5 $325,000 – $280,000 = $45,000

4.

A. | | | |
|---|---|---|
| Purchase price | $8,000 | Cost principle |
| Less: Cash discount | 160 | |
| Net purchase price | 7,840 | |
| Add: Shipping | 125 | |
| Installation | 250 | |
| Cost of asset | $8,215 | |

B. | | | |
|---|---|---|
| Purchase price | $475,000 | Cost principle |
| Add: Survey | 5,000 | |
| Landscaping | 22,500 | |
| Cost of asset | $502,500 | |

C. Cost of asset $ 61,000   Cost principle

V. Critical Thinking

Generally, there are two different approaches to this "adjustment" for inflation. One approach is to update historical cost using a price index, thereby constantly re-stating assets to reflect inflation. For example, an asset purchased at the beginning of the month for $400 would be re-stated to $800 at the month's end. A second approach ignores the rise in general prices and re-states the $400 asset at a current replacement cost at the month's end. For example, suppose the $400 asset would cost $700 to replace at the month's end. The $700 amount would be used. Both of these techniques measure inflation, but do so from different perspectives. (While the 100%-per-month inflation seems absurd, remember that in 1994, in certain parts of Eastern Europe, inflation was running at 1000% per day!)

VI. Demonstration Problems

Demonstration Problem #1 Solved and Explained

1. *Entity concept.* A fundamental assumption under GAAP accounting is that business-related transactions are always accounted for separately from the transactions of other organizations and the personal transactions of the owners. If personal and business accounts and records are combined, it is difficult or impossible to evaluate the activity of the business.

2. *Going-concern concept.* The facts reveal that the business remains in strong condition financially and the owners do not plan to liquidate. The going-concern concept assumes that an entity will continue long enough to recover the cost of its assets, and that both assets and liabilities should be reported in the balance sheet at their historical cost. Unless there is reason to believe that it will cease operating in the foreseeable future, the business should not report assets and liabilities at their estimated liquidation or market values.

3. *Matching principle.* The matching principle governs the reporting of revenue and expenses and is the cornerstone of the adjustment process. By recording expenses and revenues when cash is paid or received, the bookkeeper is not recording and linking the transaction in the proper accounting period, and may well be distorting reported net income. Revenues should be recorded when earned, expenses recorded when incurred.

4. *Disclosure principle.* A firm should report information (good or bad) that would help financial statement users make knowledgeable decisions about a company. Although no lawsuits have yet been filed in the short period since the accident occurred, a material negative outcome is clearly a possibility. Most companies disclose contingent liabilities in footnotes to the financial statements.

5. *Cost principle.* GAAP requires that assets such as land be recorded at their acquisition cost even though the value of the asset may change. Although it has its critics, the cost principle provides a verifiable, objective, and definite means of recording assets at their exchange price. This reduces subjectivity in the recording process and improves the reliability of financial statement reporting.

6. *Materiality concept.* Insignificant items of information that would not cause a financial statement user to change a decision are not required to be reported in strict compliance with GAAP. Although the stapler could technically be depreciated over its economic life, the cost of recording and preparing depreciation schedules would likely outweigh any reporting benefits that would be achieved by doing so. A $7 stapler should be expensed in its year of purchase.

7. *Comparability principle.* The comparability principle states that accounting information should be comparable over time (period to period) for a single firm and among different firms in a similar line of business. Frequent changes in accounting methods confuse statement users and make it difficult for them to analyze a firm's performance.

8. *Revenue principle.* The revenue principle provides guidance on the timing of the recording of revenue and the amount of revenue to record in each accounting period. The contractor is violating the revenue principle by recording revenue before it is earned. GAAP provides four methods of recognizing revenue (Sales, Collection, Installment, and Percentage-of-Completion). In all of them, revenue is recorded when earned and not before.

9. *Reliability principle.* The reliability principle states that accounting information must be dependable, that is, verifiable by objective evidence. The realtor's memory of approximate cost is not dependable.

10. *Time-period concept.* The time-period concept assumes that the economic life of all entities can be divided into periods and directs that accounting information be reported at regular intervals.

11. *Conservatism concept.* In an effort to counterbalance management optimism, accountants have adopted a number of practices which are conservative in nature. These practices typically result in earlier reporting of expenses and later reporting of revenues, both of which defer the reporting of net income.

Demonstration Problem #2 Solved and Explained

Collection Method

	Collections	Costs	Income
19X1	$ 5,000,000	$ 5,100,000	$ (100,000)
19X2	16,000,000	13,400,000	2,600,000
19X3	9,000,000	6,200,000	2,800,000
Totals	$30,000,000	$24,700,000	$5,300,000

The collection method uses the receipt of cash as the basis for recognizing revenue. The actual costs incurred are then deducted from the cash receipts each year to determine the amount of income.

Completed Contract Method

	Revenues	Costs	Income
19X1	0	0	0
19X2	0	0	0
19X3	30,000,000	24,700,000	5,300,000
Totals	$30,000,000	$24,700,000	$5,300,000

The completed contract method records revenue only when the contract has been completed. Therefore, Quality Construction ignores the cash received during the three years and waits to record the $30 million in19X3, the year the contract was completed. As the matching principle dictates the recognition of expenses on a similar basis, the project's total costs are recognized during 19X3 as well.

Percentage of Completion Method

	Actual Costs	Total Estimated Costs	% Annual Completion	Total Revenue	Annual Revenue	Annual Income
19X1	$ 5,100,000	$24,000,000	21.25	$30,000,000	$ 6,375,000	$1,275,000
19X2	13,400,000	24,000,000	55.80	30,000,000	16,740,000	3,340,000
19X3	6,200,000	24,000,000	balance	30,000,000	6,885,000	685,000
Totals	$24,700,000	$24,000,000		$30,000,000	$30,000,000	$5,300,000

The percentage-of-completion method recognizes revenue as the work is performed. In order to do this, you need to estimate the total project cost at the start of construction. In our case, the total estimated cost was $24 million (200 homes at $120,000 estimated cost each). Total revenue is spread out over the life of the contract using a fraction, the denominator of which is the total estimated costs (this remains constant over the 3 years) while the numerator is the actual costs incurred each year. As the actual costs incurred will never exactly total the estimated costs, the percentage applied the final year of the project is whatever number is necessary to total 100%.

Notice that the revenue-recognition method used does not determine the total amount of income earned on the project. This amount is the same (in our example, $5.3 million) in all three methods. The method used simply determines how much of the $5.3 million is recognized each year during the project's life.

Chapter 13

Accounting for Partnerships

 ## Chapter Overview

*I*n Chapter 1 you were introduced to the three legal forms of business organization: sole proprietorships, partnerships, and corporations. Since then, the focus has been on either sole proprietorships or corporations. We now turn our attention to the third type, partnerships. This topic can be covered in one chapter because the differences are not all that great and most of the topics covered so far apply to all three forms. The specific learning objectives for this chapter are:

1. Identify the characteristics of a partnership
2. Account for partners' initial investments in a partnership
3. Allocate profits and losses to the partners by different methods
4. Account for the admission of a new partner to the business
5. Account for the withdrawal of a partner from the business
6. Account for the liquidation of a partnership
7. Prepare partnership financial statements

Chapter Review

1.
2.
3.

OBJECTIVE 1
Identify the characteristics of a partnership.

A **partnership** is an association of two or more persons who are co-owners of a business for profit. Partners frequently draw up a **partnership agreement**, also called **articles of partnership.** This agreement is a contract between the partners which sets forth the duties and rights of each partner.

The **characteristics of a partnership** are: *Do not need written*

1. **Limited life:** The addition or withdrawal of a partner dissolves the partnership.
2. **Mutual agency:** Every partner has the authority to obligate the business to contracts within the scope of regular business operations.
3. **Unlimited liability:** If the partnership cannot pay its debts, the partners are personally responsible for payment.
4. **Co-ownership:** Assets of the business become the joint property of the partnership.
5. **No partnership income taxes:** The net income of a partnership is divided among the partners, who individually pay income taxes on their portions of the partnership's income.
6. **Partners' owner's equity accounts:** Separate owner's equity accounts will be set up for each partner, both a Capital account and Withdrawal account.

OBJECTIVE 2
Account for partners' initial investments in a partnership.

Partners may invest assets and liabilities in a business. The simplest investment to account for is cash:

Cash	XX	
Partner's Name, Capital		XX

Assets other than cash are recorded at the current market value. Suppose Craine invests land in a partnership. The land cost $60,000 several years ago and has a current market value of $95,000. The correct entry on the partnership's books is:

Land	95,000	
Craine, Capital		95,000

OBJECTIVE 3
Allocate profits and losses to the partners by different methods.

If there is no partnership agreement, or the agreement does not specify how profits and losses are to be divided, then the partners share profits and losses equally. If the agreement specifies a method for sharing profits, but not losses, then losses are shared in the same manner as profits.

Several methods exist to allocate profits and losses. Partners may share profits and losses according to a stated fraction or percentage. If the partnership agreement allocates 2/3 of the profits and losses to Williams's, and 1/3 to Vierra, then the entry to record the allocation of $60,000 of income is:

Income Summary	60,000	
Williams, Capital		40,000
Vierra, Capital		20,000

The partnership agreement may provide that profits and losses be allocated in proportion to the partner's capital contributions to the business. To find the income allocated to a particular partner, use this formula:

$$\text{Income allocated to a partner} = \frac{\text{Partner's capital}}{\text{Total capital}} \times \text{Net income}$$

Suppose Williams and Vierra have the capital balances listed below:

Williams, Capital	240,000
Vierra, Capital	160,000
Total Capital balances	400,000

Partnership income of $60,000 will be allocated as follows:

Williams: (240,000/400,000) × 60,000 =	36,000
Vierra: (160,000/400,000) × 60,000 =	24,000
Total income allocated to partners	60,000

The entry to record the allocation of profits is:

Income Summary	60,000	
Williams, Capital		36,000
Vierra, Capital		24,000

Sharing of profits and losses may also be allocated based on a combination of capital contributions, service to the business, and/or interest on capital contributions. The important point to remember is to follow the exact order of allocation specified by the partnership agreement.

When a loss occurs, the process does not change. Simply follow the terms of the agreement (or divide the loss equally in the absence of an agreement) in the order specified.

Partners generally make periodic withdrawals of cash from a partnership. If Vierra withdraws $5,000 from the partnership, the entry is:

Vierra, Drawing	5,000	
Cash		5,000

The drawing accounts must be closed to the capital accounts at the end of the period. If Vierra's $5,000 withdrawal is the only withdrawal during the period, the closing entry is:

Vierra, Capital	5,000	
Vierra, Drawing		5,000

OBJECTIVE 4
Account for the admission of a new partner to the business.

Remember that a partnership is dissolved when a new partner is added or an existing partner withdraws. Often a new partnership is immediately formed to replace the old partnership. CPA firms and law firms often admit new partners and have existing partners retire during the course of a year.

A new partner may be admitted into an existing partnership either by purchasing a present partner's interest or by investing in the partnership. The new partner must be approved by all the current partners in order to participate in the business.

When **purchasing a partnership interest**, the new partner pays the old partner directly, according to the terms of the purchase agreement. The purchase transaction has no effect on the partnership's books. The only entry the partnership will make is to close the old partner's capital account and open the new partner's capital account:

Old Partner, Capital	XX	
New Partner, Capital		XX

A person may also be admitted to a partnership by directly **investing in the partnership.** This investment can be a simple investment, and is recorded as:

Cash and Other assets	XX	
New Partner, Capital		XX

The new partner's interest in the business will equal:

$$\textbf{New partner's interest} = \frac{\textbf{New partner's capital}}{\textbf{Total capital}}$$

Note that sharing of profits and losses is determined by the new partnership agreement, and not by the proportion of total capital allotted to the new partner.

Successful partnerships frequently require incoming partners to pay a **bonus** to existing partners. In this situation, the incoming partner will pay more for a portion of the partnership interest than the amount of capital he receives. The difference, which is a bonus to the existing partners, is computed by a three-step calculation:

1)   Total capital before new partner's investment
    + New partner's investment
    = Total capital after new partner's investment

2)   New partner's capital = Total capital after new partner's investment x
                  New partner's interest in the partnership

3)   Bonus to existing partners = New partner's capital – New partner's capital

The entry on the partnership books to record the transaction is:

Cash	XX	
New Partner, Capital		XX
Old Partners, Capital		XX

Note that the bonus paid by the new partner is credited to the old partner's Capital account. The allocation of the bonus to existing partners is based on the partnership agreement of the existing partners.

In some cases, a potential new partner may bring substantial future benefits to a partnership, such as a well-known reputation. In this situation, the existing partners may offer the newcomer a partnership share that includes a bonus. The calculation is similar to the calculation for a bonus to the existing partners:

1)   Total capital before new partner's investment
    + New partner's investment
    = Total capital after new partner's investment

2)   New partner's capital = Total capital after new partner's investment x
                  New partner's interest in the partnership

3)   Bonus to new partners = New partner's capital – New partner's investment

The entry on the partnership books to record the transaction is:

Cash and Other Assets	XX	
Old Partners, Capital	XX	
New Partner, Capital		XX

Note that the bonus paid to the new partner is debited to the old partners' Capital accounts. The allocation of the bonus to the new partner is based on the partnership agreement of the existing partners.

Partners may **withdraw from a partnership** due to retirement, partnership disputes, or other reasons. The withdrawing partner may sell his or her interest or may receive the appropriate portion of the business directly from the partnership in the form of cash, other partnership assets, or notes.

The first step is to determine whether the partnership assets are to be valued at book value or market value. If assets are to be valued at market value, they must be revalued, often by an independent appraiser. Increases in asset values are debited to asset accounts and credited to the partners' capital accounts (according to the profit-and-loss sharing ratio). Decreases in asset values are debited to the partners' capital accounts and credited to asset accounts. The revalued assets then become the new book value of the assets.

A partner may withdraw from a partnership at book value, at less than book value, or at more than book value. (Remember that book value may or may not be equal to current market value, depending upon whether the assets have been revalued or not.) A partner willing to withdraw at less than book value may be eager to leave the partnership. A partner withdrawing at more than book value may be collecting a bonus from the remaining partners, who may be eager to have the partner withdraw.

Withdrawal at book value is recorded as:

Withdrawing Partner, Capital	XX	
Cash, Other Assets, or Note Payable		XX

Withdrawal at less than book value is recorded by:

Withdrawing Partner, Capital	XX	
Cash, Other Assets, or Note Payable		XX
Remaining Partners, Capital		XX

When a partner withdraws at less than book value, the difference between the withdrawing partner's capital and the payment to the withdrawing partner is allocated to the remaining partners based on the new profit-and-loss ratio.

Withdrawal at more than book value is recorded by:

Withdrawing Partner, Capital	XX	
Remaining Partners, Capital	XX	
Cash, Other Assets, or Note Payable		XX

When a partner withdraws at more than book value, the difference between the payment to the withdrawing partner and the withdrawing partner's capital is allocated to the remaining partners based on the new profit-and-loss ratio.

The death of a partner also dissolves the partnership. The books are closed to determine the deceased partner's capital balance on the date of death. Settlement with the partner's estate is made according to the partnership agreement. The entry is:

Deceased Partner, Capital	XX	
Liability Payable to Estate		XX

OBJECTIVE 6
Account for the
liquidation of a
partnership.

Liquidation is the process of going out of business and involves three basic steps:

1. Selling the partnership assets and allocating gains or losses to the partners' capital accounts based on the profit-and-loss ratio.
2. Paying the partnership liabilities.
3. Distributing the remaining cash to the partners based on their capital balances.

When selling assets, gains result in credits (increases) to partners capital accounts. Losses result in debits (decreases) to partners' capital accounts.

The general work sheet for liquidation of a partnership is:

	Cash	+	Noncash Assets	= Liabilities +	Capital	
Balances before sale of assets	XX		XX	XX	XX	
Sale of assets and sharing of gains and (losses)	XX		(XX)		XX (XX)	if gain if loss
Balances after sale of assets	XX		-0-	XX	XX	
Payment of liabilities	(XX)			(XX)		
Balances after payment of liabilities	XX		-0-	-0-	XX	
Disbursement of cash to partners	(XX)				(XX)	
Ending balances	-0-		-0-	-0-	-0-	

Occasionally, allocation of losses on the sale of assets results in a capital deficiency for one or more partners. The deficient partner should contribute personal assets to eliminate the deficiency. If not, the deficiency must be allocated to the remaining partners.

OBJECTIVE 7
Prepare
partnership
financial
statements.

Partnership financial statements are similar to the financial statements of a proprietorship. The exceptions are that a partnership income statement includes a section showing the division of net income to the partners, and the owners' equity section of the balance sheet includes accounts for each partner.

Test Yourself

All the self-testing materials in this chapter focus on information and procedures that your instructor is likely to test in quizzes and examinations.

I. Matching *Match each numbered term with its lettered definition.*

1. partnership agreement or articles of partnership
2. capital deficiency
3. unlimited personal liability
4. dissolution
5. liquidation

6. mutual agency
7. bonus
8. limited partner
9. general partner

A. a contract among partners specifying such things as the name, location, and nature of the business; the name, capital investment, and the duties of each partner; and the method of sharing profits and losses by the partners

B. a debit balance in a partner's capital account

C. ending of a partnership

D. the ability of every partner to bind the business to a contract within the scope of the partnership's regular business operations

E. the process of going out of business

F. when partnership (or a proprietorship) cannot pay its debts with business assets, the partners (or the proprietor) must use personal assets to meet the debt

G. a partner in a limited partnership whose liability is unlimited

H. a partner in a limited partnership whose liability is limited

I. results when assets contributed (or withdrawn) do not equal the amount credited (or debited) to a partner's capital account

II. Multiple Choice *Circle the best answer.*

1.   Which of the following provisions will *not* be found in the partnership agreement?
     A.   liquidation procedures
     B.   profit-and-loss ratio
     C.   withdrawals allowed to partners
     D.   dividends payable to partners

2.   Which of the following does *not* result in dissolution of a partnership?
     A.   addition of a new partner
     B.   withdrawal of a partner
     C.   marriage of a partner
     D.   death of a partner

3.   Assets and liabilities contributed by a partner to a partnership are recorded at:
     A.   expected future value
     B.   fair market value
     C.   original cost
     D.   book value

4.   Profits and losses are usually shared by partners according to:
     A.   verbal agreements
     B.   the balance in partners' equity accounts
     C.   partners' personal wealth
     D.   the partnership agreement

5.   When a partner takes money out of the partnership, the partner's:
     A.   Drawing is credited
     B.   Drawing is debited
     C.   Capital is debited
     D.   Capital is credited

6.   A new partner may be admitted to a partnership:
     A.   only by investing in the partnership
     B.   only by purchasing a partner's interest
     C.   by purchasing common stock of the partnership
     D.   either by investing in the partnership or by purchasing a partner's interest

7.   In a partnership liquidation, a gain from the sale of assets is allocated to the:
     A.   payment of partnership liabilities
     B.   partners based on their capital balances
     C.   partner with the lowest capital balance
     D.   partners based on their profit-and-loss ratio

8. If a partner has a debit balance in his capital account and is personally insolvent, then the other partners:

    A. absorb the deficiency based on their personal wealth

    B. absorb the deficiency based on their capital balances

    C. absorb the deficiency based on their profit-and-loss ratio

    D. sue the insolvent partner's spouse

9. ABC partnership shares profits and losses in a 5:4:3 ratio, respectively. This means:

    A. partner A receives 5/12 of the profits

    B. partner A receives 5/9 of the profits

    C. partner B receives 1/4 of the profits

    D. partner C receives 1/3 of the profits

10. In a limited partnership, which of the following is false?

    A. there must be more than one partner

    B. there must be at least one general partner

    C. all partners have unlimited liability

    D. some partners have limited liability

 ## III. Completion *Complete each of the following statements.*

1. If the partnership agreement does not specify a profit-and-loss ratio, profits and losses are allocated _____.

2. The five characteristics of a partnership are: 1) _____,
2) _____, 3) _____,
4) _____, and 5) _____.

3. The difference between a partnership and sole proprietorship is that a partnership has _____ owners, while a sole proprietorship has_____owners.

4. _____ refers to the ability of any partner to contract on behalf of the partnership.

5. A _____ occurs when a new partner is admitted or an existing partner leaves a partnership.

6. A partnership undergoes _____ when it ceases operations and settles all its affairs.

7. A debit balance in a partner's capital account is called

_____.

8. The steps in liquidating a partnership are:

1)_____

2)_____

3)_____

4)_____

9. A partner with limited liability is called a _____.

10. When liquidating, cash is distributed to the partners according to the

_____.

 # IV. Exercises

1. Abbott and Costello formed a partnership. Abbott contributed cash of $9,000, and land with a fair market value of $65,000 that had cost $14,000. The partnership also assumed Abbott's note payable of $24,000. Costello contributed $20,000 in cash, equipment with a fair market value of $14,000 that had cost $22,000, and the partnership assumed his accounts receivable of $3,200.

Make journal entries to show each partner's contribution to the business.

GENERAL JOURNAL

Date	Accounts and Explanation	PR	Debit	Credit

2. Arthur and Anderson formed a partnership. Arthur invested $75,000 and Anderson invested $50,000. Arthur devotes most of his time on the road developing the business, while Anderson devotes some of his time to managing the home office and the rest of his time watching television. They have agreed to share profits as follows:

- The first $50,000 of profits is allocated based on the partner's capital contribution.
- The next $50,000 of profits is allocated 3/4 to Arthur and 1/4 to Anderson based on their service to the partnership.
- Any remaining amount is allocated equally.

A.   If the partnership profits are $110,000, how much will be allocated to Arthur, and how much will be allocated to Anderson? Use the format below.

B.   If the partnership has a loss of $70,000, how much will be allocated to Arthur, and how much will be allocated to Anderson? Use the format on the next page.

C.   If the partnership profits are $62,000, how much will be allocated to Arthur, and how much will be allocated to Anderson? Use the format on the next page.

A.

	Arthur	Anderson	Total

B.

	Arthur	Anderson	Total

C.

	Arthur	Anderson	Total

3. Mac and Donald are partners in a fast food restaurant. Their capital balances are $18,000 and $12,000, respectively. They share profits and losses equally. They admit King to a one-fourth interest with a cash investment of $6,000. Make the journal entry to show the admission of King to the partnership.

GENERAL JOURNAL

Date	Accounts and Explanation	PR	Debit	Credit

4. Jose, Kim, and Lonnie are partners with capital balances of $15,000, $45,000, and $30,000, respectively. They share profits and losses equally. Kim decides to retire.

A. Make the journal entry to show Kim's retirement if she is allowed to withdraw $25,000 in cash.

GENERAL JOURNAL

Date	Accounts and Explanation	PR	Debit	Credit

B. Make the journal entry to show Kim's retirement if she is allowed to withdraw $45,000 in cash.

GENERAL JOURNAL

Date	Accounts and Explanation	PR	Debit	Credit

C.   Make the journal entry to show Kim's retirement if she is allowed to withdraw $55,000 in cash.

GENERAL JOURNAL

Date	Accounts and Explanation	PR	Debit	Credit

5.   The following balance sheet information is given for Slim-An-Nunn Company:

Cash	16,000	Liabilities	28,000
Noncash assets	56,000	Slim, Capital	6,000
		An, Capital	24,000
		Nunn, Capital	14,000
Total assets	72,000	Total liabilities and capital	72,000

Slim, An, and Nunn use a profit and loss ratio of 3:4:1, respectively. Assume that any partner with a deficit in his or her capital account is insolvent.

Prepare the journal entries for liquidation assuming the noncash assets are sold for $20,000.

GENERAL JOURNAL

Date	Accounts and Explanation	PR	Debit	Credit

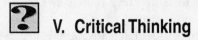 **V. Critical Thinking**

Review the information in Exercises 5. Assume all information is the same except Slim is a limited partner. Prepare journal entries to record the liquidation.

GENERAL JOURNAL

Date	Accounts and Explanation	PR	Debit	Credit

 VI. Demonstration Problems

Demonstration Problem #1

The partnership of Groucho and Harpo is considering admitting Zeppo as a partner on April 1, 19X4. The partnership general ledger includes the following balances on that date:

Cash	25,000	Total liabilities	30,000
Other assets	55,000	Groucho, Capital	15,000
		Harpo, Capital	35,000
Total assets	80,000	Total liabilities and capital	80,000

Groucho's share of profit and losses is 40%, and Harpo's share is 60%.

Required

1. Assume that Zeppo pays Harpo $50,000 to acquire Harpo's interest of the business, and that Groucho has approved Zeppo as a new partner. See the formats on the next page.

   a. Prepare the journal entries for the transfer of owner's equity on the partnership books.

   b. Prepare the partnership balance sheet immediately after Zeppo is admitted as a partner.

2. Suppose Zeppo becomes a partner by investing $50,000 cash to acquire a one-fourth interest in the business. See the formats on the next page.

   a. Prepare a schedule to compute Zeppo's capital balance. Record Zoppo's investment in the business.

   b. Prepare the partnership balance sheet immediately after Zeppo is admitted as a partner.

Requirement 1

a. (Journal entry)

Date	Accounts and Explanation	PR	Debit	Credit

b. (Balance sheet)

Groucho, Harpo, and Zeppo
Balance Sheet
April 1, 19X4

Requirement 2

a.   *Computation of Zeppo's capital balance:*

(Journal entry)

Date	Accounts and Explanation	PR	Debit	Credit

b.   (Balance sheet)

Groucho, Harpo, and Zeppo
Balance Sheet
April 1, 19X4

Demonstration Problem #2

The partnership of R, S, and T is liquidating. The partnership agreement allocated profits to the partners in the ratio of 3:2:1. In liquidation, the noncash assets were sold in a single transaction for $120,000 on August 31, 19X4. The partnership paid the liabilities the same day. The partnership accounts are presented at the top of the liquidation schedule on the next page.

1. Complete the schedule summarizing the liquidation transactions. See the format on the next page. You may wish to refer to the partnership liquidation exhibits in the text. Assume that T invests cash of $4,000 in the partnership in partial settlement of any capital account deficiency. This cash is distributed to the other partners. The other partners must absorb the remainder of the capital deficiency

2. Journalize the liquidation transactions. See the formats on pages 323 and 324.

Requirement 1 (summary of liquidation transaction)

	Cash	+	Noncash Assets	=	Liabilities	+	R(1/2)	+	S(1/3)	+	T(1/6)
									Capital		
Balance before sale of assets	30,000		240,000		120,000		90,000		50,000		10,000
a) Sale of assets and sharing of loss											
Balances											
b) Payment of liabilities											
Balances											
c) T's investment of cash to share part of his his deficiency											
Balances											
d) Sharing of deficiency by remaining partners in ratio of 3/5 to 2/5											
Balances											
e) Distribution of cash to partners											
Balances											

Requirement 2 (journal entries to record the liquidation transactions)

a.

GENERAL JOURNAL

Date	Accounts and Explanation	PR	Debit	Credit

b.

GENERAL JOURNAL

Date	Accounts and Explanation	PR	Debit	Credit

c.

GENERAL JOURNAL

Date	Accounts and Explanation	PR	Debit	Credit

d.

GENERAL JOURNAL

Date	Accounts and Explanation	PR	Debit	Credit

e.

GENERAL JOURNAL

Date	Accounts and Explanation	PR	Debit	Credit

Solutions

I. Matching

1. A   2. B   3. F   4. C   5. E   6. D   7. I   8. H   9. G

II. Multiple Choice

1. **D**   Dividends are distributions of earnings paid by corporations to their shareholders. It is a term that is strictly applicable to corporate accounting and as such cannot apply to partnership accounting.

2. **C**   The marriage of a partner is an event of the partner's personal life and has no direct bearing on the partnership entity. All of the other items listed cause a dissolution of the partnership.

3. **B**   Using fair market value is appropriate to accurately measure exactly what each partner is bringing into the partnership.

4. **D**   The partnership agreement can specify the distribution of profits and losses in any manner the partners have agreed to.

5. **B**   Withdrawing money from the partnership requires a credit to cash which is balanced with a debit to the partner's Drawing account. The balance of the partner's Drawing account will be closed to his Capital account at the end of the period.

6. **D**   Of the items listed, answer C "purchasing common stock of the partnership" is inappropriate since partnerships do not have stock; answer A and B are incorrect because of the use of the word "only" in the answers.

7. **D**   Gains and losses incurred in liquidation are distributed as are any other gains and losses, in accordance with the partnership agreement.

8. **C**   The deficiency in a partner's capital account balance is distributed as if it were a loss, in accordance with the partnership agreement.

9. **A**   To determine a partner's fractional share, create a denominator by summing the integers $(5 + 4 + 3 = 12)$ and use the partner's ratio as the numerator. Thus, A receives 5/12, B receives 4/12 or 1/3, and C receives 3/12 or 1/4.

10. **C**   The key distinction is the limitation of liability by at least one of the partners, who is identified as a limited partner.

III. Completion

1. equally
2. limited life, mutual agency, unlimited liability, co-ownership of property, no partnership income taxes
3. two or more, one
4. mutual agency
5. dissolution
6. liquidation
7. deficit
8. close the books, sell the assets, pay the debts, distribute the cash (order is important)
9. limited partner
10. the balance in the capital accounts (*not* the profit/loss ratio)

IV. Exercises

1.

Date	Accounts and Explanation	PR	Debit	Credit
	Land		65,000	
	Cash		9,000	
	Notes Payable			24,000
	Abbott, Capital			50,000
	Cash		20,000	
	Equipment		14,000	
	Account Receivable		3,200	
	Costello, Capital			37,200

2.

A.

	Arthur	Anderson	Total
Total net income			$110,000
Sharing of first $50,000 of net income, based on capital contribution:			
Arthur (75,000/125,000) x (50,000)	30,000		
Anderson (50,000/125,000) x (50,000)		20,000	
Total			50,000
Net income remaining for allocation			60,000
Sharing of the next $50,000 based on service:			
Arthur (3/4 x 50,000)	37,500		
Anderson (1/4 x 50,000)		12,500	
Total			50,000
Net income remaining for allocation			10,000
Remainder shared equally:			
Arthur (1/2 x 10,000)	5,000		
Anderson (1/2 x 10,000)		5,000	
Total			10,000
Net income remaining for allocation			-0-
Net income allocated to the partners	72,500	37,500	110,000

B.

	Arthur	Anderson	Total
Total net income (loss)			($70,000)
Sharing of first $50,000 of net income (loss), based on capital contribution:			
Arthur (50,000/125,000) x (50,000)	(30,000)		
Anderson (50,000/125,000) x (50,000)		(20,000)	
Total			(50,000)
Net income (loss) remaining for allocation			(20,000)
Sharing of the remainder based on service:			
Arthur (3/4 x 20,000)	(15,000)		
Anderson (1/4 x 20,000)		(5,000)	
Total			(20,000)
Net income (loss) remaining for allocation			-0-
Net income (loss) allocated to the partners	(45,000)	(25,000)	(70,000)

C.

	Arthur	Anderson	Total
Total net income			$62,000
Sharing of first $50,000 of net income, based on capital contribution:			
Arthur (50,000/125,000) x (50,000)	30,000		
Anderson (50,000/125,000) x (50,000)		20,000	
Total			50,000
Net income remaining for allocation			12,000
Sharing of the remainder based on service:			
Arthur (3/4 x 12,000)	9,000		
Anderson (1/4 x 12,000)		3,000	
Total			12,000
Net income remaining for allocation			-0-
Net income allocated to the partners	39,000	23,000	62,000

3.

GENERAL JOURNAL

Date	Accounts and Explanation	PR	Debit	Credit
	Cash		6,000	
	Mac, Capital [1/2 x (9,000 – 6,000)]		1,500	
	Donald, Capital		1,500	
	King, Capital [1/4 x (18,000 + 12,000 + 6,000)]			9,000

4.

A.

GENERAL JOURNAL

Date	Accounts and Explanation	PR	Debit	Credit
	Kim, Capital		45,000	
	Cash			25,000
	Jose, Capital			10,000
	Lonnie, Capital			10,000

B.

GENERAL JOURNAL

Date	Accounts and Explanation	PR	Debit	Credit
	Kim, Capital		45,000	
	Cash			45,000

C.

GENERAL JOURNAL

Date	Accounts and Explanation	PR	Debit	Credit
	Kim, Capital		45,000	
	Jose, Capital		5,000	
	Lonnie, Capital		5,000	
	Cash			55,000

5.

GENERAL JOURNAL

Date	Accounts and Explanation	PR	Debit	Credit
	Cash		20,000	
	Slim, Capital		13,500	
	An, Capital		18,000	
	Nunn, Capital		4,500	
	Noncash assets			56,000

Loss on sale = 36,000 (56,000 – 20,000). Therefore,
  Slim = 36,000 x 3/8 = 13,500
  An   = 36,000 x 4/8 = 18,000
  Nunn= 36,000 x 1/8 = 4,500

	Liabilites	28,000	
	Cash		28,000
	An, Capital	6,000	
	Nunn, Capital	1,500	
	Slim, Capital		7,500

Slim's Deficit = 7,500 (6,000 – 13,500)
  An   = 4/5 x 7,500 = 6,000
  Nunn = 1/5 x 7,500 = 1,500

	Nunn, Capital	8,000	
	Cash		8,000
	An's balance = 0(24,000 – 18,000 – 6,000=0)		

V. Critical Thinking

GENERAL JOURNAL

Date	Accounts and Explanation	PR	Debit	Credit
	Cash		20,000	
	Slim, Capital		6,000	*
	An, Capital		24,000	**
	Nunn, Capital		6,000	
	Noncash assets			56,000

* Because Slim is a limited partner, the amount of loss he must absorb is limited to the balance in his capital account.

** After debiting Slim's account for $6,000, the remaining loss is distributed between An and Nunn, as follows:

  An   = 30,000 x 4/5 = 24,000
  Nunn = 30,000 x 1/5 = 6,000

	Liabilites	28,000	
	Cash		28,000
	Nunn, Capital	8,000	
	Cash		8,000

VI. Demonstration Problems

Demonstration Problem #1 Solved and Explained

Requirement 1

a.

Date	Accounts	Debit	Credit	Explanation
July 1	Harpo, Capital	35,000		Debit closes Harpo's account
	Zeppo, Capital		35,000	Credit opens Zeppo's account

To transfer Harpo's equity in the partnership to Zeppo.

Note that the book value of Harpo's capital account ($35,000) is transferred, not the price Zeppo paid ($50,000) to buy into the business. Since the partnership received no cash from the transaction, the entry would be the same no matter what Zeppo paid Harpo for the interest.

b.

Groucho and Zeppo
Balance Sheet
April 1, 19X4

Cash	25,000	Total liabilities	30,000
Other assets	55,000	Groucho, Capital	15,000
		Zeppo, Capital	35,000
Total assets	$80,000	Total liabilities and capital	$80,000

Requirement 2

a.
Computation of Zeppo's capital balance:

Partnership capital before Zeppo is admitted (15,000 + 35,000)	$ 50,000
Zeppo's investment in the partnership	50,000
Partnership capital after Zeppo is admitted	$100,000
Zeppo's capital in the partnership (100,000 x 1/4)	$ 25,000

Date	Accounts and Explanation	PR	Debit	Credit
July 1	Cash		50,000	
	Zeppo, Capital			25,000
	Groucho, Capital (40% of $25,000)			10,000
	Harpo, Capital (60% of $25,000)			15,000
	To admit Zeppo as a business partner with a one-fourth interest in the business.			

Note that Groucho's capital account increased by $10,000 and Harpo's capital account increased by $15,000. These amounts represent Groucho and Harpo's proportionate share of the $25,000 amount by which Zeppo's $50,000 payment exceeded his $25,000 capital account credit. When a partner is admitted by investment in the partnership, often the investment exceeds the new partner's capital account credit and the original partners share proportionately in the difference.

b.

Groucho, Harpo, and Zeppo
Balance Sheet
April 1, 19X4

Cash (25,000 + 50,000)	75,000	Total liabilities	30,000
Other assets	55,000	Groucho, Capital	25,000
		Harpo, Capital	50,000
		Zeppo, Capital	25,000
Total assets	$130,000	Total liabilities and capital	$130,000

Points to Remember

1. Partners may specify any profit or loss sharing method they desire. Common arrangements include:

   a. Sharing equally - unless the partners agree otherwise, profits and losses are required by law to be divided equally

   b. Sharing based on a stated fraction

   c. Sharing based on capital contributions

   d. Sharing based on salaries and interest

   e. Sharing based on a combination of the above and/or other factors

   Be alert to problems requiring an allocation of profits and losses when the capital account balances are given for each partner, but nothing is specified about the sharing method. When the sharing method is not specified, each partner receives an equal share.

2. New partners are often admitted to established partnerships. Technically, a new partnership is formed to carry on the former partnership's business, and the old partnership ceases to exist (it is dissolved). Although the old partnership dissolves, the business is not normally terminated, nor are the assets liquidated.

   Be sure you can distinguish between the admission of a partner by purchase of a partner's interest (Requirement 1) and admission by making a direct investment in the partnership (Requirement 2).

Demonstration Problem #2 Solved and Explained

Requirement 1 (summary of liquidation transactions)

	Cash	+	Noncash Assets	=	Liabilities	+	R(1/2)	+	Capital S(1/3)	+	T(1/6)
Balance before sale of assets	30,000		240,000		120,000		90,000		50,000		10,000
a) Sale of assets and sharing of loss	120,000		(240,000)				(60,000)		(40,000)		(20,000)
Balances	150,000		-0-		120,000		30,000		10,000		(10,000)
b) Payment of liabilities	(120,000)				(120,000)						
Balances	30,000		-0-		-0-		30,000		10,000		(10,000)
c) T's investment of cash to share part of his deficiency	4,000										4,000
Balances	34,000		-0-		-0-		30,000		10,000		(6,000)
d) Sharing of deficiency by remaining partners in ratio of 3/5 to 2/5							(3,600)		(2,400)		6,000
Balances	34,000		-0-		-0-		26,400		7,600		-0-
e) Distribution of cash to partners	(34,000)						(26,400)		(7,600)		
Balances	-0-		-0-		-0-		-0-		-0-		-0-

Requirement 2 (journal entries to record the liquidation transactions)

a.

GENERAL JOURNAL

Date	Accounts and Explanation	PR	Debit	Credit
	Cash		120,000	
	R, Capital [(240,000 – 120,000) x 3/6]		60,000	
	S, Capital [(240,000 – 120,000) x 2/6]		40,000	
	T, Capital [(240,000 – 120,000) x 1/6]		20,000	
	Noncash Assets			240,00
	To record the sale of noncash assets in liquidation, and to distribute loss to partners.			

b.

GENERAL JOURNAL

Date	Accounts and Explanation	PR	Debit	Credit
	Liabilities		120,000	
	Cash			120,000
	To pay liabilities in liquidation.			

c.

GENERAL JOURNAL

Date	Accounts and Explanation	PR	Debit	Credit
	Cash		4,000	
	T, Capital			4,000
	T's contribution to pay part of the captial deficiency in liquidation.			

After posting the entries above, T's capital account reveals a $6,000 deficiency, indicated by its debit balance:

T, Capital

Loss on sale 20,000	Bal. 10,000
	Investment 4,000
Bal. 6,000	

d.

GENERAL JOURNAL

Date	Accounts and Explanation	PR	Debit	Credit
	R, Capital ($6,000 x 3/5)		3,600	
	S, Capital ($4,000 x 2/5)		2,400	
	T, Capital			6,000
	To allocate T's capital deficiency to the other partners in their profit and loss ratio.			

Prior to T's withdrawal from the partnership, the partners shared profits and losses as follows:

Ratio: R 3 = 1/2
           S 2 = 1/3
           T 1 = 1/6

The remaining partners are required to absorb the deficiency left by a partner who is unable to contribute sufficient capital to cover the deficiency. After a $4,000 contribution, T's deficiency was reduced to $6,000. Note that between R and S, profits and losses are shared in the ratio of 3 to 2 (or 60% and 40%). As a result, T's uncovered deficiency is allocated to R and S by reducing their capital accounts by $3,600 ($6,000 x 60%) and $2,400 ($6,000 x 40%), respectively.

e.

GENERAL JOURNAL

Date	Accounts and Explanation	PR	Debit	Credit
	R, Capital		26,400	
	S, Capital		7,600	
	Cash			34,000
	To distribute cash to partners on liquidation of partnership.			

At this point, the cash and capital accounts of the partners appear as follows:

Cash

Bal.	30,000	Payment of liabilites	120,000
Sale of assets	120,000		
T's contribution	4,000		
Bal.	34,000	Final distribution	34,000
Bal.	0		

R, Capital

Loss on sale	60,000	Bal.	90,000
Loss on T	3,600		
Final distribution	26,400	Bal.	26,400
		Bal.	0

S, Capital

Loss on sale	40,000	Bal.	50,000
Loss on T	2,400		
Final distribution	7,600	Bal.	7,600
		Bal.	0

Chapter 14

Corporate Organization,
Paid-in Capital,
and the Balance Sheet

 Chapter Overview

In Chapter 13 you learned about the partnership form of organization. In this chapter, we begin an in-depth discussion of the corporate form of organization. Because the corporate form is more complex than either sole proprietorships or partnerships, our discussion of corporations continues in Chapter 15, 16, and 17. Therefore, an understanding of the topics in this chapter is important before continuing to the next chapters. The specific learning objectives for this chapter are:

1. Identify the characteristics of a corporation
2. Record the issuance of stock
3. Prepare the stockholders' equity section of a corporation balance sheet
4. Account for the incorporation of a going business
5. Account for cash dividends
6. Compute two profitability measures: return on assets and return on stockholders' equity
7. Distinguish among market value, redemption value, liquidation value, and book value
8. Account for a corporation's income tax

Chapter Review

OBJECTIVE 1
Identify the characteristics of a corporation.

1. A corporation is a **separate legal entity** chartered and regulated under state law. The owners' equity of a corporation is held by stockholders as shares of stock.

2. A corporation has **continuous life**. A change in ownership of the stock does not affect the life of the corporation.

3. **Mutual agency of owners is not present** in corporations. A stockholder cannot commit a corporation to a binding contract (unless that stockholder is also an officer of the corporation).

4. Stockholders have **limited liability**. That is, they have no personal obligation for the debts of the corporation.

5. **Ownership and management are separated.** Corporations are controlled by boards of directors who appoint officers to manage the business. Boards of directors are elected by stockholders. Thus, stockholders are not obligated to manage the business; ownership is separate from management.

6. **Corporations pay taxes:** state franchise taxes and federal and state income taxes. Corporations pay dividends to stockholders who then pay personal income taxes on their dividends. This is considered double taxation of corporate earnings.

Corporations come into existence when a **charter** is obtained from a relevant state official. **Bylaws** are then adopted. The stockholders elect a **board of directors**, who appoint the officers of the corporation. (Review Exhibit 14-2 in your text.)

Owners receive **stock certificates** for their investment. The basic unit of investment is a **share.** A corporation's outstanding stock is the shares of its stock that are held by stockholders. Stockholders' equity is reported differently than owners' equity of a proprietorship or a partnership because corporations must report the sources of their capital. These sources are **paid-in or contributed capital** from sale of stock, and **retained earnings.** Generally, paid-in capital is not subject to withdrawal. Retained Earnings is the account that at any time is the sum of earnings accumulated since incorporation, minus any losses, and minus all dividends distributed to stockholders. Revenues and expenses are closed into Income Summary and then Income Summary is closed to Retained Earnings. To close net income, debit Income Summary and credit Retained Earnings. To close net loss, debit Retained Earnings and credit Income Summary.

Stockholders have four basic **rights:**

1. to participate in management by **voting** their shares,

2. to receive a proportionate share of any **dividend,**

3. to receive a proportionate share of the remaining assets after payment of liabilities in the event of liquidation, and

4. to maintain a proportionate ownership in the corporation (**preemptive right**).

Stock may be **common or preferred** and have a **par value or no-par value. Par value** is an arbitrary value that a corporation assigns to a share of stock. Different classes of common or preferred stock may also be issued. Each class of common or preferred stock is recorded in a separate general ledger account. Preferred stockholders receive their dividends before common stockholders and take priority over common stockholders in the receipt of assets if the corporation liquidates.

The corporate charter specifies the number of shares a corporation is authorized to issue. The corporation is not required to issue all the stock it is authorized to issue.

If a corporation sells common stock for a cash receipt equal to the par value, the entry to record the transaction is:

Cash	XX	
Common Stock		XX

Par value is usually set low enough so that stock will not be sold below par. A corporation usually sells its common stock for a price above par value, that is, at a premium. The **premium** is also paid-in capital, but is recorded in a separate account called **Paid-In Capital in Excess of Par Value**. A premium is not a gain, income, or profit to the corporation. A corporation cannot earn a profit or incur a loss by buying or selling its own stock. The entry to record stock issued at a price in excess of par value is:

Cash	XX	
Common Stock		XX
Paid-in Capital in Excess of Par — Common Stock		XX

If no-par common stock has no stated value, the entry is the same as for a cash selling price equal to par value (above). Accounting for no-par common stock with a stated value is identical to accounting for par-value stock. When a corporation receives non-cash assets as an investment, the assets are recorded by the corporation at their current market value.

Accounting for preferred stock follows the same pattern as accounting for common stock. The difference is that instead of the word "Common," the word "Preferred" will appear in the titles of the general ledger accounts.

OBJECTIVE 3
Prepare the
stockholders'
equity section of
a corporation
balance sheet.

Preferred stock always appears before common stock in the stockholders' equity section of the balance sheet.

The format of the stockholders' equity section of the balance sheet is:

Stockholders' Equity

Paid-in capital:	
Preferred stock, $ par, number of shares	
authorized, number of shares issued	XX
Paid-in capital in excess of par – preferred stock	XX
Common stock, $ par, number of shares	
authorized, number of shares issued	XX
Paid-in capital in excess of par – common stock	XX
Total paid-in capital	XX
Retained earnings	XX
Total stockholders' equity	XX

To account for the incorporation of an existing proprietorship or partnership, we close the owners' equity accounts of the prior entity and set up the stockholders' equity accounts of the corporation.

If common stock is issued with par value equal to the owners' equity balances, the entry to record the incorporation of the business is:

Owners, Capital	XX	
Common Stock		XX

The costs of organizing a corporation include legal fees, taxes, and any **underwriting** fees associated with selling the stock. These costs are debited to an intangible asset account entitled **Organization Cost**. Organization Cost is amortized over a period which is ordinarily between 5 years (the IRS minimum) and 40 years (the GAAP maximum).

A **dividend** is a distribution of cash to the stockholders of a corporation. A corporation must have Retained Earnings and sufficient cash in order to declare a dividend. A dividend must be declared by the board of directors before the corporation can pay it. Once a dividend has been declared, it is a legal liability of the corporation.

On the **date of declaration** the board also announces the **date of record** and the **payment date**. Those owning the shares on the date of record will receive the dividend. The payment date is the date the dividends are actually mailed.

OBJECTIVE 5
Account for
cash dividends.

When a dividend is declared, this entry is recorded:

Retained Earnings	XX	
Dividends Payable		XX

Dividends Payable is a current liability.

The date of record falls between the declaration date and the payment date and requires no journal entry. The dividend is usually paid several weeks after it is declared. When it is paid, this entry is recorded:

Dividends Payable	XX	
Cash		XX

Preferred stockholders have priority over common stockholders for receipt of dividends. In other words, common stockholders do not receive dividends unless the total declared dividend is sufficient to pay the preferred stockholders first.

Preferred stock usually carries a stated percentage rate or a dollar amount per share. Thus, if par value is $100 per share, 6% preferred stockholders receive a $6 ($100 x 6%) annual dividend. Stockholders holding "$3 preferred" stock would receive a $3 annual cash dividend regardless of the par value of the stock. The dividend to common stockholders will equal:

Common dividend = Total dividend – Preferred dividend

A dividend is passed when a corporation fails to pay an annual dividend to preferred stockholders. Passed dividends are said to be in arrears. **Cumulative preferred stock** continues to accumulate annual dividends until the dividends are paid. Therefore, a corporation must pay all dividends in arrears to cumulative preferred stockholders before it can pay dividends to other stockholders.

Dividends in arrears are not liabilities, but are disclosed in notes to the financial statements. Preferred stock is considered cumulative unless it is specifically labeled as noncumulative. Noncumulative preferred stock does not accumulate dividends in arrears.

Holders of **participating preferred stock** first receive the preferred dividend and then share in any extra common dividend over and above the initial dividend.

Convertible preferred stock can be exchanged by the holder for another class of stock. Suppose you have 200 shares of preferred stock and each share can be converted to 4 shares of common stock. If the market value of 800 shares of common stock exceeds the market value of 200 shares of convertible preferred stock, conversion would be to your advantage.

The entry to record conversion, assuming that the par value of the preferred stock is greater than the par value of the common stock, is:

Preferred stock	XX	
Common stock		XX
Paid-in capital in excess of par –		
common stock (if applicable)		XX

1. Rate of return on total assets = $\dfrac{\text{Net income + Interest expense}}{\text{Average total assets}}$

The return on total assets (or return on assets) measures how successfully the company was in using its (average) assets to earn a profit.

2. Rate of return on common stockholders' equity = $\dfrac{\text{Net income – Preferred dividends}}{\text{Average common stockholders' equity}}$

The denominator, average common stockholders' equity, is equal to total stockholders' equity minus preferred equity.

The rate of return on common stockholders' equity also measures profitability of the company. The return on equity should always be higher than the return on assets.

Market value (market price) is the price at which a person could buy or sell a share of the stock. Daily newspapers report the market price of many publicly traded stocks.

Sometimes preferred stock can be redeemed by the corporation for a stated amount per share. This amount, which is set when the stock is issued, is called **redemption value**.

Preferred stock may also be issued with a liquidation value. This is the amount the corporation agrees to pay preferred stockholders if the company liquidates. Dividends in arrears are added to liquidation value to determine the amount to be paid if liquidation occurs.

Book value is the amount of stockholders' equity per share of stock. If only common stock is outstanding:

$$\text{Book value} = \frac{\text{Total stockholders' equity}}{\text{Number of shares outstanding}}$$

If both preferred and common stock are outstanding, preferred stockholders' equity must be calculated first. If preferred stock has no redemption value, then total preferred equity in the equation below is equal to the balance in Preferred Stock. If preferred stock has a redemption value, then total preferred equity in the equation below equals the total redemption value (redemption value per share x number of preferred shares).

$$\text{Preferred book value} = \frac{\text{Total preferred equity + Dividends in arrears}}{\text{Number of preferred shares outstanding}}$$

$$\text{Common book value} = \frac{\text{Total equity – (Total preferred equity + Dividends in arrears)}}{\text{Number of common shares outstanding}}$$

Because corporations have a distinct legal identity (they have the right to contract, to sue, and be sued—just as individuals have these rights), their income is taxed just like individuals. However, unlike individuals, the amount of tax actually paid will differ from the expense incurred for the period (for individuals, these amounts are generally the same). The difference results from the following:

Income tax expense is calculated by multiplying the applicable tax rate times the amount of pre-tax accounting income as reported on the income statement while income tax payable is calculated by multiplying the applicable tax rate times the amount of taxable

OBJECTIVE 6
Compute two profitability measures: return on assets and return on stockholders' equity.

OBJECTIVE 7
Distinguish among market value, redemption value, liquidation value, and book value.

OBJECTIVE 8
Account for a corporation's income tax.

income as reported on the corporate tax return. Because these results will differ, a third
account, **Deferred Income Tax**, is used to reconcile the entry, as follows:

Income Tax Expense	XX	
Income Tax Payable		XX
Deferred Income Tax		XX
(When the expense is greater than the liability.)		
Income Tax Expense	XX	
Deferred Income Tax	XX	
Income Tax Payable		XX
(When the expense is less than the liability.)		

Test Yourself

All the self-testing materials in this chapter focus on information and procedures that your
instructor is likely to test in quizzes and examinations.

I. Matching *Match each numbered term with its lettered definition.*

1. authorized stock	16. board of directors
2. book value	17. bylaws
3. chairperson of the board	18. charter
4. convertible stock	19. common stock
5. cumulative stock	20. deficit
6. dividends in arrears	21. dividends
7. revenue from donations	22. limited liability
8. liquidation value	23. paid-in capital
9. market value	24. organization cost
10. outstanding stock	25. par value
11. participating preferred stock	26. preemptive right
12. preferred stock	27. premium on stock
13. stockholders' equity	28. proxy
14. retained earnings	29. income tax expense
15. deferred income tax	30. income tax payable

A. an account that reconciles the difference between income tax expense and income tax payable

B. a corporation's capital that is earned through profitable operation of the business

C. a corporation's capital from investments by the stockholders

D. a debit balance in the retained earnings account

E. a group elected by the stockholders to set policy for a corporation and to appoint its officers

F. a legal document that expresses a stockholder's preferences and appoints another person to cast his vote

G. the account created when a corporation receives a gift from a donor who receives no ownership interest in the company

H. a stockholder's right to maintain a proportionate ownership in a corporation

I. an arbitrary amount assigned to a share of stock

J. an elected person on a corporation's board of directors who is usually the most powerful person in the corporation

K. cumulative preferred dividends that the corporation has failed to pay

L. distributions by a corporation to its stockholders

M. means that the most that a stockholder can lose on his investment in a corporation's stock is the cost of the investment

N. owners' equity of a corporation

O. preferred stock whose owners may receive dividends beyond the stated amount or stated percentage

P. preferred stock that may be exchanged by the stockholders, if they choose, for another class of stock in the corporation

Q. preferred stock whose owners must receive all dividends in arrears before the corporation pays dividends to the common stockholders

R. pre-tax accounting income times the tax rate

S. shares of stock in the hands of stockholders

T. stock that gives its owners certain advantages such as the priority to receive dividends and the priority to receive assets if the corporation liquidates

U. the amount that a corporation agrees to pay a preferred stockholder per share if the company liquidates

V. the amount of owners' equity on the company's books for each share of its stock

W. taxable income times the tax rate

X. the constitution for governing a corporation

Y. the costs of organizing a corporation, including legal fees, taxes, fees paid to the state, and charges by promoters for selling the stock

Z. the document that gives the state's permission to form a corporation

AA. the excess of the issue price of stock over its par value

BB. the most basic form of capital stock

CC. the price for which a person could buy or sell a share of stock

DD. the maximum number of shares of stock a corporation may issue

II. Multiple Choice *Circle the best answer.*

1. The corporate board of directors is:
   A. appointed by the state
   B. elected by management
   C. elected by the stockholders
   D. appointed by corporate officers

2. A stockholder has no personal obligation for corporation liabilities. This is called:
   A. mutual agency
   B. limited agency
   C. transferability of ownership
   D. limited liability

3. Stockholders may vote on corporate matters without attending the annual meeting by using a:
   A. proxy
   B. computer
   C. corporate right
   D. substitute

4. A stock certificate shows all of the following except:
   A. additional paid-in capital
   B. stockholder name
   C. par value
   D. company name

5. The ownership of stock entitles common stockholders to all of the following rights except:
   A. right to receive guaranteed dividends
   B. voting right
   C. preemptive right
   D. right to receive a proportionate share of assets in a liquidation

6. When a corporation declares a cash dividend:
   A. liabilities decrease, assets decrease
   B. assets decrease, retained earnings decreases
   C. assets decrease, retained earnings increases
   D. liabilities increase, retained earnings decrease

7. When a corporation pays a cash dividend:
   A. liabilities decrease, assets increase
   B. assets decrease, retained earnings decrease
   C. liabilities decrease, assets decrease
   D. retained earnings decrease, liabilities increase

8. When a company issues stock in exchange for assets other than cash, the assets are recorded at:
   A. market value
   B. original cost
   C. book value
   D. replacement cost

9. Dividends Payable is a(n):
   A. expense
   B. current liability
   C. paid-in capital account
   D. stockholders' equity account

10. Dividends in arrears on preferred stock are reported:
    A. on the balance sheet
    B. as a reduction of retained earnings
    C. on the income statement
    D. as a footnote to the financial statements

III. Completion   *Complete each of the following statements.*

1. Every corporation issues _____ stock.

2. Organization cost is a(n) _____ asset.

3. Preferred stockholders have preference over common stockholders in
   _____ and _____.

4. Dividends are declared by _____.

5. Taxable income times the applicable tax rate equals _____.

6. Stockholders' equity minus preferred equity equals _____.

7. The date of _____ determines who receives the dividend.

8. The date of _____ establishes the liability to pay a dividend.

9. The cost to buy or sell shares of stock is called the _____ value.

10. Corporations come into existence when a _____ is approved by the _____ government.

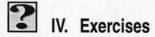 **IV. Exercises**

1. Festival Corporation declared a cash dividend of $1.50 a share on common stock on June 1. The dividend was paid on June 30 to stockholders of record on June 20. Festival Corporation has 75,000 shares of common stock outstanding.

Prepare the journal entry on June 1.

Date	Accounts and Explanation	PR	Debit	Credit

Prepare the journal entry on June 20.

Date	Accounts and Explanation	PR	Debit	Credit

Prepare the journal entry on June 30.

Date	Accounts and Explanation	PR	Debit	Credit

2. The charter of Berger Corporation authorizes the issuance of 25,000 shares of preferred stocks and 300,000 shares of common stock. During the first month of operation, Berger Corporation completed the following stock-issuance transactions:

March 1   Issued 40,000 shares of $1 par common stock for cash of $15 per share.

March 10 Issued 5,000 shares of 6%, no-par preferred stock with a stated value of $50 per share. The issue price was $60 per share.

March 28 Received inventory valued at $25,000 and equipment with a market value of $60,000 in exchange for 2,000 shares of $1 par common stock.

Retained earnings has a balance of $95,000. Prepare the stockholders' equity section of the Berger Corporation balance sheet at the end of the first month.

3. Mullins Muffin Corporation has 2,000 shares of $50 par, cumulative and nonpartici-pating, 8% preferred stock outstanding. There were no dividends in arrears at the end of 19X3, and no dividends were paid in 19X4 or 19X5. Mullins Muffin also has 10,000 shares of $5 par common stock outstanding.

   A. If Mullins Muffin pays a total of $60,000 in dividends in 19X6, how much will each class of stockholders receive?

   B. If Mullins Muffin pays a total of $20,000 in dividends in 19X6, how much will each class of stockholders receive?

4. The balance sheet of Winter House Corporation reports total stockholders' equity of $719,500, consisting of the following:

   a. Redeemable preferred stock; redemption value $22,000; 400 shares issued and outstanding.

   b. Common stockholders' equity, 15,500 shares issued and outstanding.

   c. Winter House has paid preferred dividends for the current year and there are no dividends in arrears.

   Compute the book value per share of the preferred stock and the common stock.

5. Viera-Wood Corporation reported pre-tax income of $176,000 on their income statement and $141,000 taxable income on their tax return. Assuming a corporate tax rate of 35%, present the journal entry to record Viera-Wood taxes for the year.

Date	Accounts and Explanation	PR	Debit	Credit

 V. Critical Thinking

Review the information in Exercise 3, assuming the preferred stock is participating, and recalculate your answers to Questions A and B.

_____

_____

_____

_____

_____

_____

_____

_____

 VI. Demonstration Problems

Demonstration Problem # 1

On January 1, 19X4, California authorized Video Productions, Inc. to issue 50,000 shares of $50 par preferred stock and 250,000 shares of common stock with a $1 par value. During its start-up phase, the company completed the following selected transactions related to its stockholders' equity:

1/4 Paid fees and incorporation taxes of $800 to the State of California to obtain its charter and file all required documents for incorporation. Incurred $4,000 in legal fees related to the incorporation procedure.

1/9 Issued 2,500 shares of common stock to the promoters who organized the corporation. Their fee was $20,000.

1/10 Sold 30,000 shares of common stock at $14 per share.

1/11 Sold 4,000 shares of preferred stock at $65 per share.

1/17 Issued 18,000 shares of common stock in exchange for land valued at $310,000.

1/24   An old building and small parcel of land were donated to the corporation by a town for a future office site that would employ 60 people. The site value was $45,000; the building was worthless.

1/31   Earned a small profit for January and closed the $3,800 credit balance of Income Summary into the Retained Earnings account.

Required

1. Record the transactions in the general journal. See the format below.
2. Post the journal entries into the equity accounts provided on the next page.
3. Prepare the stockholders' equity section of Video Productions, Inc. balance sheet at Jan. 31, 19X4. See the format on the next page.
4. Compute the book value per share of the preferred stock and the common stock. The preferred stock has a liquidation value of $55 per share. No dividends are in arrears. Use the space on the next page.

Requirement 1 (journal entries)

Date	Accounts and Explanation	PR	Debit	Credit

Requirement 2 (postings)

_____|_____	_____|_____

_____|_____	_____|_____

_____|_____

Requirement 3 (stockholders' equity section)

Video Productions, Inc.
Balance Sheet – Stockholders' Equity Section
January 31, 19X4

Requirement 4 (book value per share)

Demonstration Problem #2

Wilcox Corporation has the following capital structure: 5,000 shares of $25 par, 4% preferred stock authorized and outstanding, and 100,000 authorized shares of $2 par common stock, 20,000 shares issued. During years X1 through X4, the corporation declared the following dividends:

X1	$ 0
X2	2,000
X3	40,000
X4	120,000

A.   Assume the preferred stock is noncumulative and nonparticipating, calculate the amount of dividends per share for each share of stock for each year.

Year	Dividend Amount	Preferred	Common

B.   Assume the preferred stock is cumulative and participating, calculate the amount of dividends per share for each year for each share of stock.

Year	Dividend Amount	Preferred	Common

Solutions

I. Matching

1. DD	2. V	3. J	4. P	5. Q	6. K	7. G	8. U	9. CC	10. S
11. O	12. T	13. N	14. B	15. A	16. E	17. X	18. Z	19. BB	20. D
21. L	22. M	23. C	24. Y	25. I	26. H	27. AA	28. F	29. R	30. W

II. Multiple Choice

1. C   Each share of common stock usually gives the stockholder one vote in the election of the board of directors.

2. D   Recall that mutual agency is a characteristic of partnerships not present in corporations. Transferability of ownership is a characteristic that the corporate form of organization simplifies as compared with partnerships. Limited agency has no meaning.

3. A   Most stockholders of large corporations do not attend the annual meeting and exercise their right to vote by using a proxy, a legal document that expresses the stockholders preferences and appoints another person to cast his votes.

4. A   Additional paid-in capital is the excess of the price paid to the corporation over the par value of the stock.

5. A   Dividends represent the distribution of the earnings of the corporation and are not guaranteed.

6. D   The declaration of a dividend reduces Retained Earnings and increases the liability account, Dividends Payable.

7. C   The payment of a cash dividend results in cash being paid to the stockholders to settle the liability created by the declaration of the dividend.

8. A   When capital stock is issued in exchange for non-cash assets, the transaction should be recorded at fair market value.

9. B   The declaration of a dividend by the board of directors creates a current liability.

10. D   Dividends in arrears is not a liability since a dividend must be declared to create a liability. However, dividends in arrears do impair the amount of capital available to common stockholders. Dividends in arrears are usually disclosed by a footnote.

III. Completion

1. common (A corporation may also issue preferred stock, but that is optional.)
2. intangible (Organization cost is an asset that cannot be seen or felt, but future periods will benefit from the amounts expended to organize the corporation.)
3. receiving dividends and in event of a liquidation
4. the board of directors
5. Income Tax Payable
6. common stockholders' equity
7. record
8. declaration
9. market
10. charter; state

IV. Exercises

1.

Date	Accounts and Explanation	PR	Debit	Credit
6/1	Retained Earnings		112,500	
	Dividends Payable			112,500
	(75,000 shares x $1.50)			
6/20	No entry			
6/30	Dividends Payable		112,500	
	Cash			112,500

2.

Stockholders' Equity

Paid-in capital:

Preferred stock, 6%, no-par, $50 stated value, 25,000 shares authorized, 5,000 shares issued	250,000
Paid-in capital in excess of par – preferred stock	50,000
Common stock, $1 par, 300,000 shares authorized, 42,000 shares issued	42,000
Paid-in capital in excess of par – common stock	643,000
Total paid-in capital	985,000
Retained earnings	95,000
Total stockholders' equity	1,080,000

3.

    A.   Preferred: 3 years x 2,000 shares x $50 par x 8% = $24,000

              Common: $60,000 – $24,000 = $36,000

    B.   Preferred: 3 years x 2,000 shares x $50 par x 8% = $24,000

           Since $20,000 is less than the $24,000 preferred stockholders must receive before common stockholders receive anything, all $20,000 goes to the preferred stockholders.

4.

Preferred book value = $\dfrac{\text{Total preferred equity + Dividends in arrears}}{\text{Number of preferred shares outstanding}}$

Preferred book value = $\dfrac{\$22,000 + \$0}{400} = \$55$

Common book value = $\dfrac{\text{Total equity – (Total preferred equity + Dividends arrears)}}{\text{Number of common shares outstanding}}$

Common book value = $\dfrac{\$719,500 – (\$22,000 + \$0)}{15,500} = \$45.00$

5.

Date	Accounts and Explanation	PR	Debit	Credit
	Income Tax Payable		61,600	
	Income Tax Payable			49,350
	Deferred Income Tax			12,250

Income Tax Expense = $176,000 x 35% = $61,600
Income Tax Payable = $141,000 x 35% = $49,350
Deferred Income Tax = $61,600 – $49,350 = $12,250

V. Critical Thinking

When preferred stock is participating, it means the preferred stockholders are entitled to dividends in excess of their stated amount but only after the common stockholders have received a dividend proportionate to the preferred stock. Therefore, your answer to question B does not change as there is no excess. In fact, the $20,000 is not enough to meet the preferred requirement.

However, the amounts for Question A are as follows:

    Preferred: 3 years x 2,000 shares x $50 par x 8% = $24,000

Now allocate an 8% dividend to common, as follows:

    8% x $5 par x 10,000 shares = $4,000 (Note: Common stock is never cumulative!)

Of the total dividend of $60,000, $28,000 ($24,000 to preferred and $4,000 to common) has been allocated. A balance of $32,000 remains ($60,000 – $28,000). The $32,000 is allocated as follows:

    Preferred: 2,000 shares x $50 par = $100,000
    Common: 10,000 shares x $5 par =   50,000
    Total   = $150,000

Preferred gets 100,000/150,000 x $32,000   = $21,333
Common gets 50,000/150,000 x $32,000   =   10,667
Total   = $32,000

Therefore, preferred is given $45,333 ($24,000 + $21,333) and common is given $14,667 ($4,000 + $10,667) or, on a per share basis,

Preferred = $45,333/2,000 = $22.67 per share
Common = $14,667/10,000 = $1.47 per share

VI. Demonstration Problems

Demonstration Problem #1 Solved and Explained

Requirement 1 (journal entries)

1/4   Organization Cost ($800 + $4,000)   4,800
          Cash   4,800
      Legal fees and state incorporation fee to organize the corporation.

Legal fees, taxes, fees paid to the state, and charges by promoters for selling stock are recorded in an account called Organization Cost. This account is an intangible asset and is reported in the balance sheet along with patents, trademarks, and goodwill. It will be amortized over its estimated useful life.

1/9   Organization Cost   20,000
          Common Stock (2,500 shares x $1 par)   2,500
          Paid-in Capital in Excess of Par – Common
             Stock (2,500 shares x $7 premium)   17,500
      Promoter fee for selling stock in corporation.

The sale (or issuance in return for services provided) of common stock at a price in excess of its par value requires the recording of the amount received above par ($7 per share) in a premium account. Note that the firm's paid-in capital increased by $20,000, the total value of the services provided. Both the premium and par value of the stock are part of the paid-in capital.

1/10 Cash   420,000
          Common Stock (30,000 x $1)   30,000
          Paid-in Capital in Excess of Par – Common
             Stock (30,000 x $13)   390,000
      Sold common stock at $14 per share.

The receipt of cash is recorded by debiting Cash for the amount received and crediting Common Stock for the number of shares times the par value of the stock (30,000 x $1). The balance is recorded in the premium account, Paid-in Capital in Excess of Par – Common Stock.

1/11 Cash (4,000 x $65)   260,000
          Preferred Stock (4,000 x $50)   200,000
          Paid-in Capital in Excess of Par – Preferred
             Stock (4,000 x $15)   60,000
      Issued preferred stock at a premium.

Preferred Stock is credited for the shares times par (4,000 x $50). The balance is recorded in the premium account, Paid-in Capital in Excess of Par – Preferred Stock.

1/17	Land	310,000	
	Common Stock (18,000 x $1)		18,000
	Paid-in Capital in Excess of Par – Common		
	Stock ($310,000 – $18,000)		292,000
	To issue common stock at a premium price.		

When a corporation issues stock in exchange for an asset other than cash, it debits the asset received (in this case, land) for its fair market value and credits the capital accounts as it would do if cash were the asset received.

1/24	Land	45,000	
	Revenue from Donations		45,000
	To record land received as a donation from the town.		

The donation of land by a town is a gift. The donor receives no ownership interest in the company in return. The donation is recorded by debiting the asset received at its current market value and by crediting Revenue from Donations. Since the building is worthless, the debit should be made to the Land account. Note that Revenue from Donations is reported on the income statement as Other Revenue.

1/31	Income Summary	3,800	
	Retained Earnings		3,800
	To close Income Summary by transferring net income into Retained Earnings.		

At the end of each month or year, the balance of the Income Summary account is transferred to Retained Earnings. Video Productions, Inc. earned a small profit in January. The closing entry will debit Income Summary (to reduce it to zero) and credit Retained Earnings (increasing stockholders' equity to reflect profitable operations).

Requirement 2 (postings)

Preferred Stock			Common Stock	
	1/11 200,000			1/9 2,500
	Bal. 200,000			1/10 30,000
				1/17 18,000
				Bal. 50,500

Paid-in Capital in Excess of Par – Preferred Stock			Paid-in Capital in Excess of Par – Common Stock	
	1/11 60,000			1/9 17,500
	Bal. 60,000			1/10 390,000
				1/17 292,000
				Bal. 699,500

Retained Earnings	
	1/31 3,800
	Bal. 3,800

Requirement 3 (stockholders' equity section)

Video Productions, Inc.
Balance Sheet – Stockholders' Equity Section
January 31, 19X4

Stockholders' equity:

Preferred stock, 6%, $50 par, 50,000 shares authorized	$ 200,000
Paid-in capital in excess of par – Preferred stock	60,000
Common stock, $1 par, 250,000 shares authorized	50,500
Paid-in capital in excess of par – Common stock	699,500
Total paid-in capital	1,010,000
Retained earnings	3,800
Total stockholders' equity	$1,013,800

Requirement 4 (book value per share)

Preferred:

Liquidation value (4,000 shares x $55)	$220,000
Cumulative dividends in arrears	0
Stockholders' equity allocated to preferred	220,000
Book value per share ($220,000/4,000 shares)	$55.00

Common:

Total stockholders' equity	$1,013,800
Less: Stockholders' equity allocated to preferred	220,000
Stockholders' equity allocated to common	793,800
Book value per share ($793,800/50,500 shares)	$15.72

Calculated as follows:

Date	No. of Shares	Transactions
1/9	2,500	Issued
1/11	30,000	Issued
1/17	18,000	Issued
	50,500 shares	

Demonstration Problem #2 Solved and Explained

A.   Preferred stock is noncumulative and nonparticipating;

Year	Dividend Amount	Preferred	Common
X1	$0	$0	$0
X2	$2,000	$0.40 per share ($2,000/5,000 shares)	$0
X3	$40,000	$1.00 per share 5,000 shares x $25 par x 4%	$1.75 per share $35,000/20,000
X4	$120,000	$1.00 per share 5,000 shares x $25 par x 4%	$5.75 $115,000/20,000

The preferred stock is noncumulative so the shareholders are only entitled to the current years dividend, which is $1/share for a total of $5,000. Any (and all) excess goes to the common shareholders.

B.   The preferred stock is cumulative and participating.

Year	Dividend Amount	Preferred	Common
X1	$0	$0	$0

There are now $5,000 of preferred dividends in arrears.

Year	Dividend Amount	Preferred	Common
X2	$2,000	$0.40 per share ($2,000/5,000 shares)	$0

There are now $8,000 of preferred dividends in arrears.

Year	Dividend Amount	Preferred	Common
X3	$40,000	$6.45 per share	$0.39 per share

First, the preferred shares get their arrearage, which is $1 from X1 and $.60 from X2 for a total of $1.60. Then they get their 4% for X3, a total of $2.60. Now, distribute a 4% dividend to common ($0.08 per share = $2 par x 4%). A total of $14,600 has now been distributed with $25,400 remaining. Total preferred equity is $125,000 (5,000 shares x $25 par) while common equity is $40,000 (20,000 shares x $2 par), or a total of $165,000. Distribute the $25,400 remaining proportional to each class's equity:

Preferred = $125,000/$165,000 x $25,400 = $19,242 or $3.85 per share
Common = $40,000/$165,000 x $25,400 = $6,158 or 31 cents per share

Divide each result by the number of shares and add the results to the $2.60 and $.08 above.

Year	Dividend Amount	Preferred	Common
X4	$120,000	$5.30 per share ($1 + $4.30)	$1.455 ($.08 + $1.375)

Preferred has no arrearage so begin by distributing $1.00 per share to it and a comparable (4%) dividend to common ($.08 each—see above). These two amounts total $6,600 ($5,000 preferred and $1,600 for common). $113,400 remains ($120,000—$6,600). This amount is distributed proportionately, as follows:

Preferred: $125,000/$165,000 x $113,400 = $85,909 or $4.30 per share.
Common: $40,000/$165,000 x $113,400 = $27,491 or $1.375 per share.

Note: Most preferred stock is cumulative and nonparticipating. Neither term has any meaning when applied to common stock.

Chapter 15

Retained Earnings,
Dividends, Treasury Stock,
and the Income Statement

 ## Chapter Overview

*I*n Chapter 14 you learned about capital stock, cash dividends, stock values, corporate income taxes, and other topics related to corporations. We expand those topics in this chapter and learn about stock dividends, treasury stock, and prior
period adjustments, among other topics. The specific learning
objectives for this chapter are:

1. Account for stock dividends
2. Distinguish stock splits from stock dividends
3. Account for treasury stock
4. Report restrictions on retained earnings
5. Identify the elements of a corporation income statement
6. Account for prior-period adjustments
7. Prepare a statement of stockholders' equity

Chapter Review

Retained earnings is the account that holds all the corporation's net incomes less net losses and less dividends declared, accumulated over the life of the business. A deficit or debit balance means net losses have exceeded net incomes. Income Summary is closed to Retained Earnings at the end of each period. Retained Earnings is not a fund of cash.

OBJECTIVE 1
Account for stock dividends.

Corporations declare **stock dividends** instead of cash dividends when they want to conserve cash or reduce the market price per share of stock. Unlike cash dividends, stock dividends are not distributions of corporate assets. A stock dividend is a proportional distribution of the corporation's stock to its stockholders. Thus, a stock dividend affects only a corporation's stockholders' equity accounts; the results of a stock dividend are a reduction in Retained Earnings and an increase in contributed capital, and total stockholders' equity stays the same.

The effect of declaring a stock dividend is to capitalize or transfer a portion of Retained Earnings to Common Stock. In the event of a small stock dividend, a portion of Retained Earnings is also transferred to Paid-in Capital in Excess of Par - Common in order to reflect the excess of market value over par.

A **small stock dividend** is one that comprises less than 25% of shares issued. A **large stock dividend** comprises 25% or more of shares issued. Small stock dividends are accounted for at market value on the declaration date. The entry is:

Retained Earnings	XX	
Common Stock Dividend Distributable		XX
Paid-in Capital in Excess of Par - Common		XX

The amount of the debit to Retained Earnings is equal to:

No. of Shares Outstanding x Dividend % x Market Price Per Share

The credit to Common Stock Dividend Distributable is equal to:

No. of Shares Outstanding x Dividend % x Par Value Per Share

The credit to Paid-in Capital in Excess of Par - Common is equal to:

No. of Shares Outstanding x Dividend % x (Market Price – Par)

On the date of distribution of a small stock dividend, the par value of the issued stock is transferred from the dividend distributable account to the stock account:

Common Stock Dividend Distributable	XX	
Common Stock		XX

Large stock dividends (25% or more than outstanding shares) are usually accounted for at par value. On the declaration date, this entry is recorded:

Retained Earnings	XX	
Common Stock Dividend Distributable		XX

When the dividend is issued, this entry is recorded:

Common Stock Dividend Distributable	XX	
Common Stock		XX

Note that these entries are all based on par rather than on market value.

A **stock split** increases the number of outstanding shares and proportionately reduces the par value of the stock. A stock split affects only the par value of the shares and the number of shares outstanding. No account balances are affected.

OBJECTIVE 2
Distinguish stock splits from stock dividends.

Both stock splits and stock dividends increase the number of shares outstanding and may decrease the market price per share. The difference between stock splits and stock dividends is that a stock split changes the par value of the stock, while a stock dividend leaves the par value of the stock unchanged; also a stock dividend requires a transfer from Retained Earnings while a stock split requires no journal entry.

OBJECTIVE 3
Account for treasury stock.

Stock that a corporation issues and later reacquires is called **treasury stock**. Treasury stock does not receive dividends and has no voting rights. Corporations may acquire treasury stock for distribution within the company, to support or raise the market price, to try to increase net assets by buying low and selling high, or to avoid a takeover. The entry to record the purchase of treasury stock is:

Treasury Stock, Common	XX	
Cash		XX
(Shares x market price per share)		

The debit balance in the Treasury Stock account reduces total stockholders' equity. Note that treasury stock is *not* an asset, and that a corporation *never* incurs a gain or loss by dealing in its own stock.

The purchase of treasury stock does not alter the number of shares authorized or issued. To determine the number of shares outstanding, take the issued number and deduct the number of shares of treasury stock. The result is the number of shares outstanding.

When treasury stock is sold, the entry to record the transaction depends on the relationship between the selling price and the cost of the treasury stock. The entry to record the sale of treasury stock at cost is:

Cash	XX	
Treasury Stock, Common		XX

The entry to record the sale of treasury stock above cost is:

Cash (Shares x Current price)	XX	
Treasury Stock, Common (Shares x Orig. price)		XX
Paid-in Capital from Treasury Stock		XX

The entry to record the sale of treasury stock below cost is:

Cash	XX	
Paid-in Capital from Treasury Stock	XX	
Treasury Stock, Common		XX

Note that when treasury stock is sold, the Treasury Stock account is credited for the original cost of the treasury stock. Any difference between cost and selling price is recorded in the Paid-in Capital from Treasury Stock account. However, this Paid-In Capital Account cannot have a debit balance. If necessary, the Retained Earnings account may be debited if there is no balance in the Paid-In Capital account and the treasury stock's reissue price is less than its original cost.

A corporation that is replacing issues of stock or is liquidating may repurchase its own stock and retire it. Like treasury stock, retired stock produces neither a gain nor a loss.

Many corporations obtain financing through long-term loans. Creditors wish to ensure that funds will be available to repay these loans. Thus, loan agreements frequently **restrict** the amount of retained earnings that can be used to pay dividends and purchase treasury stock. These restrictions are usually reported in notes to the financial statements.

A corporation may also **appropriate** a portion of retained earnings for a specific purpose by debiting Retained Earnings and crediting Retained Earnings Appropriated.

OBJECTIVE 5
Identify the
elements of a
corporation
income
statement.

Investors may want to examine the trend of a company's earnings and the makeup of its net income. Therefore, the corporation income statement starts with income from continuing operations, follows with income or loss from discontinued operations and extraordinary gains and losses, and concludes with earnings per share of common stock. See Exhibit 15-3 in your text.

Continuing operations are expected to continue in the future. Income from continuing operations helps investors make predictions about future earnings. Income from continuing operations is shown both before and after income tax has been deducted.

When a corporation sells one of its segments, the sale is reported in a section of the income statement called **discontinued operations**. Such sales are viewed as one-time transactions, and are therefore not a future source of income. Discontinued operations is separated into an operating component and a disposal component. Each is shown net of its related tax effect. (Review Exhibit 15-4 in your text.)

Extraordinary gains and losses are both unusual and infrequent, and are reported net of tax. Extraordinary items are those that are unusual and not likely to occur in the future. Examples are natural disasters and expropriations of business assets by foreign governments.

On occasion companies change an accounting method. When this occurs, it is difficult for financial statement users to compare consecutive years' activity unless they are informed of changes. For this reason, the cumulative (total) effect of any **changes in accounting principles** is reported separately. This cumulative effect is also reported net of its related tax effect.

Earnings per share of common stock is computed for each source of income or loss: continuing operations, discontinued operations, and extraordinary items.

To compute EPS, divide net income by the weighted average number of shares of common stock outstanding.

Weighted Average = Shares outstanding x Fraction of year that shares were held

Review the example in your text to be certain that you understand how to compute the weighted average number of shares.

When preferred dividends exist, they must be subtracted from income subtotals (income from continuing operations, income before extraordinary items, and net income) in the computation of EPS. Preferred dividends are not subtracted from income or loss from discontinued operations, and they are not subtracted from extraordinary gains and losses.

Dilution must be considered if preferred stock can be converted into common stock because there is the potential for more common shares to be divided into net income. Corporations therefore provide **primary EPS** and **fully-diluted EPS** information.

Prior period adjustments usually occur as the result of correcting an error in a previous accounting period. Prior period adjustments that decrease income from a prior period are debited to Retained Earnings:

Retained Earnings	XX	
Asset or Liability account		XX

Prior period adjustments that increase prior period income are credited to Retained Earnings:

Asset or Liability account	XX	
Retained Earnings		XX

Note that, because of the matching principle, prior period adjustments *never* affect revenue or expense accounts in the current period.

Prior period adjustments net of related tax effect are reported on the Statement of Retained Earnings:

Retained earnings, beginning, as originally reported	$XX
Prior period adjustment (plus or minus)	XX
Retained earnings, beginning, as adjusted	XX
Net income for current year	XX
	XX
Dividends for current year	(XX)
Retained earnings, ending	$XX

A **statement of stockholders' equity** reports the changes in all elements of equity. Therefore, it contains any changes in stock (both preferred and common), retained earnings, and treasury stock. Review Exhibit 15-7 in your text as an example.

Test Yourself

All the self-testing materials in this chapter focus on information and procedures that your instructor is likely to test in quizzes and examinations.

I. Matching *Match each numbered term with its lettered definition.*

1. stock dividend
2. earnings per share (EPS)
3. extraordinary item
4. prior period adjustments
5. small stock dividend
6. appropriation of retained earnings
7. date of record
8. declaration date
9. large stock dividend
10. segment of a business
11. stock split
12. treasury stock
13. deficit
14. dilution
15. price-to-earnings ratio

A. a correction to Retained Earnings for an error of an earlier period
B. gain or loss that is both unusual for the company and nonrecurring
C. a significant part of a business
D. a stock dividend of 25% or more of the corporation's issued stock
E. a stock dividend of less than 25% of the corporation's issued stock
F. a proportional distribution by a corporation of its own stock that affects only the stockholders' equity section of the balance sheet
G. amount of a company's net income per share of its outstanding common stock
H. an increase in the number of outstanding shares of stock coupled with a proportionate reduction in the par value of the stock
I. date on which the board of directors announces the intention to pay a dividend
J. date on which the owners of stock to receive a dividend are identified
K. restriction of retained earnings that is recorded by a formal journal entry
L. the stock that a corporation issues and later reacquires
M. the market price of a share of stock divided by the current earnings per share
N. when a corporation has outstanding equity which may be converted to common stock
O. a debit balance in Retained Earnings

II. Multiple Choice *Circle the best answer.*

1. The correct order for pertinent dividend dates is:
   A. declaration date, record date, payment date
   B. record date, declaration date, payment date
   C. declaration date, payment date, record date
   D. record date, payment date, declaration date

2. Small stock dividends are recorded at:
   A. par value
   B. market value
   C. book value
   D. carrying value

3. The market price of a share of Nafpak Corporation's common stock is $90. If Nafpak declares and issues a 50% stock dividend, the market price will adjust to approximately:
   A. $45
   B. $180
   C. $135
   D. $60

4. The Common Stock Dividend Distributable account is reported in which section of the balance sheet?
   A. current liabilities
   B. long-term liabilities
   C. current assets
   D. stockholders' equity

5. The purchase of treasury stock will:
   A. decrease assets
   B. increase liabilities
   C. increase stockholders' equity
   D. have no effect on stockholders' equity

6. The purchase of treasury stock decreases the number of:
   A. authorized shares
   B. outstanding shares
   C. issued shares
   D. both B and C

7. When a company retires common stock:
   A. the number of shares outstanding decreases
   B. the number of shares issued is unchanged
   C. the number of shares authorized increases
   D. total assets increase

8. An appropriation of retained earnings will:
   A. decrease total retained earnings
   B. increase total retained earnings
   C. not affect total retained earnings
   D. increase total assets

9. All of the following would usually be reported as extraordinary items on the income statement *except:*
   A. a flood loss
   B. the loss on assets taken by a foreign government
   C. the loss from a strike by workers
   D. a tornado loss

10. Prior period adjustments are found on the:
    A. balance sheet
    B. income statement
    C. statement of cash flows
    D. statement of retained earnings

III. Completion *Complete each of the following statements.*

1. Earnings per share is calculated by dividing _____ by
   _____.

2. _____ stock does not receive cash dividends.

3. Extraordinary gains and losses on the income statement are both
   _____ and _____.

4. A corporation may buy treasury stock in order to:

   _____

   _____

   _____

5. Number the following income statement categories to show the order in which they should appear. Use * to indicate those categories that should be shown net of tax.

   _____ A. Discontinued Operations

   _____ B. Continuing Operations

   _____ C. Extraordinary Items

6. The P/E is the abbreviation for the _____.

7. The denominator for the P/E ratio is _____.

8. A _____ occurs when a stockholder returns shares to the corporation and receives more shares in the exchange.

9. An error affecting net income in a previous accounting period is called a _____.

10. A _____ occurs when a stockholder returns shares to the corporation and receives fewer shares in the exchange.

? IV. Exercises

1. A stockholder owns 2,000 shares of Lawlor, Inc. If the company declares and issues a 15% stock dividend, how many shares will the stockholder own?

2. Indicate the effect of each of the following transactions on Assets, Liabilities, Paid-in Capital, and Retained Earnings. Use + for increase, – for decrease, and 0 for no effect.

	Assets	Liabilities	Paid-in Capital	Retained Earnings
A. Declaration of a cash dividend	_____	_____	_____	_____
B. Payment of a cash dividend	_____	_____	_____	_____
C. Declaration of a stock dividend	_____	_____	_____	_____
D. Issuance of a stock dividend	_____	_____	_____	_____
E. A stock split	_____	_____	_____	_____
F. Cash purchase of treasury stock	_____	_____	_____	_____
G. Sale of treasury stock below cost	_____	_____	_____	_____

3. Wholesome Corporation had 400,000 shares of $5 par common stock outstanding on October 1. Prepare journal entries (using the format on the next page) for the following transactions:

10/10 Declared a 15% stock dividend. The market price was $20 per share.

10/30 Issued the stock dividend.

Date	Accounts and Explanation	PR	Debit	Credit

4. Salutary Confinement Corporation had 10,000 shares of $1 par common stock outstanding on April 1. Prepare journal entries for the following transactions:

4/4   Declared a 50% stock dividend. The market price was $60 per share.

4/26   Issued the stock dividend.

Date	Accounts and Explanation	PR	Debit	Credit

5. Prepare journal entries for the following transactions:

2/10   Purchased 800 shares of $5 par treasury stock for $24 per share.

7/1   Sold 500 shares of treasury stock for $28 per share.

12/12   Sold 300 shares of treasury stock for $16 per share.

Date	Accounts and Explanation	PR	Debit	Credit

V. Critical Thinking

Review the facts in Exercise 4 with the following changes:

4/4   Declared a 3-for-2 stock split. The market price was $60 per share.

4/26   Issued the shares.

Present the journal entries for the above stock split.

_____

_____

_____

_____

_____

_____

 VI. Demonstration Problems

Demonstration Problem #1

Digital Data Systems, Inc. reported the following stockholders' equity:

Stockholders' Equity:
   Preferred stock, 8%, $25 par value
      Authorized - 1,000,000 shares
      Issued 150,000 shares $ 3,750,000
   Common stock $1 par value
      Authorized - 5,000,000 shares
      Issued - 800,000 shares   800,000
Paid-in capital in excess of par - common   6,000,000
Retained earnings   6,855,180
Less: Treasury stock, at cost (2,000 common shares)   14,000
Total stockholders' equity $17,419,180

Required (Work space to complete each of these questions is provided on the following pages.)

1.   What was the average issue price per share of the common stock?

2.   What was the average issue price per share of the preferred stock?

3.   Assume that net income for the year was $825,000 and that issued shares of both common and preferred stock remained constant during the year. Journalize the entry to close net income to Retained Earnings. What was the amount of earnings per share?

4.   The current market price of Digital Data Systems, Inc. common stock was 22 1/2 as reported in the Wall Street Journal. Calculate the price-earnings (P/E) ratio.

5.   Journalize the issuance of 10,000 additional shares of common stock at $22.50 per share. Use the same account titles as shown in the problem.

6.   How many shares of common stock are outstanding after the 10,000 additional shares have been sold?

7. How many shares of common stock would be outstanding after the corporation split its common stock 2 for 1? What is the new par value?

8. Journalize the declaration of a stock dividend when the market price of the common stock is $22.50 per share. Consider each of the following stock dividends independently:

    a. Digital Data Systems, Inc. declares a 10% common stock dividend on shares outstanding after the 2-for-1 split.

    b. Digital Data Systems, Inc. declares a 40% common stock dividend on shares outstanding after the 2-for-1 split.

9. Journalize the following treasury stock transactions in the order given:

    a. Digital Data Systems, Inc. purchases 2,500 shares of treasury stock at $25 per share.

    b. One month later, the corporation sells 1,000 shares of the same treasury stock for $27 per share (credit Paid-in Capital from Treasury Stock Transactions).

    c. An additional 1,000 shares of treasury stock acquired in 9a are sold for $22 per share.

10. The board of directors has voted to appropriate $800,000 of retained earnings for future expansion of foreign operations. Prepare the journal entry to record this event.

Work Space

1.

2.

3.

Date	Accounts and Explanation	PR	Debit	Credit

4.

5.

Date	Accounts and Explanation	PR	Debit	Credit

6.

7.

8.

a.

Date	Accounts and Explanation	PR	Debit	Credit

b.

Date	Accounts and Explanation	PR	Debit	Credit

9.

a.

Date	Accounts and Explanation	PR	Debit	Credit

b.

Date	Accounts and Explanation	PR	Debit	Credit

c.

Date	Accounts and Explanation	PR	Debit	Credit

10.

Date	Accounts and Explanation	PR	Debit	Credit

Demonstration Problem #2

Refer to the information in Demonstration Problem #1 and complete the following:

a. Set up the balances in the following T-accounts using the information provided in the stockholders' equity section for Digital Data Systems, Inc.

Preferred Stock

Common Stock

Paid-in Capital in Excess of Par - Common Stock

Retained Earnings

Treasury Stock

b. Post the journal entries from Problem 1's instructions 3, 5, 8a, 9a, 9b, 9c, and 10 to the T-accounts on the previous page.

c. Prepare a current Stockholders' Equity section for Digital Data Systems, Inc.

 Solutions

I. Matching

1. F   2. G   3. B   4. A   5. E   6. K   7. J   8. I

9. D   10. C   11. H   12. L   13. O   14. N   15. M

II. Multiple Choice

1. A   The board of directors declares a dividend on the declaration date, to stockholders of record on the record date, that is paid on the payment date.

2. B   A small stock dividend (less than 25%) is accounted for at market value on the date of declaration.

3. **D** If the market price for one share of pre-dividend stock is $90, then approximately the same market value will apply to the 1.5 shares of post-dividend stock since the stockholder's percentage ownership in the corporation has not changed. $90 / 1.5 shares = $60 per share.

4. **D** Common Stock Dividend Distributable represents the new shares of stock that will be issued as a result of the declaration of the stock dividend.

5. **A** Treasury Stock, a contra stockholders' equity account, is acquired by purchasing it; cash is decreased and stockholders' equity is decreased.

6. **B** Treasury stock has been, and still is, authorized and issued, but it is no longer outstanding.

7. **A** When a company retires stock, it purchases its own outstanding stock and cancels the stock certificates. The number of shares issued and outstanding both decrease.

8. **C** Appropriating retained earnings has no effect on total retained earnings. It merely indicates that some retained earnings are not available for dividends.

9. **C** To be treated as an extraordinary item on the income statement, an event must be unusual and infrequent. In today's business environment, worker strikes are neither, whereas the other listed items can be considered both.

10. **D** By its definition, prior period adjustments are corrections to retained earnings for errors of an earlier period.

III. Completion

1. net income less preferred dividends; weighted average number of common shares outstanding

2. Treasury (For practical purposes, treasury stock is like unissued stock; neither is in the hands of stockholders, nor do they receive dividends.)

3. unusual in nature; infrequent in occurrence (Note that extraordinary items must be both unusual and infrequent.)

4. avoid a takeover; support the market price of the stock; distribute to employees; buy low and sell high

5. A. 2*

   B. 1   Note, however, that income from continuing operations is shown both before and after income taxes.

   C. 3*

6. price-to-earnings ratio

7. earnings per share

8. stock split

9. prior period adjustment

10. reverse split

IV. Exercises

1.

Current holdings	2,000 shares
Dividend (.15 x 2,000)	300 shares
Total	2,300 shares

2.

	Assets	Liabilities	Paid-in Capital	Retained Earnings
A. Declaration of a cash dividend	0	+	0	–
B. Payment of a cash dividend	–	–	0	0
C. Declaration of a stock dividend	0	0	+	–
D. Issuance of a stock dividend	0	0	0	0
E. A stock split	0	0	0	0
F. Cash purchase of treasury stock	–	0	0*	0*
G. Sale of treasury stock below cost	+	0	–*	–**

* While a cash purchase of treasury stock does not affect Paid-in Capital or Retained Earnings, it does reduce stockholders' equity.

** The sale may reduce one or the other, or both. In addition, the sale also increases total stockholders' equity, by the amount of the credit to Treasury Stock.

3.

Date	Accounts and Explanation	PR	Debit	Credit
10/10	Retained Earnings		1,200,000	
	(400,000 x .15 x $20)			
	Common Stock Dividend Distributable			300,000
	(400,000 x .15 x $5)			
	Paid-in Capital in Excess of Par - Common			900,000
	[400,000 x .15 x ($20 – $5)]			
10/30	Common Stock Dividend Distributable		300,000	
	Common Stock			300,000

4.

Date	Accounts and Explanation	PR	Debit	Credit
4/4	Retained Earnings		5,000	
	Common Stock Dividend Distributable			5,000
	(10,000 x .50 x $1)			
4/26	Common Stock Dividend Distributable		5,000	
	Common Stock			5,000

5.

Date	Accounts and Explanation	PR	Debit	Credit
2/10	Treasury Stock (800 x $24)		19,200	
	Cash			19,200
7/1	Cash		14,000	
	Treasury Stock (500 x $24)			12,000
	Paid-in Capital from Treasury Stock Transactions			2,000
	[($28 – 24) x 500]			
12/12	Cash (300 x $16)		4,800	
	Paid-in Capital from Treasury Stock Transactions		2,000	
	Retained Earnings		400	
	Treasury Stock (300 x $24)			7,200

The July 1 transaction resulted in a $2,000 balance in the Paid-in Capital account. This credit balance is not large enough to absorb the entire $2,400 difference between the Treasury Stock cost and its selling price (300 shares x $16). Therefore, the Paid-in Capital account is debited up to its credit balance ($2,000) and the excess is charged against Retained Earnings. The Paid-in Capital account cannot carry a debit balance.

V. Critical Thinking

No journal entries are required when a company declares a stock split. The outstanding shares are returned to the company and replaced with new shares. Each new share will have a par value of 66 2/3 cent ($1 par divided by 3/2). The total paid-in capital remains unchanged, however. The market price will drop proportionately (to $40 per share). Stock splits have the same effect on market price as large stock dividends.

VI. Demonstration Problems

Demonstration Problem #1 Solved and Explained

1. Average issue price of the common stock was $8.50 per share:

Common stock at par ($1 x 800,000 shares)	$ 800,000
Paid-in capital in excess of par - common	6,000,000
Total paid in for common stock	6,800,000
÷ number of issued shares	÷ 800,000
Average issue price	$ 8.50

2. Average issue price of the preferred stock was $25 per share:

Preferred stock at par ($25 x 150,000 shares)	$3,750,000
Paid-in capital in excess of par - preferred	0
Total paid in for preferred stock	3,750,000
÷ number of issued shares	÷ 150,000
Average issue price	$ 25.00

3.
Income Summary	825,000	
Retained Earnings		825,000

   Earnings per share is $0.66:

Net income	$ 825,000
Less: Preferred dividends (150,000 x $2)	300,000
Net income available to common stock	525,000
÷ average outstanding shares (800,000 issued – 2,000 treasury stock)	÷ 798,000
Earnings per share (rounded)	$ 0.66

4.
   The price-earnings ratio is 34 to 1:

Market price of common stock	$22.50
÷ earnings per share	÷ $ 0.66
P/E ratio (rounded to the nearest whole number)	34 times

5.

Cash (10,000 shares x $22.50 selling price)	225,000	
Common Stock (10,000 x $1)		10,000
Paid-in Capital in Excess of Par – Common		215,000
To issue common stock at a premium.		

6. Shares outstanding = 808,000
810,000 shares issued* less 2,000 shares treasury stock = 808,000
* 800,000 shares issued, plus 10,000 shares from answer 5 above.

7. Shares outstanding after 2-for-1 split = 1,616,000:
808,000 shares outstanding immediately before split x 2/1 = 1,616,000 shares outstanding
The new par value of the common stock is $0.50 ($1.00 x 1/2)

8.

a.

Retained Earnings (1,616,000 outstanding shares x 10% x $22.50)	3,636,000	
Common Stock Dividend Distributable (161,600 x $.50)		80,800
Paid-in Capital in Excess of Par - Common (161,600 shares x $22.00 premium)		3,555,200
To declare a 10% stock dividend.		

When a *small stock dividend* occurs (GAAP defines a small dividend as one for less than 25%), Retained Earnings should be capitalized for the *fair market value* of the shares to be distributed (in this case, 3,636,000). Note that 1,616,000 shares were outstanding after answer 7 above, and that the 2-for-1 stock split reduces par value to $0.50 per share. The 10% distribution was for 161,000 shares (1,616,000 x 10% = 161,600).

b.

Retained Earnings (1,616,000 outstanding shares x 40% x $0.50)	323,200	
Common Stock Dividend Distributable		323,200
To declare a 40% common stock dividend.		

When a *large stock dividend* occurs (GAAP defines a large dividend as one for 25% or more), Retained Earnings should be capitalized for the *par value* of the shares issued. 40% x 1,616,000 = 646,400 shares to be distributed x $0.50 par = 323,200.

9.

a.

Treasury Stock (2,500 x $25)	62,500	
Cash		62,500
To purchase 2,500 shares of treasury stock at $27 per share.		

b.

Cash (1,000 x $27)	27,000	
Treasury Stock (1,000 x $25)		25,000
Paid-in Capital from Treasury Stock Transactions		2,000
To sell 1,000 shares of treasury stock at $27 per share.		

c.

Cash (1,000 x $22)	22,000	
Paid-in Capital from Treasury Stock Transactions	2,000	
Retained Earnings	1,000	
Treasury Stock (1,000 x $25)		25,000
To sell 1,000 shares of treasury stock at $22 per share.		

A company does not earn income on the purchase and sale of its own stock. The sale of treasury stock results in an increase to paid-in capital, not income. Paid-in Capital from Treasury Stock Transactions is *credited* for sales in excess of cost (as in answer 9b) and *debited* for a sale below cost. If the account balance is not large enough to cover a sale below cost, it may be necessary to debit Retained Earnings (as in answer 9c).

10. Retained Earnings 800,000
       Retained Earnings Appropriated
       for Future Expansion 800,000
       To appropriate retained earnings for future expansion of foreign operations.

Demonstration Problem #2 Solved and Explained

Requirements a and b

Preferred Stock	
	Bal. 3,750,000

Common Stock	
	Bal. 800,000
	(5) 10,000
	Bal. 810,000

Paid-in Capital in Excess of Par-Common Stock	
	Bal. 6,000,000
	(5) 215,00
	(8a) 3,555,200
	Bal. 9,770,200

Retained Earnings	
(8a) 3,636,000	Bal. 6,855,180
(9c) 1,000	(3) 825,000
(10) 800,000	
	Bal. 3,243,180

Treasury Stock	
Bal. 14,000	(9b) 25,000
(9a) 62,500	(9c) 25,000
Bal. 26,500	

Common Stk. Dividend Distrib.	
	(8a) 80,800

Ret. Earnings Appropriated	
	(10) 800,000

Paid-in Cap. fm. Treasury Stock	
(9c) 2,000	(9b) 2,000

Requirement c

Stockholders' Equity:		
Preferred Stock, 8%, $25 par value		
Authorized - 1,000,000 shares		
Issued 150,000 shares	$3,750,000	
Common Stock, $0.50 par value		
Authorized - 5,000,000 shares		
Issued - 1,620,000 shares	810,000	
Common Stock Dividend Distributable	80,800	
Paid-in Capital in Excess of Par - Common	<u>9,770,200</u>	
Total Paid-in Capital		14,411,000
Retained Earnings		
Appropriated	800,000	
Unappropriated	<u>3,243,180</u>	
Total Retained Earnings		<u>4,043,180</u>
Total Paid-in Capital and Retained Earnings		18,454,180
Less: Treasury stock, at cost (4,500 common shares)		
Total Stockholders' Equity		<u>26,500</u>
		<u>$18,427,680</u>

Explanation:

All the amounts were taken directly from the ending T-account balances. These ending balances are the result of requirements a and b. Remember, the common shares split 2 for 1, thereby reducing the par value of each from $1.00 to $.50. Therefore, the ending balance in the common stock account of $810,000 must represent 1,620,000 shares ($810,000 ÷ $.50 par = 1,620,000 shares). When the common stock dividend of 161,000 shares is distributed, the total number of issued shares will increase to 1,781,600 (1,620,000 + 161,600). The Treasury Stock balance represents the original balance of $14,000 plus the 500 shares remaining from the transactions in entry 9. The total shares are now 4,500 because the original 2,000 shares were affected by the 2-for-1 split in #7 (2,000 x 2 = 4,000 + 500 = 4,500).

Chapter 16

Long-Term Liabilities

Chapter Overview

*I*n Chapters 14 and 15 you learned about topics related to stockholders' equity. Paid-in capital is a major source of funds for corporations. However, companies obtain funds from other sources as well. Hopefully, profitable operations will supply a significant amount of these funds. Corporations can also obtain additional funds by borrowing. In this chapter we examine long-term liabilities, particularly bonds and leases. The specific learning objectives for the chapter are:

1. Account for basic bonds payable transactions by the straight-line amortization method
2. Amortize bond discount and premium by the effective interest method
3. Account for retirement of bonds payable
4. Account for conversion of bonds payable
5. Explain the advantages and disadvantages of borrowing
6. Account for lease transactions

The Chapter 16 Appendix covers these additional objectives:

A1. Compute the future value of an investment made in a single amount
A2. Compute the future value of an annuity-type investment
A3. Compute the present value of a single future amount
A4. Compute the present value of an annuity
A5. Determine the cost of an asset acquired through a capital lease

Chapter Review

OBJECTIVE 1
Account for basic bonds payable transactions by the straight-line amortization method.

Corporations issue **bonds** (typically in $1,000 units) to raise large amounts of money from multiple lenders. Bonds are long-term liabilities. The **bond certificate** states the 1) principal amount, 2) interest rate, 3) maturity date, and 4) dates that interest payments are due (which are generally every six months over the life of the bond).

Term bonds mature at the same time. **Serial bonds** mature in installments over a period of time. Unsecured bonds are called **debentures. Secured bonds** may be referred to as mortgage bonds (i.e., used to purchase a building). The owners of a secured bond have the right to take specified assets of the issuer in the event of default.

Bonds are often traded on bonds markets. Bond prices are quoted at a percentage of their maturity value. For example, a $10,000 bond selling for 97 would sell for $9,700.

Four factors set the **price of bonds:** 1) the length of time until the bond matures, 2) the company's ability to meet interest and principal payments, 3) the maturity value, and 4) the rates of other available investment plans.

A basic understanding of the concept of **present value** is necessary to understand bond prices. When companies borrow money, they have to pay interest on the debt. To the lender, this represents the time value of money. Therefore, a lender would not be interested in giving up $500 today only to receive $500 five years from now. If the lender wants to receive $500 years from now, the question is, how much would the lender be willing to give up today to do so? The answer to the question represents the present value of that future amount ($500). Present value is discussed in detail in the Chapter 16 Appendix.

The price at which bonds are sold is determined by the **contract interest (stated) rate** and the **market (effective) interest rate.** The contract rate is the amount (expressed as a percent) listed on the bond certificate. The market rate is the amount that potential investors are currently demanding for their money. When the contract rate is less than the market rate, the bonds have to be sold at less than their face value (called a **discount**) to attract investors. Conversely, when the contract price is greater than the market rate, the bonds will sell at a **premium.**

The simplest transaction occurs when bonds are issued on an interest date and no difference exists between the stated rate and the market rate. Debit Cash and credit Bonds Payable. When interest is paid, debit Interest Expense and credit Cash. When the bonds mature and are paid off, debit Bonds Payable and credit Cash.

When **bonds are issued between interest dates** (or sold "plus accrued interest"), the corporation collects the accrued interest from the purchaser, in addition to the selling price of the bonds. Debit Cash, credit Bonds Payable, and credit Interest Payable.

The first interest payment is recorded with a debit to Interest Expense, a debit to Interest Payable, and a credit to Cash (for the full 6 months' interest payment).

Interest payments are not prorated based on the issue date. The interest payment to the purchaser is composed of the accrued interest collected from the purchaser plus the interest expense from the sale date to the next interest date; in other words, the full 6 months' interest.

Issuing Bonds at a Discount

If the market interest rate is higher than the stated rate of a bond issue, then the issuer must **sell the bonds at a discount,** that is, at less than face value, in order to attract buyers. The entry debits Cash, debits Discount on Bonds Payable, and credits Bonds Payable.

Discount on Bonds Payable is a contra account to Bonds Payable. On the balance sheet, the discount balance is subtracted from Bonds Payable to equal the book value or carrying amount of the bond issue. The issuer will have to repay the face value of the bonds when they mature. Therefore, a discount is additional interest expense to the issuer.

The discount is allocated to Interest Expense over the life of the bonds, in accordance with the matching principle. **Straight-line amortization** of the discount is computed by dividing the discount by the number of accounting periods during the life of the bonds. On each interest date, the entry to record interest expense debits Interest Expense, credits Cash, and credits Discount on Bonds Payable. Therefore, the total cost to the corporation of borrowing the money is the sum of the interest payments plus the discount.

Issuing Bonds at a Premium

If the market rate is lower than the stated rate of a bond issue, then the issuer can **sell the bonds at a premium**, that is, for more than face value. The entry debits Cash, credits Bonds Payable, and credits Premium on Bonds Payable. **Premium on Bonds Payable** is added to Bonds Payable on the balance sheet to show the book value or carrying amount. The issuer will have to repay only the face value of the bonds when they mature. Therefore, a premium is treated as a reduction of the issuer's interest expense. The premium is allocated to reduce interest expense over the life of the bonds, in accordance with the matching principle.

Straight-line amortization of the premium is computed by dividing the premium by the number of accounting periods during the life of the bonds. On each interest date, the entry to record interest expense debits Interest Expense, debits Premium on Bonds Payable, and credits Cash.

Adjusting entries are prepared to accrue interest and amortize the discount or premium for the period from the last interest date to the end of the accounting period. Debit Interest Expense, credit Interest Payable, and either debit Premium on Bonds Payable or credit Discount on Bonds Payable.

OBJECTIVE 2
Amortize bond discount and premium by the effective interest method.

GAAP requires that discounts and premiums be amortized using the **effective interest method.** However, when the difference between the straight-line and effective interest methods is not material, either method may be used.

The objective of the effective interest method is to match interest expense as a constant percentage of the changing carrying value of the bonds rather than as a constant amount each period. The effective interest rate is the market rate in effect when the bonds are sold. Three steps are followed when using the effective interest method:

1. Interest expense is calculated by multiplying the effective interest rate by the carrying value of the bonds. (This amount changes each period.)
2. The cash paid to bondholders is calculated by multiplying the stated interest rate by the principal amount of the bonds. (This amount is the same each period.)
3. The difference between the interest expense and the cash paid is the amount of discount or premium amortized.

Remember that amortization of bond discount or premium will change the carrying value of the bonds before the next calculations are made. If a premium is amortized, the carrying value of the bonds will decrease; if a discount is amortized, the carrying value will increase.

Carefully study Exhibits 16-5 and 16-6 in your text in order to understand the effective interest method.

As with straight-line amortization, adjusting entries must be prepared for a partial period from the last interest date to the end of the accounting period in order to accrue interest and amortize bond discount or premium. Debit Interest Expense, credit Interest Payable, and either debit Premium on Bonds Payable or credit Discount on Bonds Payable.

OBJECTIVE 3
Account for the retirement of bonds payable.

Sometimes corporations retire bonds prior to the maturity date. **Callable bonds** may be retired at the option of the issuer. **Noncallable bonds** may be bought back on the open market and retired. If interest rates have dropped, the issuer may compare the book value of the bonds to the market price to decide whether to retire the bonds. When bonds are retired and the bonds were initially sold at either a premium or discount, the entry to retire the bonds must also remove the unamortized premium or discount from the books. A **gain (or loss) on retirement** results when the carrying value of the bonds is greater (or lesser for a loss) than the cash paid for the bonds. Any gain or loss on the retirement of bonds payable is an **extraordinary item** according to GAAP.

OBJECTIVE 4
Account for conversion of bonds payable.

Bonds that can be converted into common stock are called **convertible bonds.** Investors will convert the bonds when the stock price of the issuing company increases to the point that the stock has a higher market value than the bonds. The entry transfers the bond carrying amount into stockholders' equity:

Bonds Payable	XX	
Premium on Bonds Payable (if applicable)	XX	
Discount on Bonds Payable (if applicable)		XX
Common stock		XX
Paid-in Capital in Excess of Par - Common		XX

Note that both Premium and Discount cannot appear in the same entry. Also, there will never be a gain or loss recorded on the conversion of bonds. The credit to Paid-in Capital is the difference between the carrying value of the bonds (Bonds Payable + Premium or Bonds Payable – Discount) and the par value of the shares issued.

OBJECTIVE 5
Explain the advantages and disadvantages of borrowing.

Advantages of borrowing:

1. Borrowing does not affect ownership; bondholders are creditors, not stockholders.
2. Interest on debt is deductible for tax purposes.
3. Trading on the equity usually increases EPS. This means that the corporation earns a return on the borrowed funds that is greater than the cost of the borrowed funds.

Disadvantages of borrowing:

1. High interest rates.
2. Interest on debt must be paid; dividends on stock are optional.

A **lease** is a rental agreement in which the tenant (lessee) agrees to make rent payments to the property owner (lessor) in exchange for the use of some asset. **Operating leases** are usually short-term or cancelable. To account for an operating lease, the lessee debits Rent Expense and credits Cash for the amount of the lease payment.

Capital leases are long-term and noncancelable. Accounting for capital leases is similar to accounting for the purchase of an asset. Debit the asset leased, credit Cash for the initial payment, and credit Lease Liability for the present value of future lease payments. Because the leased asset is capitalized, it must be depreciated. Leased assets are usually depreciated over the term of the lease. Debit Depreciation Expense and credit the asset's Accumulated Depreciation account.

At year-end, interest is accrued on the lease liability. Debit Interest Expense and credit Lease Liability. Lease payments are recorded with a debit to Lease Liability and a credit to Cash.

FASB 13 sets the **guidelines for capital leases.** Only one of the following criteria is required to be present to classify the lease as capital:

1. The lease transfers title (ownership) to the lessee at the end of the lease term.
2. The lease contains a bargain purchase option.
3. The term of the lease is 75% or more of the estimated useful life of the asset.
4. The present value of the lease payments is 90% or more of the market value of the leased asset.

Operating leases are defined by exception; i.e., operating leases are only those that fail to meet all four of these criteria.

In the past, companies were attracted to operating leases because they were not required to list the lease as a liability on the balance sheet—in other words, the company had the use of an asset (or service) without the related debt showing (called **off-balance-sheet financing**). This practice has been curtailed.

Pensions and **post-retirement benefits** are other types of liabilities found on balance sheets. **Pensions** are compensation paid to employees after retirement, usually based on a variety of factors, including length of service. Companies are required to report the present value of promised future pension payments to retirees. If the plan assets exceed this amount, the plan is overfunded. Conversely, the fund could be underfunded if assets are less.

In addition to pensions, companies are required to report the present value of future payments to retirees for other benefits. The largest of these is health care. At the end of each period, companies accrue the expense and the liability of post-retirement benefits based on information about the current work force.

Chapter 16 Appendix

Time Value of Money: Future Value and Present Value

 Appendix Overview

OBJECTIVE A1
Compute the future value of an investment made in a single amount.

Because you can earn interest on your money over time, the value of invested funds is greater in the future than it is today. This refers to the **time value of money.** To determine what a **future value** will be, you simply apply an interest rate to the amount of your investment and calculate the amount of interest. Add this result to your original amount and the sum becomes the future value at the end of one interest period. Repeat this process for additional interest periods, remembering to add in the interest each time. Therefore, there are three factors involved in determining a future value: 1) the amount of the original investment, 2) the length of time, and 3) the interest rate. Obviously the longer the time, the more calculations are involved. Fortunately, mathematical tables are available to ease your task. Review Exhibit 16A-2 carefully. This is the table used to determine a future value of a single investment, again assuming time and interest rate.

OBJECTIVE A2
Compute the future value of an annuity-type investment.

Instead of investing a single amount for a specific period, you might wish to invest multiple amounts over time. This is an example of an **annuity-type investment.** In other words, you invest identical amounts for several years—what will the future value of these multiple investments be? Of course, you could calculate each individually and add the results, or you can consult mathematical tables, which do the multiple calculations for you. Review Exhibit 16-A3 carefully. This is the table used to determine a future value of multiple investments, again assuming time and interest rate. This table is used to answer questions like "If I start setting aside (investing) $500 each year for the next 10 years, what will it be worth assuming I can invest this money at 8%?" Exhibit 16-A3 shows the value 14.487 at the intersection of 10 years and 8%. Multiply this value by your annual investment ($500) and the result is $7,243.50.

OBJECTIVE A3
Compute the present value of a single future amount.

Another way to look at present and future values is to begin with the future value and work backwards. In other words, in order to have X amount sometime in the future, how much would one need to set aside today? Again, assumptions need to be made about the time and the interest rate (this is always true).

As with the preceding discussions, you could calculate the result manually, but the longer the period of time, the more calculations you would have to complete. As before, mathematical tables are available to use. Study Exhibit 16A-6 carefully.

Rather than determining the present value of a single amount, you may be interested in the **present value of an annuity-type investment.** In other words, what is the present value of an investment that will give you the same fixed amount over a number of periods? As with earlier discussions, this value can be calculated manually, but it is time-consuming. Once again, tables are available to simplify the process. Study Exhibit 16A-7 carefully.

IMPORTANT: BEFORE PROCEEDING, BE CERTAIN YOU UNDERSTAND IN WHICH CIRCUMSTANCES YOU USE WHICH TABLE. This distinction is vital to understanding the topics that follow.

This chapter examines long-term liabilities, primarily bonds payable. What is a bond? It is a way for a company to borrow funds. When a company issues a bond, what happens? The company promises to pay the face value of the bond at maturity and, during the life of the bond, the company also promises to pay a fixed amount of interest periodically. The face value at maturity is a single value, whereas the interest payments are like an annuity. Therefore, when a company issues bonds, it needs to know what price should be asked (remember, bond prices are quoted as percentages of face value) in order to attract investors. To determine this price, consult the appropriate tables—in this case, 16A-6 and 16A-7 in your text. Using the market rate of interest, the first table will give you the present value of a future single amount, the second the present value of an annuity. Sum the results and you have an estimate of the market price of the bonds. The market rate of interest is used because this is the rate potential investors will demand for the use of their funds. If the market rate is higher than the contract (or stated) rate of interest, the bonds will have to be sold at a discount to attract investors. Conversely, if the market rate is lower than the contract rate, the bonds will sell at a premium.

OBJECTIVE A5
Determine the
cost of an asset
acquired
through a
capital lease.

Earlier you learned about capital leases. When a company acquires an asset with a capital lease, the company needs to record the asset at "cost." What is the cost when the lease requires payments over the life of the lease? Using present value tables, specifically Exhibit 16A-7, you can value the asset because the fixed payments over the life of the lease are like annuities, and you want to determine the present value (i.e., cost) of all those payments.

Test Yourself

All the self-testing materials in this chapter focus on information and procedures that your instructor is likely to test in quizzes and examinations. *Questions followed by the letter "A" refer to topics in the chapter appendix.*

I. Matching   *Match each numbered term with its lettered definition.*

1. bond discount
2. bond premium
3. callable bonds
4. contract interest rate
5. debentures
6. lessee
7. stated interest rate
8. market interest rate
9. registered bonds
10. trading on the equity
11. off-balance-sheet financing
12. bond indenture

13. bonds payable
14. capital lease
15. convertible bonds
16. lease
17. lessor
18. mortgage
19. operating lease
20. serial bonds
21. term bonds
22. underwriter
23A. annuity

A. a rental agreement in which the tenant agrees to make rent payments to the property owner in exchange for the use of the asset
B. another name for the contract interest rate
C. acquisition of assets or services with debt that is not reported on the balance sheet
D. bonds for which the owners receive interest checks from the issuing company
E. bonds that may be exchanged for the common stock of the issuing company at the option of the investor
F. bonds that mature in installments over a period of time
G. bonds that the issuer may pay off at a specified price whenever the issuer desires
H. bonds that all mature at the same time for a particular issue
I. borrower's promise to the lender to transfer the legal title to certain assets if the debt is not paid on schedule
J. contract under which bonds are issued

K.   earning more income than the interest on the borrowed amount

L.   excess of a bond's maturity (par) value over its issue price

M.   excess of a bond's issue price over its maturity (par) value

N.   groups of notes payable issued to multiple lenders, called bondholders

O.   interest rate that investors demand in order to lend their money

P.   a lease agreement that meets any one of four special criteria

Q.   organization that purchases bonds from an issuing company and resells them to clients, or sells the bonds for a commission and agrees to buy all unsold bonds

R.   the property owner in a lease agreement

S.   the tenant in a lease agreement

T.   the interest rate that determines the amount of cash interest the borrower pays

U.   unsecured bonds backed only by the good faith of the borrower

V.   usually a short-term or cancelable rental agreement

W.   a fixed amount paid (or received) over a number of periods

 ## II. Multiple Choice *Circle the best answer.*

1.   A $10,000 bond quoted at 101 1/8 has a market price of:

   A. $10,000

   B. $10,112.50

   C. $10,011.25

   D. $101.25

2.   All of the following affect the market price of bonds except:

   A.   bond holder's credit rating

   B.   bond issuer's credit rating

   C.   market interest rate

   D.   length of time to maturity

3A. The present value of a future amount does not depend on the:

   A.   interest rate

   B.   convertibility of a bond

   C.   amount of the future payment

   D.   length of time until the future payment is made

4.   The interest rate demanded by investors in order to lend their money is the:

   A.   contract rate

   B.   issue rate

   C.   effective rate

   D.   stated rate

5. The premium on a bond payable:
   A. increases the interest expense only in the year the bonds are sold
   B. increases the interest expense over the life of the bonds
   C. reduces interest expense only in the year the bonds mature
   D. is a liability account that is amortized (to expense) over the life of the bonds

6. The book value of Bonds Payable on the balance sheet equals:
   A. Bonds Payable + Discount on Bonds Payable or + Premium on Bonds Payable
   B. Bonds Payable − Discount on Bonds Payable or − Premium on Bonds Payable
   C. Bonds Payable + Discount on Bonds Payable or − Premium on Bonds Payable
   D. Bonds Payable − Discount on Bonds Payable or + Premium on Bonds Payable

7. When bonds are issued at a premium, their carrying amount:
   A. decreases from issuance to maturity
   B. increases from issuance to maturity
   C. remains constant over the life of the bonds
   D. decreases when the market interest rate increases

8. Gains and losses from early retirement of debt are reported:
   A. as operating gains and losses on the income statement
   B. as increases or decreases to Retained Earnings on the statement of retained earnings
   C. as extraordinary items on the income statement
   D. in the footnotes to the financial statements

9. When a convertible bond is exchanged for common stock:
   A. stockholders' equity increases
   B. liabilities increase
   C. revenues increase
   D. expenses increase

10. Which of the following is not reported on the balance sheet?
    A. capital lease
    B. pension liabilities
    C. post-retirement benefit liabilities
    D. operating leases

III. Completion *Complete each of the following statements.*

1. When the market interest rate is _____ than the stated rate, bonds will sell at a premium.

2. When the premium on bonds payable is reduced, the book value of bonds payable _____.

3. Gains or losses on early retirement of debt are _____ and reported separately on the income statement.

4. The liability to make _____ lease payments is not reported on the balance sheet.

5. If a lease transfers ownership of assets at the end of the lease term, the lease is a(n) _____ lease.

6. The _____ method of interest amortization results in the same amount of discount/premium amortization for identical periods of time.

7. Accruing pension and post-retirement benefit liabilities is an example of the _____ principle.

8 When the market interest rate is greater than the stated rate, the bonds will sell at a _____.

9. Convertible bonds give the _____ the right to convert the bonds to common stock.

10. When the effective interest method of amortization is used, the total amount of interest expense over the life of the bonds is _____.

11A. A(n) _____ is a fixed sum of money received over a number of periods.

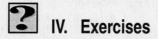

IV. Exercises

1. ABC Inc. issued $1,000,000 in 15-year bonds with a stated interest rate of 8%. The bonds were issued at par on April 1, 1996. Interest is paid October 1 and April 1.

   Give the journal entries for:
   A. Issuance of the bonds on April 1, 1996.
   B. Payment of interest on October 1, 1996.
   C. Maturity payment of bonds on April 1, 2011.

	Date	Accounts and Explanation	Debit	Credit
A.				
B.				
C.				

2.   Minifield Corporation issued $500,000 in 7-year bonds with a stated interest rate of 8%. The bonds were sold on January 1, 1996 for $477,956 to yield 9%. Interest is paid July 1 and January 1. Minifield uses the effective interest method to amortize Discount on Bonds Payable. (Assume a December 31 year-end.)

Record the journal entries for:

A.   Issuance of bonds on January 1, 1996.

B.   Payment of interest on July 1, 1996.

C.   Accrual of interest and related amortization on December 31, 1996 (year-end)

D.   Payment of interest on January 1, 1997

E.   Maturity payment of bonds on January 1, 2003.

	Date	Accounts and Explanation	Debit	Credit
A.				
B.				
C.				
D.				
E.				

3. Langston Corporation issued $500,000 in 7-year bonds with a stated interest rate of 8%. The bonds were sold on January 1, 1996 for $477,956 to yield 9%. Interest is paid July 1 and January 1. Langston uses the straight-line method to amortize Discount on Bonds Payable. (Assume an October 31 year-end.)

Record the journal entries for:
A. Issuance of bonds on January 1, 1996.
B. Payment of interest on July 1, 1996.
C. Accrual of interest and related amortization on October 31, 1996 (year-end)
D. Payment of interest on January 1, 1997
E. Maturity payment of bonds on January 1, 2003.

	Date	Accounts and Explanation	Debit	Credit
A.				
B.				
C.				
D.				
E.				

4. Tucker Corporation issued $500,000 in 7-year bonds with a stated interest rate of 8%. The bonds were sold on January 1, 1996 for $558,420 to yield 6%. Interest is paid July 1 and January 1. Tucker uses the effective interest method to amortize Premium on Bonds Payable. (Assume a December 31 year-end.)

Record the journal entries for:

A. Issuance of bonds on January 1, 1996.

B. Payment of interest on July 1, 1996.

C. Accrual of interest and related amortization on December 31, 1996 (year-end)

D. Payment of interest on January 1, 1997

E. Maturity payment of bonds on January 1, 2003.

	Date	Accounts and Explanation	Debit	Credit
A.				
B.				
C.				
D.				
E.				

V. Critical Thinking

Review the information in Exercises 3 and 4 above and assume, in each case, that each $1,000 bond is convertible, at the option of the holder, into 31.25 shares of the corporation's common stock. Determine when an investor should seriously consider exercising the option to convert the bonds to stock.

_____

_____

_____

_____

_____

_____

_____

_____

_____

 ## VI. Demonstration Problems

Demonstration Problem #1

On February 1, 1995, Infomercial, Inc. issued $50,000,000 of 8% bonds at 102 3/4. The market rate on that date was approximately 7%. The bonds mature in 20 years. Interest is paid each July 31 and January 31.

Required (Work space provided on the next page.)

1. Record the issuance of the bonds.

2. Record the July 31, 1995 interest payment and straight-line amortization on premium or discount.

3. Accrue interest and amortize premium or discount as of December 31, 1995, the last day of the reporting year for Infomercial, Inc. Use straight-line amortization.

4. Show how the bonds would be reported on the balance sheet at the year end, 1995.

5. Record the payment of interest and amortization of the premium or discount on January 31, 1996. Use straight-line amortization.

Date	Accounts and Explanation	Debit	Credit
1.			
2.			
3.			

4.			

Date	Accounts and Explanation	Debit	Credit
5.			

Demonstration Problem #2

McClain's Corporation has outstanding an issue of 10% callable bonds that mature in 2006. The bonds were dated January 1, 1996, and pay interest each July 1 and January 1. Additional bond data:

a. Fiscal year-end for McClain Corporation: September 30.

b. Maturity value of the bonds: $500,000.

c. Contract interest rate: 10%.

d. Interest is paid 5% semiannually, $25,000 ($500,000 x .05)

e. Market interest rate at time of issue: 9% annually, 4.5% semiannually.
   Issue price: 106.

Required

1. Complete the interest method amortization table through January 1, 1998. Round pennies to the nearest dollar. You may use the Summary Problem in Chapter 16 of the text as a guide. See the form below.

2. Using the amortization table that you have completed and the form on the next page, record the following transactions:

    a.   Issuance of the bonds on January 1, 1996.

    b.   Payment of interest and amortization of premium on July 1, 1996.

    c.   Accrued interest and amortization of premium as of September 30, 1996.

    d.   Payment of interest and amortization of premium on January 1, 1997.

    e.   Retirement of the bonds on January 2, 1997. Callable price of bonds was 108.

Requirement 1

	A	B	C	D	E
Semi-annual Interest Date	Interest Payment (5% of Maturity Value)	Interest Expense (4.5% of Preceding Bond Carrying Value)	Premium Amortiza-tion (A – B)	Premium Account Balance (D – C)	Bond Carrying Value ($500,000 + D)
___	___	___	___	___	___
___	___	___	___	___	___
___	___	___	___	___	___
___	___	___	___	___	___
___	___	___	___	___	___
___	___	___	___	___	___

Requirement 2

Date	Accounts and Explanation	Debit	Credit
a.			
b.			
c.			
d.			
e.			

Solutions

I. Matching

1. L   2. M   3. G   4. T   5. U   6. S   7. B   8. O   9. D   10. K
11. C   12. J   13. N   14. P   15. E   16. A   17. R   18. I   19. V   20. F
21. H   22. Q   23A. W

II. Multiple Choice

1. B   The number 101 1/8 means 101.125% (or 1.01125) of the face value: $10,000 x 101.125% = $10,112.50.

2. A   Since anyone may be a bondholder, it does not make sense that a bondholder's credit rating would affect the market price of the bond. All the other listed items do affect the market price of the bond.

3A. B   Interest rate, amount of payment, and length of time until payment all affect present value whether or not the bond is convertible.

4. C   Effective rate of interest and market rate of interest are synonymous.

5. D   Amortization of the premium on bonds payable serves to reduce the recorded amount of interest expense over the life of the bonds.

6. D   The book value or carrying amount of a bond is equal to the face amount of the bond minus the unamortized discount or plus the unamortized premium.

7. A   The carrying amount of a bond is the face amount of the bond plus (minus) unamortized premium (discount). Since the balance of the premium (discount) account is amortized over the life of the bond, it moves toward zero. Accordingly, the carrying amount of bonds issued at a premium (discount) decreases (increases) over time.

8. C   GAAP identifies gains and losses on early retirement of debt as an extraordinary item.

9. A   The conversion of a bond to common stock converts a liability to stockholders' equity, which increases stockholders' equity.

10. D   Of the items listed, only "operating lease" is not reported on the balance sheet. Operating leases are generally short-term rental agreements that transfer none of the rights of ownership.

III. Completion

1. lower (When market rate > stated rate, then discount; when market rate < stated rate, then premium)

2. decreases (The book value or carrying value amount of a bond is equal to the face amount of the bond plus [minus] the unamortized premium [discount].)

3. extraordinary (Though they do not meet the normal "infrequent and unusual" requirement for other extraordinary items, GAAP specifies that such gains and losses are extraordinary items.)

4. operating (Operating leases are normally short-term and transfer none of the rights of ownership to the lessee. Accordingly, neither an asset nor a liability is recorded for such leases.)

5. capital (Capital leases require that the lessee record the leased property as an asset and the obligation to make future lease payments as a liability.)

6. straight-line (This method divides the amount of the discount/premium by the number of time periods, resulting in the same figure each period.)

7. matching

8. discount (because the lender expects a greater return on the loan than the stated rate provides)

9. lender (not the borrower; convertibility make the bonds more attractive to prospective lenders because of the potential for greater returns)

10. a constant percentage (as compared with the straight-line method, where the amount of discount/premium is constant). The effective rate is required, although the straight-line method can be used if the difference between the results of the two methods is not material.

11A. annuity

IV. Exercises

1.	A.	Cash	1,000,000	
		Bonds Payable		1,000,000
	B.	Interest Expense ($1,000,000 x.08 x 6/12)	40,000	
		Cash		40,000
	C.	Bonds Payable	1,000,000	
		Cash		1,000,000
2.	A.	Cash	477,956	
		Discount on Bonds Payable	22,044	
		Bonds Payable		500,000
	B.	Interest Expense (477,956 x .09 x 6/12)	21,508	
		Cash (500,000 x .08 x 6/12)		20,000
		Discount on Bonds Payable		1,508

New book value of bonds = Bonds Payable – Discount on Bonds Payable
= 500,000 – (22,044 – 1,508) = 479,464

C. Interest Expense (479,464 x .09 x 6/12)   21,576
    Interest Payable (500,000 x .08 x 6/12)   20,000
    Discount on Bonds Payable   1,576

New book value of bonds = Bonds Payable – Discount on Bonds Payable
       = 500,000 – (20,536 – 1,576) = 481,040

D. Interest Payable   20,000
    Cash   20,000

E. Bonds Payable   500,000
    Cash   500,000

Note that after the last interest payment, the account Discount on Bonds Payable has a zero balance.

3. A. Cash   477,956
   Discount on Bonds Payable   22,044
    Bonds Payable   500,000

B. Interest Expense (20,000 + 1,575)   21,575
    Cash (500,000 x .08 x 6/12)   20,000
    Discount on Bonds Payable   1,575
     (22,044/14 interest payments)

C. Interest Expense (13,333 + 1,050)   14,383
    Interest Payable (500,000 x .08 x 4/12)   13,333
    Discount on Bonds Payable (22,044/14 x 2/3)   1,050
  Note: In this exercise, the year-end is October 31, not December 31.

D. Interest Expense [(20,000 – 13,333) + 525]   7,192
   Interest Payable   13,333
    Cash (500,000 x .08 x 6/12)   20,000
    Discount on Bonds Payable (22,044/14 x 1/3)   525

E. Bonds Payable   500,000
    Cash   500,000

4. A. Cash   558,420
    Bonds Payable   500,000
    Premium on Bonds Payable   58,420

B. Interest Expense (558,420 x .06 x 6/12)   16,753
   Premium on Bonds Payable   3,247
    Cash (500,000 x .08 x 6/12)   20,000

New book value of bonds = Bonds Payable + Premium on Bonds Payable
      = 500,000 + (58,420 – 3,247) = 555,173

C. Interest Expense (555,173 x .06 x 6/12)   16,655
   Premium on Bonds Payable   3,345
    Cash (500,000 x .08 x 6/12)   20,000

New book value of bonds = 500,000 + (55,173 – 3,345) = 551,828

| D. | Interest Payable | 20,000 | |
| | Cash | | 20,000 |

| E. | Bonds Payable | 500,000 | |
| | Cash | | 500,000 |

Note that after the last interest payment, the account Premium on Bonds Payable has a zero balance.

V. Critical Thinking

If each $1,000 bond can be converted into 31.25 shares of common stock, then a quick calculation indicates an investor should seriously think about converting when the market price of the stock reaches $32 per share ($1,000 divided by 31.25 shares). However, this assumes the investor paid face value for the bonds. In Exercise 3, investors purchased the bonds at a discount of 95.59% of face value or $955.91 for each $1,000 bond. Therefore, investors in Langston's bonds could consider converting at a lower price of approximately $30.59 per share ($955.91 divided by 31.25). In Exercise 4, the investors paid a premium for the bonds because they were purchased at 111.68% of face value ($558,420 divided by $500,000). These investors would not be interested in converting until the price rose to $35.74 ($1,116.80 divided by 31.25 shares).

VI. Demonstration Problems

Demonstration Problem #1 Solved and Explained

(Amounts rounded to nearest dollar)

Requirement 1

2/1/1995	Cash	51,375,000	
	Bonds Payable		50,000,000
	Premium on Bonds Payable		1,375,000
	(Selling price = 102 3/4% x $50,000,000 = $51,375,000)		

Requirement 2

7/31/1995	Interest Expense	1,965,625	
	Premium on Bonds Payable	34,375	
	Cash		2,000,000
	(Interest = $50,000,000 x 8% x 6/12 = $2,000,000)		

The straight-line method of interest amortization ignores the market rate of interest at the time the bonds are sold. To amortize, you divide the amount of the premium (or discount) by the total number of interest payments.

Requirement 3

12/31/1995	Interest Expense	1,638,021	
	Premium on Bonds Payable	28,646	
	Interest Payable		1,666,667
	(Interest Payable = $50,000,000 x .08 x 5/12 = $1,666,667)		
	(Premium on Bonds Payable = $1,375,000/20 x 5/12 = $28,646)		

Requirement 4

Bonds Payable		50,000,000	
Premium on Bonds Payable		1,311,979	51,311,979

(Premium on Bonds Payable = $1,375,000 − $34,375 − $28,646 = $1,311,979)

Requirement 5

1/31/1996	Interest Expense	327,604	
	Premium on Bonds Payable	5,729	
	Interest Payable	1,666,667	
	Cash		2,000,000

This may seem a difficult transaction, but it is not if you separate it and THINK. The bondholders are owed $2,000,000. This is your credit to cash ($50,000,000 x .08 x 6/12). In Requirement 3, you accrued $1,666,667 as Interest Payable. This is your debit to the same account. Also in Requirement 3, you recorded five months of premium amortization ($28,646). You now need to amortize one additional month, or $5,729 (six months' amortization is $34,375 - see Requirement 2; therefore, one month's amortization is $34,375 / 6 = $5,729). The debit to Interest Expense reconciles the entry.

Demonstration Problem #2 Solved and Explained

Requirement 1

	A	B	C	D	E
Semi-annual Interest Date	Interest Payment (5% of Maturity Value)	Interest Expense (4.5% of Preceding Bond Carrying Value)	Premium Amortization (A − B)	Premium Account Balance (D − C)	Bond Carrying Value ($500,000 + D)
1/1/96				30,000	530,000
7/1/96	25,000	23,850	1,150	28,850	528,850
1/1/97	25,000	23,798	1,202	27,648	527,648
7/1/97	25,000	23,744	1,256	26,392	526,392
1/1/98	25,000	23,688	1,312	25,080	525,080

As the premium is amortized, the carrying amount moves toward the maturity value.

Requirement 2

a.	1/1/96	Cash ($500,000 x 106/100)	530,000	
		Premium on Bonds Payable		30,000
		Bonds Payable		500,000
		To issue 10%, 10-year bonds at premium.		

The bonds were sold at 106, indicating that investors were willing to pay a premium of $30,000 to earn 10% interest on $500,000 of principal over a 10 year period. This is to be expected because the bond is paying 10% annual interest at a time when the market rate of interest is only 9%.

b.   7/1/96   Interest Expense ($25,000 – $1,150 amortization) 23,850
              Premium on Bonds Payable   1,150
                Cash   25,000
              To pay interest and amortize bond premium for six months.

Note that the amortization of the premium has the effect of reducing interest expense from the stated rate ($25,000) to the market rate ($23,850). If the bond is sold at a discount, the interest expense is increased from the stated rate to the market rate.

c.   9/30/96   Interest Expense ($12,500 – $601 amortization)   11,899
               Premium on Bonds Payable ($1,202 x 3/6)   601
                 Interest Payable   12,500
               To accrue three months' interest and amortize three months' premium.

d.   1/1/97   Interest Expense ($12,500 – $601 amortization)   11,899
              Interest Payable   12,500
              Premium on Bonds Payable ($1,202 x 3/6)   601
                Cash   25,000
              To pay semiannual interest, part of which was accrued, and amortize three months' premium on bonds payable.

In this entry, six months of interest is actually paid to the bondholders on January 1. Note, however, that only half (three months' worth) of the interest is current accounting period expense; the remaining amount represents the payment of the September 30 accrual of three months' interest.

e.   1/2/97   Bonds Payable   500,000
              Premium on Bonds Payable   27,648
              Extraordinary Loss on Retirement on Bonds   12,352
                Cash ($500,000 x 108/100)   540,000
              To record the retirement of bonds payable at 108, retired before maturity.

This entry removes the bonds payable and related premium account from the corporate records, and records the extraordinary loss on retirement. The carrying value of the bonds ($527,648) is less than the cost to call the bonds ($540,000), resulting in the $12,352 loss. Had the price paid to call the bonds been less than the carrying value, the entry would have recorded an extraordinary gain. Extraordinary gains and losses are reported separately on the income statement.

Points to Remember

The interest rate stated on a debt instrument such as a corporate bond will typically differ from the actual market rate of interest when the bond is ultimately issued to the public. This occurs because of the lag in time that frequently occurs between the approval of the bond by the corporation (and regulatory agencies), its actual printing and finally its issuance to the public. Rather than reprint the bond and potentially miss the rapidly changing market interest rate again, bonds are sold at a discount or premium. Occasionally, bonds are sold at face amount.

A bond is sold at a discount when the stated interest rate of the bond is below the current market rate. A premium is paid when the contract rate is higher than interest rates paid by comparable investments.

Premiums and discounts are, in effect, an adjustment to the interest rates. Thus, premiums and discounts should be amortized over the life of the bond. A few things should be noted:

1. A good rule to remember is that Bonds Payable are always recorded at the face amount of the bond. Premiums and discounts are recorded in separate accounts.

2. The actual interest paid to the bondholders at the periodic payment dates (generally semiannually) will always be the face value of the bond multiplied by the stated interest rate. A discount or premium will not affect these periodic cash payments.

3. The carrying amount (or book value) of a bond is conceptually similar to the book value of a fixed asset. Premiums are added to the face amount of bonds payable, and discounts are subtracted.

$$
\begin{array}{l}
\text{Bonds Payable} \\
+ \text{ Bond Premiums or} \\
\underline{- \text{ Bond Discount}} \\
= \text{Carrying Value}
\end{array}
$$

Note that bonds sold at a premium will have a carrying amount greater than the face amount owed and discounted bonds will have a smaller value. In both cases, the carrying value will always move toward the face amount of the bond as the discount or premium is amortized. (Because of this, it is possible to quickly double-check your amortization entries—be sure the bond carrying value is moving in the right direction.)

Chapter 17

Investments and Accounting
for International Operations

 ## Chapter Overview

*I*n Chapters 14 and 15, you learned about capital stock from the perspective of the issuing corporation. In Chapter 16 the focus was on long-term liabilities and how corporations account for bonds payable and other obligations. Now we expand these topics but change the perspective. Corporations frequently purchase stocks and bonds as short-term or long-term investments. In addition, we learn about parent and subsidiary relationships and foreign currency transactions. The specific learning objectives for this chapter are:

1. Account for trading investments in stock by the market value method

2. Use the equity method for stock investments

3. Consolidate parent and subsidiary balance sheets

4. Account for investments in bonds

5. Account for transactions stated in a foreign currency

6. Compute a foreign-currency translation adjustment

Chapter Review

OBJECTIVE 1

Account for trading investments in stock by the market value method.

Stocks are traded in markets. Prices are quoted in dollars and one-eighth fractions of a dollar (occasionally you will see quotes in 1/16 and even 1/32 of a dollar). The owner of a stock is the investor. The corporation that issues the stock is the investee.

Stock investments are assets to the investor. **Short-term investments** are 1) liquid (readily convertible to cash) and 2) expected to be converted to cash within one year. **Long-term investments** are 1) expected to be held for longer than one year or 2) not readily marketable. Stock investments fall into two categories: 1) trading securities or 2) available-for-sale securities. It is important you understand the distinction between the two types! **Trading securities** are always classified as current assets because the investor's intent is to hold them for only a short time in the hopes of earning profits on price changes. When a stock investment is acquired but the intent is not to capture profits from price changes immediately, the investment is classified as an **available-for-sale security.** Trading securities, by definition, are always current assets, whereas available-for-sale securities could be either current or long-term.

As with all assets, trading securities are recorded at cost. Thereafter, however, they are reported at their **current market value.** Any cash dividends received are credited to an appropriate revenue account. Stock dividends do not trigger an entry. Rather, the portfolio is updated to reflect the additional shares. At the end of the accounting period, the market value of the securities is determined and compared with the balance in the short-term investment accounts. If the market value is greater, the following adjusting entry is recorded for the difference:

Trading Investment in ABC Corporation   XX
    Holding Gain on Trading Investments   XX

The debit increases the balance in the account, the credit is reported as Other Revenue and Gains on the income statement.

When the market value of a trading security is lower than the balance in the account, the adjustment is:

Holding Loss on Trading Investments   XX
    Trading Investment in ABC Corporation   XX

The Holding Loss is reported on the income statement as Other Expenses and Losses.

Available-for-sale securities use a combination of the cost and market value method. This topic is covered in detail in more advanced accounting courses.

OBJECTIVE 2

Use the equity method for stock investments.

The **equity method** is used when an investor holds between 20% and 50% of an investee's voting stock because the investor may exert significant influence on the investee's business decisions.

The investment is recorded at cost. Debit Investment and credit Cash.

The investor records his proportionate ownership of the investee's net income and dividends. If the investor owns 40% of the voting stock, the investor will record 40% of the net income as revenue and will receive 40% of the dividends. The share of income is recorded with a debit to the Investment account and a credit to Equity Method Investment Revenue. The receipt of cash dividends reduces the investment. Therefore, the dividend is recorded with a debit to Cash and a credit to the Investment account.

When the equity method is used and an investment is sold, the gain (or loss) on sale is the difference between the proceeds and the balance in the investment account.

Joint ventures, regardless of the percentage owned, also use the equity method.

OBJECTIVE 3
Consolidate parent and subsidiary balance sheets.

An investor who owns more than 50% of an investee's voting stock has a controlling (majority) interest. The investor is called the **parent company,** and the investee is called the **subsidiary.**

Consolidation accounting combines the financial statements of two or more companies that are controlled by the same owners. The assets, liabilities, revenues, and expenses of the subsidiary are added to the parent's accounts.

A separate set of books for the consolidated entity does not exist. The consolidation is accomplished by the use of a work sheet such as Exhibit 17-7 in your text. Transactions that affect both the parent and the subsidiary must be eliminated from the consolidation. These transactions are called **intercompany transactions** and include loans between parent and subsidiary, the parent's investment in the subsidiary, and the subsidiary's equity accounts.

Goodwill is recorded during the consolidation process if the parent buys the subsidiary for a price above book value.

A **minority interest** will appear on the consolidated balance sheet when the parent company owns more than 50% but less than 100% of the subsidiary's stock. Minority interest usually is recorded as a liability on the consolidated balance sheet. Study Exhibit 17-8 in your text to see how minority interest is recorded in the worksheet for the consolidated balance sheet.

Consolidated income is equal to the net income of the parent plus the parent's proportionate interest in the subsidiary's net income.

OBJECTIVE 4
Account for investments in bonds.

Investors purchase bonds issued by corporations. The investor can purchase short-term (current asset) or long-term (long-term investment) bonds.

Investments in bonds are further classified as **trading, available-for-sale,** or **held to maturity** securities. Bonds acquired as trading or available-for-sale securities follows the same guidelines as stock investments.

For long-term bond investments, any premium or discount amount created at purchase is amortized directly to the Investment account (there is no separate Premium or Discount account for bond investments).

Carefully review Exhibit 17-10 in your text. It presents an excellent summary of the rules governing stock and bond investments.

OBJECTIVE 5
Account for transactions stated in a foreign currency.

International accounting deals with business activities that cross national boundaries. Each country uses its own national currency; therefore, a step has been added to the transaction: one currency must be converted into another.

The price of one nation's currency stated in terms of another country's currency is called the **foreign currency exchange rate.** The conversion of one currency into another currency is called **translation.** Exchange rates are determined by supply and demand. The main factors influencing the supply and demand for a particular country's currency are: 1) the import/export ratio, the ratio of a country's imports to its exports, and 2) the rate of return available in the country's capital markets.

A strong currency is rising relative to other nations' currencies, and a weak currency is falling relative to other currencies.

When Company A in Country A purchases goods from Company B in Country B, the transaction price may be stated in the currency of either country. Suppose the transaction is stated in Country A's currency. The transaction requires two steps:

1. The transaction price must be translated for recording in the accounting records of Company B.

2. When payment is made, Company B may experience a foreign-currency translation gain or loss. This gain or loss results when there is a change in the exchange rate between the date of the purchase on account and the date of the subsequent payment of cash.

Note that there will be no foreign-currency gain or loss for Company A because the transaction price was stated in the currency of Country A.

The net amount of Foreign-Currency Transaction Gains and Losses are combined for each accounting period and reported on the income statement as Other Revenue and Expense.

Hedging is a means of protecting the company from foreign currency transaction losses by purchasing a **futures contract,** the right to receive a certain amount of foreign currency on a particular date.

OBJECTIVE 6
Compute a foreign-currency translation adjustment.

United States companies with foreign subsidiaries must consolidate the subsidiary financial statements into their own for external reporting. This can cause two problems:

1. GAAP may be different in the foreign country.

2. When the foreign subsidiary's financial statements are translated into dollars, there may be a translation adjustment.

A **foreign currency translation adjustment** arises because of changes in exchange rates over time. Assets and liabilities are translated using exchange rates as of the balance sheet date. Stockholders' equity, including revenues and expenses, are translated using the exchange rates that were in effect when those transactions were executed. (This results in stockholders' equity not equaling assets minus liabilities.) The adjustment necessary to bring the subsidiary's balance sheet back into balance ("translation adjustment") is reported as part of stockholders' equity on the consolidated balance sheet.

Test Yourself

All the self-testing materials in this chapter focus on information and procedures that your instructor is likely to test in quizzes and examinations.

I. Matching   *Match each numbered term with its lettered definition.*

1. consolidated statements
2. joint ventures
3. controlling interest
4. cost method for investments
5. equity method for investments
6. foreign currency exchange rate
7. foreign currency translation gain or loss
8. hedging
9. long-term investment

10. trading securities
11. minority interest
12. parent company
13. available-for-sale securities
14. strong currency
15. subsidiary company
16. translation adjustment
17. weak currency
18. market value method

A. a separate entity or project owned and operated by a small group of businesses
B. adjustment to equity section of consolidated balance sheet that includes a foreign currency
C. stocks and bonds held for the short-term with the intent of realizing profits from increases in prices
D. combine the balance sheets, income statements, and other financial statements of the parent with those of the majority-owned subsidiaries into an overall set as if the separate entities were one
E. currency whose exchange rate is rising relative to other nations' currencies
F. investee company in which a parent owns more than 50% of the voting stock
G. investor company that owns more than 50% of the voting stock of a subsidiary company
H. stocks and bonds not held with the intent of realizing profits from increases in prices
I. method used to account for investments in which the investor can significantly influence the decisions of the investee
J. method used to account for short-term investments in stock, and for long-term investments when the investor holds less than 20% of the investee's voting stock
K. ownership of more than 50% of an investee company's voting stock
L. results from changes in the exchange rate between the date of the purchase on account and the date of subsequent payment

M. separate asset category reported on the balance sheet between current assets and plant assets

N. strategy to avoid foreign currency transaction losses

O. subsidiary company's equity that is held by stockholders other than the parent company

P. the price of one country's currency stated in terms of another country's monetary unit

Q. currency whose exchange rate is decreasing relative to other nations' currencies

R. method used to value trading securities on the balance sheet

 II. Multiple Choice *Circle the best answer.*

1. A stock is listed in the *Wall Street Journal* as having a High of 65 1/4, a Low of 63, a Close of 63 1/2, and a Net Change of +1 1/4. What was the previous day's closing price?

   A. $66.50

   B. $61.75

   C. $64.75

   D. $62.25

2. Assets listed as Short-Term Investments on the balance sheet are:

   A. only liquid

   B. listed on a national stock exchange

   C. only intended to be converted to cash within one year

   D. liquid and intended to be converted to cash within one year

3. Trading securities are reported on the balance sheet at:

   A. current cost

   B. historical cost

   C. lower of cost or market

   D. market value

4. Intercompany payables and receivables are eliminated in the consolidated entries so that:

   A. assets will not be overstated

   B. liabilities will not be understated

   C. stockholders' equity will not be understated

   D. net income will not be overstated

5. All of the following accounts are eliminated in the consolidated work sheet entries *except:*

   A. investment in subsidiary

   B. subsidiary's cash

   C. subsidiary's common stock

   D. subsidiary's retained earnings

6. The minority interest account is usually classified as a(n):
   A. revenue
   B. expense
   C. liability
   D. asset

7. The rate at which one unit of a currency can be converted into another currency is called the foreign currency:
   A. market rate
   B. interest rate
   C. exchange rate
   D. conversion rate

8. A strong currency has an exchange rate that is:
   A. inelastic with respect to other nations' currencies
   B. inelastic with respect to its balance of trade
   C. increasing relative to other nations' currencies
   D. decreasing relative to other nations' currencies

9. Available-for-sale securities are:
   A. stock investments only
   B. bond investments only
   C. the same as held-to-maturity investments
   D. those other than trading securities

10. A holding gain (or loss) results from:
    A. available-for-sale securities
    B. trading securities
    C. held-to-maturity securities
    D. any of the above

III. Completion *Complete each of the following statements.*

1. The price at which stock changes hands is determined by the _____ .

2. Two main factors that determine the supply and demand for a particular currency are the country's _____ and _____ .

3. Investments in stock are initially recorded at _____ .

4. The _____ method is used to account for investments when the investor can significantly influence the actions of the investee.

5. A(n) _____ is ownership of at least 50% of the voting stock of a company.

6. Goodwill is a(n) _____ asset.

7. A change in the currency exchange rates between the date of purchase and the date of payment will result in a(n) _____ .

8. _____ only result from trading securities.

9. When a parent owns less than 100% of a subsidiary, the other owners are called the _____ .

10. Holding gains and losses are reported on the _____ as _____ .

IV. Exercises

1. P Company purchased 15% of S Corporation on January 1, 19X7 for $96,000. S earned income of $24,000 and paid dividends of $8,000 during 19X7.

   A. What method should be used to account for the investment in S?

   B. How much revenue will be recorded by P in 19X7 from the investment in S?

   C. What is the balance in the Investment account at the end of 19X7?

2. Taco Company purchased 40% of Bell Corporation on January 1, 19X6 for $630,000. Bell Corporation earned income of $145,000 and paid dividends of $60,000 during 19X6.

   A. What method should be used to account for the investment in Bell Corporation?

   B. How much revenue will be recorded by Taco Company in 19X6 from the investment in Bell Corporation?

   C. What is the balance in the Investment account at the end of 19X6?

3. Peanut Company invested in Brittle Corporation on January 1, 19X4 by purchasing 60% of the total stock of Brittle Corporation for $675,000. Brittle Corporation had common stock of $400,000 and retained earnings of $725,000.

    A. What method should be used to account for the investment in Brittle Corporation?

    B. What amount of Minority Interest will appear on a consolidated balance sheet prepared on January 1, 19X4?

    C. If Peanut Company owes Brittle Corporation $72,000 on a note payable, prepare the two elimination entries in general journal form.

Date	Accounts and Explanation	Debit	Credit

4. Hunter Company purchased 100% of the common stock of Prey Corporation for $1,315,000. Prey Corporation showed Common Stock of $280,000 and Retained Earnings of $510,000. Compute the amount of goodwill resulting from the purchase.

5. Prepare journal entries for the following trading security transactions.

3/12   Purchased 250 shares of Patsy Corporation at 47 1/2. The commission was $95.

6/18   Received a 10% stock dividend.

8/28   Sold 100 shares of Patsy Corporation for $60. The commission was $65.

Date	Accounts and Explanation	Debit	Credit

6. Prepare journal entries for the following foreign currency transactions. Use the form on the next page.

10/21   Sold merchandise on account to a British company. The price was 450 pounds sterling, and the exchange rate was $1.51. (The symbol for pounds sterling is £.)

12/12   Received payment from the British company. Today's exchange rate is $1.48.

12/14   Purchased merchandise on account from a Canadian company. The price was $2,500 Canadian. The exchange rate is $0.80.

12/31   Today's exchange rate for Canadian dollars is $0.78. Today is also the end of the accounting period.

2/12   Paid cash for the December 14 purchase. The exchange rate today is $0.75.

Date	Accounts and Explanation	Debit	Credit

7. On August 31, 19X5 McKillop Corporation paid 94 3/4 for 9 percent bonds of Kelly, Inc., as an available-for-sale short-term investment. The maturity value of the bonds is $200,000, and they pay interest on April 30 and October 31.

Record McKillop's purchase of the bond investment, the receipt of semiannual interest on October 31, and the accrual of interest revenue on December 31.

Date	Accounts and Explanation	Debit	Credit

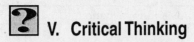

V. Critical Thinking

Examine the information in Exercise 7 above. For each date, indicate what would change if:

1. the bonds were acquired as a trading security
2. the bonds were acquired as a hold-to-maturity security (assume bonds mature on April 30, 19X8)

_____

_____

_____

_____

_____

_____

_____

_____

_____

_____

_____

_____

VI. Demonstration Problems

Demonstration Problem # 1 (Work space for parts 1-4 is provided on the following pages.)

1. At what amount should the following trading securities be reported? All of the investments represent less than 5% of the investee's stock.

Stock	Investment Cost	Current Market Value
IBM	62,500	48,000
Intel	40,000	105,000
Wal-Mart	94,000	182,000

2. Assume that the investor firm above has cash of $59,250 and accounts receivable of $161,080, net of allowance. Prepare the current assets section of the balance sheet.

3. On January 1, Investor paid $425,000 to acquire a 12% long-term common stock investment in FusionNow, Inc., a mini-fusion reactor manufacturer. On December 31, FusionNow, Inc. announced annual earnings of $158,000, as well as declared and paid-out cash dividends totaling $80,000. Prepare the January 1 and December 31 entries on the books of Investor. Assume that Investor received its share of the cash dividend on December 31.

4. Assume the same facts as in #3 except that $1,590,000 was paid for a 45% interest. Post each appropriate entry into a T-account entitled Investment in FusionNow, Inc., Common Stock and calculate the account balance after all entries have been posted.

5. Parent Corporation paid $375,000 for 90% of the common stock of Subsidiary Corporation. Subsidiary owes Parent $60,000 on an intercompany note payable. Complete the following work sheet:

	Parent Company	Subsidiary Company	Eliminations Debit	Eliminations Credit	Consolidated Amounts
Assets:					
Cash:	58,000	26,000			
Note receivable from Subsidiary	60,000	-			
Investment in Subsidiary	375,000	-			
Goodwill	-	-			
Plant & equipment, net	218,000	328,000			
Other assets	37,000	92,000			
Total	748,000	446,000			
Liabilities and Stockholders' Equity:					
Accounts payable	38,000	41,000			
Notes Payable	170,000	125,000			
Minority interest					
Common stock	500,000	110,000			
Retained earnings	40,000	170,00			
Total	748,000	446,000			

1. _____

   _____

   _____

   _____

   _____

2.

3.

Date	Accounts and Explanation	Debit	Credit

4.

Date	Accounts and Explanation	Debit	Credit

Investment in FusionNow, Inc., Common Stock

Demonstration Problem #2

At the beginning of the year, HyTech Corporation held the following trading securities in its portfolio:

	Market Value
500 shares Apex, Inc.	41 1/8 ea.
1,000 shares Comex Corporation.	18 1/2 ea.
1,200 shares Durables, Inc.	34 1/4 ea.
750 shares Trintour Inc.	78 ea.
400 shares Vellux	26 3/8 ea.
820 shares Zontac Corporation	104 3/4 ea.

During the current year, the following occurred:

On February 10, HyTech received a 26¢/share dividend on the Apex stock. Shortly thereafter, Apex shares increased to $48 1/2 so the security was sold on March 1, less a brokerage commission of $325.

Comex Corporation declared a 10% stock dividend in late March. The additional shares were received on April 14. This security remained in HyTech's portfolio at year end, when they were trading at $22 per share.

Quarterly dividends of 17.5¢/share were received on the Durables stock on March 24 and June 24. On July 8 the shares were sold for 29 1/2 per share, less a brokerage commission $485.

On June 20, Trintour announced a 4-for-1 stock split. The new shares were received on July 30. On October 4, when the stock was trading at $24.25 per share, half of the shares were sold, less a $485 commission. The balance remained in the portfolio at the end of the year when they were trading at $21 per share.

The Vellux shares remained in the portfolio throughout the year; no dividends were received during the year and the stock was trading at $25 per share at year end.

The Zontac shares also remained in the company's portfolio throughout the year. Quarterly dividends of $1.06 were received throughout the year. On December 31 the shares were trading at 101 1/8.

For each security, determine the gain or loss for the year and combine them to determine the net gain/loss for the entire portfolio.

_____

_____

_____

_____

_____

_____

_____

_____

_____

_____

_____

_____

_____

_____

_____

_____

_____

_____

_____

_____

_____

_____

_____

_____

_____

Solutions

I. Matching

1. D 2. A 3. K 4. J 5. I 6. P 7. L 8. N 9. M
10. C 11. O 12. G 13. H 14. E 15. F 16. B 17. Q 18. R

II. Multiple Choice

1. D The High is the previous day's highest price, the Low is the lowest price of the previous day. The Close is the last price at which the stock traded yesterday. Net Change is the increase (+) or decrease (–) in the Close compared to the previous day. The previous day's close is 63 1/2 – 1 1/4 or $63.50 – $1.25 = $62.50.

2. D Note that besides the determinable liquidity of the investment, the intent of management determines an investment's classification as a Short-Term Investment.

3. D GAAP requires trading securities to be reported in the balance sheet at market value.

4. A Failure to eliminate intercompany payables and receivables would result in the overstatement of both assets and liabilities of the consolidated entity. Accordingly, of the items listed, only A is correct.

5. B Elimination is not intended to do away with the assets and liabilities of the subsidiary. The intent of elimination is to do away with only those things that would double up or be counted twice if not eliminated, such as intercompany payables and receivables and the investment in subsidiary and subsidiary stockholders' equity.

6. C The Minority Interest account represents the ownership interest of parties outside of the Parent-Subsidiary relationship. In actual practice it is most often reported as part of the liability section on the balance sheet.

7. C The exchange rate is used to convert currencies.

8. C Strong currencies are those that increase relative to other currencies.

9. D Available-for-sale securities are stock investments other than trading securities and bond investments other than trading securities and held-to-maturity securities.

10. B Holding gains (or losses) are a result of the market value method applied to trading securities.

III. Completion

1. market (The market allows buyers and sellers with opposing interests to arrive at a price acceptable to both.)
2. import/export ratio; rate of return available in its capital markets
3. cost
4. equity
5. controlling interest
6. intangible
7. foreign-currency transaction gain or loss
8. holding gain and losses
9. minority interest
10. income statement; Other Revenues and Expenses

IV. Exercises

1. A. cost method
   B. .15 x $8,000 = $1,200
   C. $96,000 (cost)

2. A. equity method
   B. .40 x $145,000 = $58,000
   C. $630,000 + $58,000 − (.40 x $60,000) = $664,000

3. A. consolidation method
   B. .40 x ($400,000 + $725,000) = $450,000
   C.

(1) Note Payable to Brittle	72,000	
Note Receivable from Peanut		72,000
(2) Common stock (Brittle)	400,000	
Retained earnings (Brittle)	725,000	
Investment in Brittle		675,000
Minority Interest		450,000

(Note: Refer to Exhibit 17-8 in your text.)

4. $1,315,000 − ($280,000 + $510,000) = $525,000

5.

| 3/12 | Short-term Investment in Patsy Corporation Common Stock | 11,970 | |
| | Cash [(250 shares x $47.50) + $95] | | 11,970 |

6/18 Memo: Received 25 shares of Patsy Corporation in a stock dividend
= (250 shares x 0.10)
New cost per share = $11,970 / 275 shares = $43.53 (rounded)

8/28	Cash [100 shares x $60) − $65]	5,935	
	Short-term Investment in Patsy Corporation Common Stock (100 shares x $43.53)		4,353
	Gain on Sale of Investment		1,582

6.	10/21	Accounts Receivable	679.50	
		Sales		679.50
		(£450 x $1.51)		
	12/12	Cash (£450 x $1.48)	666.00	
		Foreign-Currency Transaction Loss	13.50	
		Accounts Receivable		679.50
	12/14	Purchases	2,000	
		Accounts Payable		2,000
		($2,500 x $.80)		
	12/31	Accounts Payable	50	
		Foreign-Currency Transaction Gain		50
		[$2,000 – ($2,500 x $.78)]		
	2/12	Accounts Payable	1,950	
		Foreign-Currency Transaction Gain		75
		Cash ($2,500 x $.75)		1,875
7.	8/31	Short-term Investment in Bonds	189,500	
		Interest Receivable	6,000	
		Cash		195,500
		($200,000 x .9475 = $189,500)		
		($200,000 x .09 x 4/12 = $6,000)		
	10/31	Cash	9,000	
		Interest Receivable		6,000
		Interest Revenue		3,000
		($200,000 x .09 x 6/12 = $9,000)		
		($200,000 x .09 x 4/12 = $6,000)		
	12/31	Interest Receivable	3,000	
		Interest Revenue		3,000
		($200,000 x .09 x 2/12 = $3,000)		

V. Critical Thinking

1. If the bonds were acquired as a trading security, an adjusting entry on 12/31 would be necessary. If, on 12/31, the market price of the bonds was greater than 94 3/4, a holding gain would be recorded. If the market price was less than 94 3/4, a holding loss would be recorded.

2. If the bonds were acquired as a hold-to-maturity security, the entries would be:

8/31/X5	Long-term Investment in Bonds	189,500.00	
	Interest Receivable	6,000.00	
	Cash		195,500.00

10/31/X5	Cash	9,000.00	
	Long-term Investment in Bonds	656.25	
	Interest Receivable		6,000.00
	Interest Revenue		3,656.25

In addition to the cash receipt of interest, the bond discount needs to be amortized. The discount ($200,000 – $189,500 = $10,500) is amortized over the remaining life of the bonds (8/31/X5 to 4/30/X8 = 32 months). Thus, $10,500 / 32 months = $328.125 per month. Two months (8/31/X5 to 10/31/X5) = $328.125 x 2 = $656.25. This amount is recorded as additional interest revenue and an increase in the carrying value of the long-term investment. Usually, a contra-asset account (Discount on Bonds Receivable) is not established.

12/31/X5	Interest Receivable	3,000.00	
	Long-term Investment in Bonds	656.25	
	Interest Revenue		3,656.25

To accrue two months' interest receivable and amortize two months' bond discount (see above for calculations).

VI. Demonstration Problems

Demonstration Problem #1 Solved and Explained

1. The investments should be reported at $335,000 because trading securities are reported at their market value.

2. Current assets:

Cash	$ 59,250
Short-term investments, at market	335,000
Accounts receivable, net of allowance	161,080
	$555,330

3. 1/1   Investment in FusionNow, Inc.

Common Stock	425,000	
Cash		425,000

To purchase 12% investment in FusionNow, Inc. stock.

12/31   Cash ($80,000 dividend paid

x 12% owned)	9,600	
Dividend Revenue		9,600

To record receipt of FusionNow, Inc. dividend income.

Accounting for long-term investments requires use of the cost method when the investor owns less than 20% of the investee's voting stock. The investment is recorded at cost, reported earnings do not require a journal entry on Investor's books, and dividend revenue is recorded for Investor's portion of total dividend ($80,000 x 12%).

4. 1/1   Investment in FusionNow, Inc.

Common Stock	1,590,000	
Cash		1,590,000

To purchase a 45% investment in FusionNow, Inc. common stock.

12/31   Investment in FusionNow, Inc.

Common Stock	71,100	
Equity Method Investment Revenue		71,100

To record 45% of FusionNow, Inc. net income
($158,000 net income x 45% ownership = $71,100).

12/31   Cash ($80,000 dividend paid x 45% ownership)   36,000

Investment in FusionNow, Inc.		
Common Stock		36,000

To record dividends declared and paid.

Investment in Fusion Now, Inc., Common Stock

1/1	1,590,000		
12/31	71,100	12/31	36,000
Bal.	1,625,100		

When an investor owns between 20% and 50% of a corporation's voting common stock, the investor may affect decisions regarding the investee's operations. Because the investor often can exert influence on dividend policy, product lines, sources of supply, and similar important matters, the equity method should be used in accounting for these investments. Initially, the investment is recorded at its $1,590,000 cost. The December 31 entry adjusts the Investment account upward for the investor's portion of the investee's net income. The Investor account is decreased for dividends paid on the investment. In this way, the success (or failure) of the influenced business is included in the investor's accounting for the investment.

5.

	Parent Company	Subsidiary Company	Eliminations Debit	Eliminations Credit	Consolidated Amounts
Assets:					
Cash:	58,000	26,000			84,000
Note receivable from Subsidiary	60,000	-		(a) 60,000	
Investment in Subsidiary	375,000	-		(b) 375,000	
Goodwill	-	-	(b) 123,000		123,000
Plant & equipment, net	218,000	328,000			546,000
Other assets	37,000	92,000			129,000
Total	748,000	446,000			882,000
Liabilities and Stockholders' equity:					
Accounts payable	38,000	41,000			79,000
Notes Payable	170,000	125,000	(a) 60,000		235,000
Minority interest				(b) 28,000	28,000
Common stock	500,000	110,000	(b) 110,000		500,000
Retained earnings	40,000	170,000	(b) 170,000		40,000
Total	748,000	446,000	463,000	463,000	882,000

Entry (a) eliminated Parent's $60,000 intercompany note receivable against the note payable owed by the Subsidiary. Note that the consolidated total represents the amount owed to outside creditors ($170,000 owed by Parent + $125,000 owed by Subsidiary) less $60,000 intercompany debt = $235,000 owed to outsiders.

Entry (b) eliminates Parent's $375,000 investment balance against the $280,000 in Subsidiary's equity. Parent acquired a 90% interest, so the minority interest is $28,000 (10% x $280,000). Goodwill is the difference between the investment ($375,000) and 90% of the Subsidiary's Common Stock and Retained Earnings, or $123,000 ($375,000 – 90% x $280,000).

Demonstration Problem #2 Solved and Explained

The easiest way to solve this problem is to record the journal entries for each security, as follows:

Apex

2/10	Cash	130	
	Dividend Revenue		130
	26¢ x 500 shares		

3/1	Cash	23,925	
	Trading Security - Apex		20,562.50
	Gain on Sale of Trading Security		3,362.50

Comex

No journal entries during the year; however, we need to adjust this security to its year-end market value. We now hold 1,100 shares (the original 1,000 plus the 10% stock dividend received on April 14).

12/31	Trading Security - Comex	5,700	
	Holding Gain - Trading Security		5,700

This security was valued at $18,500 (1,000 shares x 18 1/2 per share). It is now worth $24,200 (1,100 shares x $22 per share). Trading securities are valued at their market value as of the balance sheet date, so a $5,700 gain is adjusted into the records.

Durables

3/24	Cash	210	
	Dividend Revenue		210
	(1200 shares x 17.5¢/share)		

6/24	Cash	210	
	Dividend Revenue		210
	(as above)		

7/8	Cash	34,915	
	Loss on Sale of Trading Security	6,185	
	Trading Security - Durables		41,100

This security was valued at $41,100. It sold for $35,400 less a commission of $485, resulting in a Loss on Sale of $6,185.

Trintour

7/30   No entry upon receipt of the new shares, just a memo indicating we now hold 3,000 shares, not 750.

10/4   Cash   35,890
     Trading Security - Trintour   29,250
     Gain on Sales of Trading Security   6,640

This one requires a little thought. At the beginning of the year this security was worth $58,500 (750 shares x $78 per share). Then the stock split 4 for 1 so we ended up with 3,000 shares. We then sold half (1,500 shares) for $24.25 per share, less a $485 commission, or 1,500 x $24.25 = $36,375 – $485 = $35,890 realizing a gain of $6,640, the difference between the cash received and 50% of the original market value. The remaining 1,500 shares are still in the portfolio at year's end, so an adjusting entry is required, as follows:

12/31   Trading Security - Trintour   2,250
     Holding Gain - Trintour   2 ,250

The holding gain results from the current market value of the remaining shares of $31,500 (1,500 shares x $21 per share) less last years market value $29,250.

Vellux

12/31   Holding Loss - Vellux   550
     Trading Security - Vellux   550

The Holding Loss is the difference between last year's market value and this year's (26 3/8 – 25 = $1.375 x 400 shares = $550).

Zontac

Cash   3,476.80
   Dividend Revenue   3,476.80

This would actually be four separate transactions of $869.20 each (820 shares x $1.06 ea.).

12/31   Holding Loss - Zontac   2,972.50
     Trading Security - Zontac   2,972.50

The Holding Loss is the difference between last year's market value and this year's (104 3/4 – 101 1/8 = 3 5/8 x 820 shares).

Summary of Gains and Losses

Apex:	Dividend Revenues	$ 130.00	
	Gain on Sale	3,362.50	$ 3,492.50
Comex:	Holding Gain		5,700.00
Durables:	Dividend Revenues	420.00	
	Loss on Sale	(6,185.00)	(5,765.00)
Trintour:	Gain on Sale	6,640.00	
	Holding Gain	2,250.00	8,890.00
Vellux:	Holding Loss		(550.00)
Zontac:	Dividend Revenues	3,476.80	
	Holding Loss	(2,972.50)	504.30
	Net Gain		$12,271.80

Chapter 18

Statement of Cash Flows

 Chapter Overview

*I*n earlier chapters, reference has been made to the statement of cash flows. However, the primary financial statement emphasis has been on the income statement and balance sheet. Many people think the cash flows statement is more important, as demonstrated by the opening vignette to this chapter in your text. It is certainly the most complex of the published financial statements. The specific learning objectives for this chapter are:

1. Identify the purposes of the statement of cash flows
2. Distinguish among operating, investing, and financing activities
3. Prepare a statement of cash flows by the direct method
4. Use the financial statements to compute the cash effects of a wide variety of business transactions
5. Prepare a statement of cash flows by the indirect method

A1. Prepare a work sheet for the statement of cash flows

Chapter Review

Cash flows are cash receipts and cash payments. The **statement of cash flows** reports all these receipts and disbursements under three categories (operating, investing, and financing) and shows the reasons for changes in the cash balance. The statement is used to:

1. Predict future cash flows
2. Evaluate management decisions
3. Determine the ability to pay dividends to stockholders and interest and principal to creditors
4. Show the relationship of net income to changes in the business's cash

The term cash is used to include **cash equivalents** which are highly liquid short-term investments (such as T-bills and money market accounts).

Operating activities create revenues and expenses in the entity's major line of business. Operating activities include:

1. Collections from customers
2. Payments to suppliers and employees
3. Interest revenue and expense
4. Taxes
5. Dividends received on investments

Operating activities are always listed first because they are the largest and most important source of cash for a business.

Investing activities increase or decrease the assets that the business works with. Investing activities include:

1. Buying and selling plant assets and investments
2. Lending money to others and collecting principal repayments

Investing activities are critical because they help determine the future course of the business.

Financing activities obtain the funds from investors and creditors needed to launch and sustain the business. Financing activities include:

1. Issuing stock
2. Treasury stock transactions
3. Paying dividends
4. Borrowing money and repaying the principal

Note that while principal payments on notes and bonds payable are a financing activity the interest payments are classified as an operating activity.

Review Exhibit 18-2 in your text and become familiar with both the format and content of a cash flow statement.

OBJECTIVE 3
Prepare a
statement of
cash flows by
the direct
method.

The statement of cash flows reports the flows from operating activities, investing activities, and financing activities, calculates net increase or decrease in cash during the year, and adds that to the previous year's Cash balance in order to arrive at the current year's Cash balance. It shows where cash came from and how it was spent.

Preparing the statement of cash flows requires these steps:

1. Identify items that affect cash
2. Classify the items as operating, investing, or financing activities
3. Determine the increase or decrease in cash for each item

OBJECTIVE 4
Use the
financial
statements to
compute the
cash effects of
a wide variety
of business
transactions.

Accounts may be analyzed for the cash effects of various transactions using the income statement amounts in conjunction with changes in the balance sheet amounts.

To determine cash flow amounts from operating activities, keep the following in mind:

Revenue/expenses for the → Adjust for the change in related → Amount for the
income statement   balance sheet accounts   cash flows statement

Cash collections from customers can be computed using Sales Revenue from the income statement and the changes in Accounts Receivable from the balance sheet:

```
COLLECTIONS                         ┌ +DECREASES IN ACCOUNTS RECEIVABLE
   FROM       =  SALES REVENUE      │            or
 CUSTOMERS                          └ –INCREASES IN ACCOUNTS RECEIVABLE
```

Payments to suppliers computation:

```
                              ┌ +INCREASE IN       ┌ +DECREASE IN
 PAYMENTS      COST OF        │  INVENTORY         │  ACCOUNTS PAYABLE
   FOR      =  GOODS          │     or       and   │     or
 INVENTORY     SOLD           └ –DECREASE IN        └ –INCREASE IN
                                 INVENTORY             ACCOUNTS PAYABLE
```

Payments for operating expenses computation:

```
                              ┌ +INCREASE IN       ┌ +DECREASE IN
              OPERATING       │  PREPAID           │  ACCRUED
 PAYMENTS     EXPENSES OTHER  │  EXPENSES          │  LIABILITIES
   FOR      = THAN SALARIES,  │     or       and   │     or
 OPERATING    WAGES, AND      │ –DECREASE IN       │ –INCREASE IN
 EXPENSES     DEPRECIATION    │  PREPAID           │  ACCRUED
                              └  EXPENSES          └  LIABILITIES
```

Remember that depreciation is not included in operating expenses because depreciation is a noncash expense.

Payments to employees computation:

```
 PAYMENTS      SALARY         ┌ +DECREASES IN SALARY AND WAGE PAYABLE
   TO       =  AND WAGE       │            or
 EMPLOYEES     EXPENSE        └ –INCREASES IN SALARY AND WAGE PAYABLE
```

Payments of interest and taxes follow the pattern for payments to employees.

For investing activities we look to the asset accounts (Plants assets, Investments, Notes receivable).

Plant asset transactions can be analyzed by first determining book value:

$$\begin{array}{l}\text{BEGINNING}\\ \text{PLANT ASSET} + \text{ACQUISITIONS} - \text{DEPRECIATION} - \begin{array}{l}\text{BOOK VALUE}\\ \text{OF PLANT}\\ \text{ASSETS SOLD}\end{array} = \begin{array}{l}\text{ENDING}\\ \text{PLANT ASSET}\\ \text{BALANCE (NET)}\end{array}\\ \text{BALANCE (NET)}\end{array}$$

In order to compute sale proceeds:

$$\text{SALE PROCEEDS} = \text{BOOK VALUE SOLD} + \text{GAIN} - \text{LOSS}$$

Acquisitions will decrease cash, while sale proceeds will increase cash.

Investments and Loans and Notes Receivable are analyzed in a manner similar to plant assets; however, there is no depreciation to account for.

Financing activities affect liability and stockholders' equity accounts.

Long-term debt can be analyzed with this equation:

$$\begin{array}{l}\text{BEGINNING}\\ \text{LONG-TERM}\\ \text{DEBT BALANCE}\end{array} + \begin{array}{l}\text{ISSUANCE}\\ \text{OF}\\ \text{NEW DEBT}\end{array} - \text{PAYMENTS} = \begin{array}{l}\text{ENDING}\\ \text{LONG-TERM}\\ \text{DEBT BALANCE}\end{array}$$

Stock transactions (other than treasury stock) can be analyzed using this equation:

$$\begin{array}{l}\text{BEGINNING}\\ \text{STOCK}\\ \text{BALANCE}\end{array} + \begin{array}{l}\text{ISSUANCE}\\ \text{OF}\\ \text{NEW STOCK}\end{array} - \text{RETIREMENTS} = \begin{array}{l}\text{ENDING}\\ \text{STOCK}\\ \text{BALANCE}\end{array}$$

Issuances increase cash while retirements decrease cash.

Treasury stock can be analyzed with this equation:

$$\begin{array}{l}\text{BEGINNING}\\ \text{TREASURY STOCK}\\ \text{BALANCE}\end{array} + \text{PURCHASES} - \begin{array}{l}\text{COST OF}\\ \text{TREASURY}\\ \text{STOCK SOLD}\end{array} = \begin{array}{l}\text{ENDING}\\ \text{TREASURY STOCK}\\ \text{BALANCE}\end{array}$$

Purchases will decrease cash. Remember, that cash is increased by the proceeds of treasury stock sold. These proceeds may differ from the cost of treasury stocks sold.

Dividend payments can be computed by analyzing Retained Earnings:

$$\begin{array}{l}\text{BEGINNING}\\ \text{RETAINED EARNINGS}\\ \text{BALANCE}\end{array} + \begin{array}{l}\text{NET}\\ \text{INCOME}\end{array} - \begin{array}{l}\text{DIVIDENDS}\\ \text{DECLARATIONS}\end{array} = \begin{array}{l}\text{ENDING}\\ \text{RETAINED EARNINGS}\\ \text{BALANCE}\end{array}$$

Remember that stock dividends must be separated from cash dividends. Also, a change in the Dividends Payable account will affect the actual cash dividends paid.

Noncash investing and financing activities

You should be aware that some investing and financing activities are noncash. Some typical noncash investing and financing activities include:

1. Acquisition of assets by issuing stock.
2. Acquisition of assets by issuing debt.
3. Payment of long-term debt by transferring investment assets to the creditor.

Noncash activities can be included in a schedule or a note to the statement of cash flows.

When the direct method of computing operating cash flows is used, FASB requires companies to include a reconciliation from net income to net cash flows. This reconciliation is identical to the indirect method.

OBJECTIVE 5
Prepare a statement of cash flows by the indirect method.

The **indirect or (reconciliation) method** reconciles net income to cash flows, and affects only the operating activities section of the statement. The investing activities and financing activities sections are identical to the sections prepared using the direct method.

To prepare the operating activities section using the indirect method, we must add and subtract items that affect net income and cash flows differently. We begin with net income from the income statement.

1. Depreciation, amortization, and depletion are noncash expenses which reduce net income. Therefore, we add them back to net income as part of our effort to arrive at cash flow from operations.
2. Gains and losses from the sale of plant assets are reported as part of net income, and the proceeds are reported in the investing activities section. To avoid counting gains and losses twice, we must remove their effect from net income. Therefore, gains are subtracted from net income, and losses are added to net income.
3. Changes in current assets and current liabilities:
   a. Increases in current assets, other than cash, are subtracted from net income.
   b. Decreases in current assets, other than cash, are added to net income.
   c. Decreases in current liabilities, other than dividends payable, are subtracted from net income.
   d. Increases in current liabilities are added to net income.

Note: Under the indirect method, only changes in current assets and current liabilities are used.

Chapter 18 Appendix

The Work Sheet Approach
to Preparing the Statement of Cash Flows

Appendix Overview

OBJECTIVE A1
Prepare a work
sheet for the
statement of
cash flows.

Work sheets are frequently used as an aid in preparing the statement of cash flows. Regardless of approach (direct or indirect), the format is the same. The work sheet has four columns, with the upper half labeled as follows:

(1) Beginning Balance Sheet Amounts	(2) (3) Transaction Analysis		(4) Ending Balance Sheet Amounts
	Debit	Credit	

The lower half of the work sheet uses only the two analysis columns and provides the amounts needed to present the statement of cash flows. For both the direct and indirect method, cash flows from investing and financing activities are analyzed in the same manner. (Remember, the two methods differ only in the presentation of cash flows from operating activities.)

For the direct method, operating activities cash flows are divided into receipts and payments, while the indirect method begins with net income and adjusts (add and subtract) that amount according to changes in current asset and current liability accounts.

For either method, the actual analysis uses debits and credits to explain the changes in balance sheet accounts which resulted in cash flows (inflows or outflows). In both methods, the final reconciling figure is the net change in cash during the period.

Review carefully Exhibits 18A-2 and 18A-3 in your text. Pay particular attention to the similarities and differences between the two work sheets.

Test Yourself

All the self-testing materials in this chapter focus on information and procedures that your instructor is likely to test in quizzes and examinations. *Questions followed by the letter "A" refer to topics in the chapter appendix.*

I. Matching *Match each numbered term with its lettered definition.*

1. cash equivalents
2. direct method
3. indirect method
4. operating activity
5. cash flows

6. financing activity
7. investing activity
8. statement of cash flows
9A. work sheet

A. a report of cash receipts and cash disbursements classified according to the entity's major activities: operating, investing, and financing

B. activity that creates revenue or expense in the entity's major line of business

C. activity that increases or decreases the assets that the business has to work with

D. activity that obtains from creditors the funds needed to launch and sustain the business or repays such funds

E. cash receipts and cash disbursements

F. format of the operating activities section of the statement of cash flows that lists the major categories of operating cash receipts and cash disbursements

G. format of the operating activities section of the statement of cash flows that starts with net income and shows the reconciliation from net income to operating cash flows

H. highly liquid short-term investments that can be converted into cash with little delay

I. a columnar tool used to analyze changes in account balances to derive the amounts for the cash flows statement

II. Multiple Choice *Circle the best answer.*

1. All of the following are uses of the statement of cash flows except:
   A. to evaluate employee performance
   B. to evaluate management decisions
   C. to predict future cash flows
   D. to relate net income to changes in cash

2. Activities which increase or decrease business assets such as machinery are called:
   A. financing activities
   B. investing activities
   C. operating activities
   D. reporting activities

3. Transactions involving capital or debt activities are called:
   A. financing activities
   B. investing activities
   C. operating activities
   D. reporting activities

4. Which of the following is considered a cash equivalent?
   A. accounts receivable
   B. inventory
   C. supplies
   D. treasury bills

5. The receipt of cash dividend revenues would be reported on the:
   A. balance sheet
   B. income statement
   C. statement of cash flows only
   D. both the income statement and the statement of cash flows

6. All of the following are examples of operating activities except:
   A. purchases from suppliers
   B. sales to customers
   C. sales of equipment
   D. recording rent expense

7. All of the following are examples of investing activities except:
   A. sale of building
   B. payment of dividends
   C. purchase of equipment
   D. receipt of cash from sale of California State bonds

8. All of the following are financing activities except:
   A. issuing stock
   B. paying dividends
   C. selling equipment
   D. long-term borrowing

9. Cash collections from customers are computed by:
   A. Sales Revenue + Increase in Accounts Receivable
   B. Sales Revenue – Increase in Accounts Receivable
   C. Sales Revenue – Decrease in Accounts Receivable
   D. Sales Revenue + Decrease in Accounts Receivable
   E. Either B or D

10A. When using a worksheet to prepare the statement of cash flows, the account balances to analyze come from the:
   A. income statement
   B. retained earnings statement
   C. balance sheet
   D. all of the above

III. Completion *Complete each of the following statements.*

1. The _____ is only the financial statement that is dated as of the end of the period.

2. The largest cash inflow from operations is _____.

3. Both the _____ method and the _____ method of preparing the statements of cash flows are permitted by the FASB.

4. Payments of dividends is a(n) _____ activity on the statement of cash flows.

5. Making loans is a(n) _____ activity on the statement of cash flows.

6. Depreciation is included in the _____ activity section on the statement of cash flows when using the indirect method.

7. The purchase of equipment is a(n) _____ activity on the statement of cash flows.

8. While permitting both methods, FASB recommends the _____ method.

9. The _____ method begins with net income.

10. The difference between the direct and indirect method is found in the _____ section of the statement of cash flows.

❓ IV. Exercises

1. Crandall Company had tax expenses of $36,000 in 19X4. The balance in Taxes Payable was $1,400 at the beginning of the year and $2,400 at the end of the year. How much cash was paid for taxes during 19X4?

2. Shimer Company had cost of goods sold of $400,000, an increase in inventory of $10,000, and an increase in Accounts Payable of $18,000 in 19X7. How much cash was paid to suppliers?

3. Walter Company had sales of $1,250,000 in 19X3. Eighty percent of sales are on credit. During the year, Accounts Receivable increased from $35,000 to $81,000. How much cash was received from customers during 19X3?

4. Craibill Company purchased machinery for $91,000, loaned $14,000 to a customer, borrowed $12,000, and sold securities that were not cash equivalents for $42,000. What was the net cash flow from investing activities?

5. In 19X9 Keller Company collected $25,000 from customers, paid interest of $1,900, received dividends of $2,000, and paid dividends of $9,000. What was the net cash flow from operating activities for 19X9?

V. Critical Thinking

Review the information in Exercises 1 and 3. Calculate the same answers using a different approach.

_____

_____

_____

_____

_____

 ## VI. Demonstration Problems

Demonstration Problem #1

The income statement, schedule of current account changes, and additional data for Smith Johnson Corporation follows:

Smith Johnson Corporation
Income Statement
For the Year Ended December 31, 19X8

Revenues:		
Net sales revenue	$1,405,000	
Dividend revenue	27,000	$1,432,000
Expenses:		
Cost of goods sold	1,081,000	
Salary expense	129,000	
Other operating expense	31,000	
Depreciation expense	55,000	
Interest expense	65,000	
Amortization expense - patents	5,000	1,366,000
Net income		$ 66,000

Additional data:

a. collections exceeded sales by $7,000.

b. dividend revenue equaled cash amounts received, $27,000.

c. payments to suppliers were $18,000 less than cost of goods sold. Payments for other operating expense and interest expense were the same as the amounts reported on the Income Statement.

d. payments to employees were less than salary expense by $4,000.

e. acquisition of plant assets totaled $130,000. Of this amount, $20,000 was paid in cash and the balance was financed by signing a note payable.

f. proceeds from the sale of land were $85,000.

g. proceeds from the issuance of common stock were $50,000.

h. full payment was made on a long-term note payable, $40,000.

i. dividends were paid in the amount of $16,000.

j. a small parcel of land located in an industrial park was purchased for $74,000.

k. current asset and liability activity changes were as follows:

	December 31	
	19X8	19X7
Cash and cash equivalents	$232,000	$ 92,000
Accounts receivable	236,000	243,000
Inventory	378,000	384,000
Prepaid expense	12,000	12,000
Accounts payable	214,000	202,000
Salary payable	11,000	7,000
Income tax payable	3,200	3,200

Required

Using the direct method, prepare the December 31, 19X8 statement of cash flows and accompanying schedule of noncash investing and financing activities for Smith Johnson Corporation.

Direct Method

Smith Johnson Corporation
Statement of Cash Flows
For the Year Ended December 31, 19X8

Demonstration Problem #2

Using the information in Problem 1, prepare a statement of cash flows and accompanying schedule of noncash investing and financing activities using the indirect method.

Indirect Method

Smith Johnson Corporation
Statement of Cash Flows
For the Year Ended December 31, 19X8

Solutions

I. Matching

1. H   2. F   3. G   4. B   5. E   6. D   7. C   8. A   9A. I

II. Multiple Choice

1. A   Replace A with "to determine ability to pay dividends and interest" and you have a list of all the purposes for the statement of cash flows.

2. B   Changes in property, plant, and equipment are investing activities.

3. A   Changes in capital and debt are investing activities.

4. D   Cash and cash equivalents are highly liquid, short-term investments that can be converted into cash with little delay and include money market investments and investments in T-bills.

5. D   Recall that the receipt of a dividend from an investment accounted for under the cost method is treated as income and accordingly will be included in the income statement. For cash flow statement purposes, the receipt of dividends is considered an operating activity and will be reflected in that portion of the statement.

6. C   Operating activities create revenues and expenses in the entity's major line of business. Equipment sales are assumed not to be this entity's major line of business.

7. B   Investing activities increase and decrease the assets the business has to work with. Payment of a dividend is a financing activity. Note that while the receipt of interest on a bond is an operating activity, buying and selling bonds is an investing activity.

8. C   Financing activities include transactions with investors and creditors needed to obtain funds to launch and sustain the business. Of the items listed, only C, an investing activity, does not fit that definition.

9. E   Sales revenue is recorded on the accrual basis. To convert this to a cash flow, the net change in accounts receivable must be considered. A decrease in accounts receivable indicates that customers have paid more than they purchased and should be added to sales. An increase in accounts receivable indicates that customers have purchased more than they paid and should be subtracted from sales.

10A. C Regardless of method, changes in balance sheet accounts are analyzed.

III. Completion

1. balance sheet (The income statement, statement of retained earnings, and statement of cash flows all cover a period of time. Only the balance sheet is as of a particular date.)
2. collections of cash from customers
3. direct, indirect (order not important)
4. financing
5. investing
6. operating (Recall from our previous discussion that depreciation is a noncash expense.)
7. investing
8. direct
9. indirect
10. operating activities

IV. Exercises

1. Note that this exercise and the next ones may be solved using what you learned in earlier chapters:

	Taxes Payable (beginning)	$ 1,400
+	Taxes Expense	36,000
=	Subtotal	37,400
−	Cash Payments	?
=	Taxes Payable (ending)	$ 2,400

$1,400 + $36,000 − x = $2,400

x = $35,000

2.

	Cost of Goods Sold	$400,000
+	Increase in Inventory	10,000
=	Subtotal	410,000
−	Increase in Accounts Payable	18,000
=	Cash paid to suppliers	$392,000

3.

Cash received from credit sales:

	Accounts Receivable (beginning)	$ 35,000
+	Credit sales (80% x 1,250,000)	1,000,000
=	Subtotal	1,035,000
−	Cash collected from customers	?
=	Accounts Receivable (ending)	$ 81,000

	Cash received from credit sales ($1,035,000 − $81,000)	$ 954,000
+	Cash collected from cash sales (20% x 1,250,000)	250,000
=	Total cash collected from customers	$1,204,000

4.

Purchase of machinery	$(91,000)
Loan made to customer	(14,000)
Sale of securities	42,000
Net cash flow from investing activities	$(63,000)

Borrowing $12,000 is not an investing activity. It is a financing activity.

5.

Collection from customers	$25,000
Interest paid	(1,900)
Dividends received	2,000
Net cash flow from operating activities	$25,100

The payment of dividends is not an operating activity. It is a financing activity.

V. Critical Thinking

Exercise 1	Tax Expense	$36,000
	*Less increase in Taxes Payable	1,000
	Payments for taxes	$35,000

*The increase in the related liability is deducted because it represents an expense which has not been paid. Similarly, a decrease in the related liability would be added. Remember, we are concerned with *cash payments*.

Exercise 3	Sales	$1,250,000
	**Less increase in Accounts Receivable	46,000
	Cash received from customers	$1,204,000

**The increase in Accounts Receivable is deducted because it represents credit sales which have not been collected. Similarly, a decrease in Accounts Receivable would be added because it represents additional credit sales collected. Remember, we are concerned with *cash receipts*.

VI. Demonstration Problems

Demonstration Problem #1 Solved and Explained

Direct Method

Smith Johnson Corporation
Statement of Cash Flows
For the Year Ended December 31, 19X8

Cash flows from operating activities:			
Receipts:			
Collections from customers		$1,412,000	(A)
Dividends received on investments in stock		27,000	(B)
Total cash receipts			$1,439,000
Payments:			
To suppliers		1,094,000	(C)
To employees		125,000	(D)
For interest		65,000	(C)
Total cash payments			1,284,000
Net cash inflow from operating activities			155,000
Cash flows from investing activities:			
Acquisition of plant assets		(20,000)	(E)
Proceeds from sale of land		85,000	(F)
Acquisition of industrial park land		(74,000)	(E)
Net cash outflow from investing activities			(9,000)
Cash flows from financing activities:			
Proceeds from common stock issuances		50,000	(G)
Payment of long-term note payable		(40,000)	(G)
Dividends		(16,000)	(G)
Net cash outflow from financing activities			(6,000)
Net increase in cash			$ 140,000
Noncash investing and financing activities:			
Acquisition of plant assets by issuing note payable			$ 110,000 (E)

Computations and Explanations

(A) The largest cash inflow from operations will almost always be the collection of cash from customers. Cash sales obviously will bring in cash immediately. Since sales on account increase Accounts Receivable (not Cash), companies need to know the actual collections from customers. Item (a) of the additional data indicates that collections from customers were more than sales by $7,000. Thus, collections must have been $1,412,000 ($1,405,000 sales plus $7,000).

(B) Dividends do not accrue with the passage of time, but rather are recorded when received. Item (b) of the additional data states that $27,000 was received, the identical amount shown in the income statement. Thus, no adjustment is necessary. Note that dividends received result in a cash inflow reported as an operating activity. Although the origin of the dividend was from an investment activity, in accordance with the FASB, dividends received were accounted for as part of operating activities because they have a direct impact on net income.

(C) Payments to suppliers is a broad category which includes all cash payments for inventory and all operating expenses except disbursements for:

1. employee compensation expense
2. interest expense
3. income tax expense

A review of Item (c) indicates that payments to suppliers were $1,094,000 ($1,063,000 + $31,000) as follows:

Cost of goods sold	$1,081,000
Less: Additional amounts owed to suppliers	18,000
Payments for inventory	1,063,000
Payments for Operating expense	31,000
Total	$1,094,000

Payments to suppliers include all payments (except those listed above as exceptions) to those who supply the business with its inventory and essential services. Note that interest payment equals interest expense, an item that is separately disclosed in the statement of cash flows.

(D) Payments to employees include all forms of employee compensation. The income statement reports the expense (including accrued amounts), whereas the statement of cash flows reports only the payments. Item (d) indicates that actual payments were $125,000, which is $4,000 less than the $129,000 reported in the income statement as salary expense.

(E) The purchase of $130,000 in plant assets used $20,000 in cash. The balance was financed with a $110,000 promissory note. Because the note is not an outflow of cash, it is separately disclosed as a noncash investing activity at the bottom of the statement of cash flows.

The $74,000 industrial park land (Item j) used $74,000 cash and is shown as a cash outflow or "use." A firm's investment in income-producing assets often signals to investors the direction the firm is taking.

(F) The receipt of $85,000 from the land sale (Item f) is essentially the opposite of the acquisition of a plant asset, and should be reported as a cash inflow from an investment transaction.

(G) Investors and other financial statement users want to know how an entity obtains its financing. The financing activities section of the cash flow statement for Smith Johnson Corporation discloses the effect of the sale of common stock (inflow of $50,000, Item g), payment of a long-term note (outflow of $40,000, Item h), and payment of cash dividends (outflow of $16,000, Item i).

Demonstration Problem #2 Solved and Explained

Indirect Method

Smith Johnson Corporation
Statement of Cash Flows
For the Year Ended December 31, 19X8

Cash flows from operating activities:		
Net income (from income statement):		$ 66,000
Add (subtract) items that affect net income and cash flow differently:		
Depreciation	$55,000	
Amortization	5,000	
Decrease in accounts receivable	7,000	
Decrease in inventory	6,000	
Increase in accounts payable	12,000	
Increase in salary payable	4,000	89,000
Net cash inflow from operating activities		155,000
Cash flows from investing activities:		
Acquisition of plant assets	(20,000)	
Proceeds from sale of land	85,000	
Acquisition of industrial park land	(74,000)	
Net cash outflow from investing activities		(9,000)
Cash flows from financing activities:		
Proceeds from common stock issuances	50,000	
Payment of long-term note payable	(40,000)	
Dividends	(16,000)	
Net cash outflow from financing activities		(6,000)
Net increase in cash		$140,000
Noncash investing and financing activities:		
Acquisition of plant assets by issuing note payable		$110,000

Note that the only reporting difference with the indirect method appears in the operating activities section. Changes in the current accounts were calculated as follows:

| | December 31, | | Effect on Cash |
	19X8	19X7	Increase (Decrease)
Current assets:			
Cash and cash equivalents	$232,000	$ 92,000	$140,000
Accounts receivable	236,000	243,000	7,000
Inventory	378,000	384,000	6,000
Prepaid expense	12,000	12,000	0
Current liabilities:			
Accounts payable	214,000	202,000	12,000
Salary payable	11,000	7,000	4,000
Income tax payable	3,200	3,200	0

Points to Remember

1. Mastery of the statement of cash flows requires a complete familiarity with both the three categories of items shown in the statement (cash inflows and outflows from operating activities, investing activities, and financing activities) and the transactions that fit within each group. You will find it beneficial to carefully review Exhibit 18-2 in the text. This exhibit details the full range of transactions you will be expected to analyze.

2. Preparing the statement of cash flows requires analysis of the accounts and of the individual line items and groupings of items found on the income statement. This is necessary because the income statement is prepared on the accrual basis, while the cash flows statement deals with the direct inflows and outflows of cash. Whenever the problem indicates that there has been an accrual of an item of income or expense, the income statement figure must be restated from its accrued amount to its cash-flow amount. The text includes a wide range of examples, as do these demonstration and practice problems.

3. You should be able, with some practice, to quickly identify the location and direction (that is, cash inflow or outflow) that a particular transaction will take on the cash flows statement. For example, the issuance of stock, the borrowing of money, and the sale of treasury stock all will result in the receipt of cash relating to a financing activity. The opposite type of transaction would result in the payment (outflow) of cash. For example, the acquisition of treasury stock or the payment of a long-term debt would result in an outflow, payment, or use of cash relating to a financing activity.

Chapter 19

Financial Statement Analysis
for Decision Making

Chapter Overview

*F*inancial statements are the primary means an outsider uses to evaluate a particular company. Once completed, the results can be compared with other companies. There are a variety of tools used to evaluate performance. In this chapter you are introduced to some of these techniques. The specific learning objectives for the chapter are:

1. Perform a horizontal analysis of comparative financial statements
2. Perform a vertical analysis of financial statements
3. Prepare common-size financial statements
4. Use the statement of cash flows in decision making
5. Compute the standard financial ratios used for decision making
6. Use ratios in decision making

Chapter Review

Financial statement analysis is based on information taken from the annual report, SEC reports, articles in the business press, and so on. The objective of financial statement analysis is to provide information to creditors and investors to help them 1) predict future returns and 2) assess the risk of those returns. Past performance is often a good indicator of future performance. Three categories of financial statement analysis are horizontal, vertical, and ratio analysis.

OBJECTIVE 1
Perform a horizontal analysis of comparative financial statements.

The study of percentage changes in comparative statements is called **horizontal analysis.** Horizontal analysis highlights changes over time. Computing a percentage change in comparative statements requires two steps:

1) Compute the dollar amount of the change from the base period to the later period, and

2) Divide the dollar amount of the change by the base period amount.

The **base period** for horizontal analysis is the year prior to the year being considered. Suppose there are three years of data. The change from Year 1 to Year 2 is:

$$\frac{\$ \text{ YEAR 2} - \$ \text{ YEAR 1}}{\$ \text{ YEAR 1}}$$

and the change from Year 2 to Year 3 is:

$$\frac{\$ \text{ YEAR 3} - \$ \text{ YEAR 2}}{\$ \text{ YEAR 2}}$$

No percentage changes are computed if the base-year amount is zero or negative.

Trend percentages are a form of horizontal analysis. They indicate the direction of business activities by comparing numbers over a span of several years. Trend percentages are computed by selecting a base year and expressing the amount of each item for each of the following years as a percentage of the base year's amount for that item.

OBJECTIVE 2
Perform a vertical analysis of financial statements.

Vertical analysis of a financial statement reveals the percentage of the total that each statement item represents. Percentages on the comparative income statement are computed by dividing all amounts by net sales. Percentages on the comparative balance sheet are shown as either: 1) a percentage of total assets, or 2) a percentage of total liabilities and stockholders' equity.

Vertical analysis of the income statement highlights changes in such items as the gross profit percentage and net income.

Vertical analysis of the balance sheet shows the composition of balance sheet items. Trend analysis can be used to highlight year-to-year percentage changes.

(Review Exhibits 19-4 and 19-5 in your text.)

Common-size statements report amounts in percentages only. The common-size statement is a form of vertical analysis. On a common-size income statement, each item is expressed as a percentage of the net sales amount. In the balance sheet, the common size is the total on each side of the accounting equation. Note that common-size percentages are the same percentages shown on financial statements using vertical analysis. (Review Exhibit 19-6 in your text.)

OBJECTIVE 4
Use the
statement of
cash flows in
decision
making.

Common-size percentages can be used to compare financial statements of different companies, or to compare one company's financial statements to industry averages. (Review Exhibit 19-7 as an example of the latter.)

The statement of cash flows presents the cash flows from operating, investing, and financing activities.

Questions to consider might include:

1. Does the company generate the majority of its cash from operations, from selling fixed assets, or from borrowing?
2. Does the company retain enough income to finance future operations?

Free cash flow is the difference between cash flows from operations and cash flows from investing. In theory, a company can increase share value by using this excess for purchasing treasury stock and paying dividends.

OBJECTIVE 5
Compute the
standard
financial ratios
used for
decision
making.

There are many, many different ratios used in financial analysis. Sometimes a ratio is used alone, but more frequently a group of ratios are calculated and used to analyze a particular issue. The ratios discussed in this section are grouped as follows:

1. Ratios that measure the ability to pay current liabilities
2. Ratios that measure the ability to sell inventory and collect receivables
3. Ratios that measure profitability
4. Ratios used to analyze stock as an investment

(See Exhibit 19-10 for a summary of these categories and ratios.)

1. **Ratios that measure the ability to pay current liabilities**

Working capital is used to measure a business's ability to meet its short-term obligations with its current assets.

WORKING CAPITAL = CURRENT ASSETS – CURRENT LIABILITIES

The **current ratio** is used to measure the availability of sufficient liquid assets to maintain normal business operations.

$$\text{CURRENT RATIO} = \frac{\text{CURRENT ASSETS}}{\text{CURRENT LIABILITIES}}$$

The **acid-test (quick) ratio** measures the ability of a business to pay all of its current liabilities if they came due immediately.

$$\text{ACID-TEST RATIO} = \frac{\text{CASH + SHORT-TERM INVESTMENTS} + \text{NET CURRENT RECEIVABLES}}{\text{CURRENT LIABILITIES}}$$

Remember: Inventory and prepaid expenses are not used to compute the acid-test ratio.

2. **Ratios that measure the ability to sell inventory and collect receivables**

Inventory turnover is a measure of the number of times a company sells an average level of inventory during a year.

$$\text{INVENTORY TURNOVER} = \frac{\text{COST OF GOODS SOLD}}{\text{AVERAGE INVENTORY}}$$

$$\text{AVERAGE INVENTORY} = \frac{\text{BEGINNING INVENTORY} + \text{ENDING INVENTORY}}{2}$$

Accounts receivable turnover measures the ability of a company to collect cash from its credit customers.

$$\text{ACCOUNTS RECEIVABLE TURNOVER} = \frac{\text{NET CREDIT SALES}}{\text{AVERAGE NET ACCOUNTS RECEIVABLE}}$$

$$\text{AVERAGE NET ACCOUNTS RECEIVABLE} = \frac{\text{BEGINNING ACCOUNTS RECEIVABLE} + \text{ENDING ACCOUNTS RECEIVABLE}}{2}$$

Days' sales in receivables measures in sales days the value of accounts receivable; it tells how many days' sales remain uncollected (in accounts receivable).

$$\text{ONE DAY'S SALE} = \frac{\text{NET SALES}}{365}$$

$$\text{DAYS' SALES IN AVERAGE ACCOUNTS RECEIVABLE} = \frac{\text{AVERAGE NET ACCOUNTS RECEIVABLE}}{\text{ONE DAY'S SALES}}$$

To compute the ratio for the beginning of the year, substitute beginning net Accounts Receivable for average net Accounts Receivable. To compute the ratio for the end of the year, substitute ending net Accounts Receivable for average net Accounts Receivable.

3. **Ratios that measure the ability to pay long-term debt**

The **debt ratio** measures the relationship between total liabilities and total assets.

$$\text{DEBT RATIO} = \frac{\text{TOTAL LIABILITIES}}{\text{TOTAL ASSETS}}$$

The **times-interest-earned ratio** measures the ability of a business to pay interest expense.

$$\text{TIMES-INTEREST-EARNED RATIO} = \frac{\text{INCOME FROM OPERATIONS}}{\text{INTEREST EXPENSE}}$$

Remember that income from operations does not include interest revenue, interest expense, or income tax expense.

4. **Ratios that measure profitability**

Return on net sales measures the relationship between net income and sales.

$$\text{RATE OF RETURN ON NET SALES} = \frac{\text{NET INCOME}}{\text{NET SALES}}$$

Return on total assets measures the success a company has in using its assets to earn a profit.

$$\text{RATE OF RETURN ON TOTAL ASSETS} = \frac{\text{NET INCOME} + \text{INTEREST EXPENSE}}{\text{AVERAGE TOTAL ASSETS}}$$

$$\text{AVERAGE TOTAL ASSETS} = \frac{\text{BEGINNING TOTAL ASSETS} + \text{ENDING TOTAL ASSETS}}{2}$$

The **rate of return on common stockholders' equity** shows the relationship between net income and common stockholders' investment in the company.

$$\text{RATE OF RETURN ON COMMON STOCKHOLDERS' EQUITY} = \frac{\text{NET INCOME} - \text{PREFERRED DIVIDENDS}}{\text{AVERAGE COMMON STOCKHOLDERS' EQUITY}}$$

$$\text{AVERAGE COMMON STOCKHOLDERS' EQUITY} = \frac{\text{BEGINNING} + \text{ENDING COMMON STOCKHOLDERS' EQUITY}}{2}$$

Earnings per share (EPS) is the amount of net income per share of the company's common stock.

$$\text{EPS} = \frac{\text{NET INCOME} - \text{PREFERRED DIVIDENDS}}{\text{NUMBER OF SHARES OF COMMON STOCK OUTSTANDING}}$$

If the number of shares outstanding has changed during the year, the denominator is changed to reflect the weighted average number of shares outstanding.

5.   **Ratios used to analyze stock as an investment**

The **price/earnings (P/E) ratio** is the ratio of the market price of a share of common stock to the company's EPS.

$$\text{PRICE/EARNINGS RATIO} = \frac{\text{MARKET PRICE PER SHARE OF COMMON STOCK}}{\text{EARNINGS PER SHARE}}$$

Dividend yield is the ratio of dividends per share of stock to the stock's market price per share.

$$\text{DIVIDEND YIELD ON COMMON STOCK} = \frac{\text{DIVIDENDS PER SHARE OF COMMON STOCK}}{\text{MARKET PRICE PER SHARE OF COMMON STOCK}}$$

The formula for calculating **book value per share of common stock** is:

$$\text{BOOK VALUE PER SHARE OF COMMON STOCK} = \frac{\text{TOTAL STOCKHOLDERS' EQUITY} - \text{PREFERRED EQUITY}}{\text{NUMBER OF SHARES OF COMMON STOCK OUTSTANDING}}$$

OBJECTIVE 6
Use ratios in decision making.

Ratios should be: 1) evaluated over a period of years and 2) compared with industry standards.

When a problem is found, the items used to compute the ratio should be analyzed to determine the nature of the problem. At that time, possible solutions to the problem can be suggested.

In an efficient capital market, stock prices reflect all information that is available to the public. Financial statement analysis helps to identify and evaluate the inherent risks in potential investments.

Test Yourself

All the self-testing materials in this chapter focus on information and procedures that your instructor is likely to test in quizzes and examinations.

I. Matching *Match each numbered term with its lettered definition.*

1. accounts receivable turnover
2. working capital
3. common-size statements
4. days' sales in receivables
5. dividend yield
6. inventory turnover
7. return on total assets
8. times-interest-earned ratio
9. vertical analysis

10. acid-test ratio
11. current ratio
12. debt ratio
13. horizontal analysis
14. price/earnings ratio
15. return on net sales
16. book value per share of common stockholders' equity
17. return on common stockholders' equity

A. analysis of a financial statement that reveals the relationship of each statement item to the total that is the 100 percent figure
B. common stockholders' equity divided by the number of shares of common stock outstanding
C. current assets divided by current liabilities
D. current assets minus current liabilities
E. financial statements that report only percentages (no dollar amounts)
F. measures the number of times that operating income can cover interest expense
G. measures the number of times a company sells its average level of inventory in a year
H. ratio of the market price of a share of common stock to a company's earnings per share
I. measures the success a company has in using its assets to earn a profit
J. net income minus preferred dividends, divided by average common stockholders' equity; a measure of profitability
K. ratio of average net accounts receivable to one day's sales
L. ratio of dividends per share to the stock's market price per share
M. ratio of net income to net sales; a measure of profitability
N. study of percentage changes in comparative financial statements
O. tells the proportion of a company's assets that it has financed with debt
P. tells whether an entity could pay all its current liabilities if they came due immediately
Q. the ratio of net credit sales to average net accounts receivable; it measures the ability to collect cash from credit customers

II. Multiple Choice *Circle the best answer.*

1. In vertical analysis the relationship between cost of goods sold and net sales is shown by the:
    A. income from operations percentage
    B. net income percentage
    C. gross profit percentage
    D. net sales percentage

2. Which of the following measures profitability?
    A. debt ratio
    B. current ratio
    C. dividend yield
    D. earnings per share

3. Which of the following current assets is not used to compute the acid-test ratio?
    A. accounts receivable
    B. cash
    C. prepaid expenses
    D. short-term investments

4. Which of the following is a common measure of a firm's ability to meet short-term obligations?
    A. working capital
    B. rate of return on sales
    C. net assets
    D. price/earnings ratio

5. The times-interest-earned ratio measures:
    A. profitability
    B. ability to pay interest expense on debt
    C. ability to pay current liabilities
    D. ability to collect receivables

6. The proportion of a firm's assets financed by debt is measured by the:
    A. current ratio
    B. debt ratio
    C. debt yield ratio
    D. times-interest-earned ratio

7. Assume that a company's current ratio is greater than one. If the company pays current liabilities with cash, the new current ratio:
    A. will increase
    B. will decrease
    C. will remain unchanged
    D. cannot be determined

8. The dividend yield evaluates:
   A. the ability to pay current debt
   B. profitability
   C. stock as an investment
   D. the ability to pay long-term debt

9. The excess of cash flows from operations over cash flows from investing is:
   A. a measure of profitability
   B. free cash flows
   C. a measure of short-term liquidity
   D. a measure of long-term debt paying ability

10. Book value measures:
    A. profitability
    B. short-term liquidity
    C. long-term debt paying ability
    D. stock as an investment

 III. Completion *Complete each of the following statements.*

1. The study of percentage changes in comparative financial statements is called
   _____ analysis.

2. Vertical analysis percentages on the income statement are computed by dividing all
   amounts by _____.

3. Vertical analysis percentages on the balance sheet are computed by dividing all
   amounts by _____.

4. Working capital is _____.

5. _____ and _____ are the two most common

   measures of firm size.

6. Leverage _____ the risk to common stockholders.

7. The _____ ratio indicates the market price of one dollar of earnings.

8. The rate of return on total assets equals _____.

9. The most widely quoted of all financial statistics is _____.

10. The _____ is the recorded accounting value
    of each share of common stock outstanding.

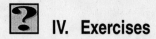 IV. Exercises

1. Net income was $75,000 in Year 1, $100,000 in Year 2, and $80,000 in Year 3. What were the percentage changes in net income?

2. Analytic, Inc. had the following information for 19X5:

Cost of goods sold	$400,000
Beginning inventory	30,000
Ending inventory	60,000
Net credit sales	725,000
Beginning accounts receivable	75,000
Ending accounts receivable	85,000

A. What is inventory turnover?

B. What is the accounts receivable turnover?

C. What is the days' sales in average receivables?

3. The following information is given for Roberts Corporation for 19X2:

Net sales	$ 825,000
Net income	60,000
Average common stockholders' equity	3,150,000
Average total assets	4,225,000
Interest expense	75,000
Preferred dividends	20,000
Common dividends	55,000
Common stock outstanding	240,000 shares

A. What is the rate of return on net sales?

B. What is the rate of return on total assets?

C. What is the rate of return on common stockholders' equity?

4. The following information is given for Maxie Mfg. Corporation:

Assets:

Cash	$ 60,000
Marketable securities	118,000
Accounts receivable	214,000
Inventory	141,000
Equipment	420,000
Total Assets	$953,000

Liabilities and Stockholders' Equity:

Accounts payable	$105,000
Salary payable	17,000
Long-term bonds payable	165,000
Common stock	200,000
Retained earnings	466,000
Total Liabilities and Stockholders' Equity	$953,000

A. What is the current ratio?

B. What is the acid-test (quick) ratio?

C. What is the debt ratio?

5. Calvin Mark Inc. has a price/earnings ratio of 18, dividends of $3.00 per share, and earnings per share of $2.57?

A. What is the market price per share?

B. What is the dividend yield?

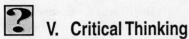 **V. Critical Thinking**

The operating cycle is the length of time between the purchase of merchandise and its conversion to cash following the sale and receipt of payment. (You were introduced to the operating cycle in Chapter 5.) Using the information in Exercise 2 above, calculate the operating cycle for Analytic, Inc.

_____

_____

_____

_____

_____

_____

_____

_____

 VI. Demonstration Problems

Demonstration Problem # 1

The Clorox Company, headquartered in Oakland, California, manufactures household products including Kingsford Charcoal briquettes, K. C. Barbecue sauces, and laundry whitening products (Clorox bleach). Figures from their 1993 annual report (slightly modified for ease of presentation) follow:

The Clorox Company
Statement of Consolidated Earnings
For Year Ended June 30, 1993

	(In thousands)
Net sales	$1,634,171
Cost and expenses	
Cost of products sold	724,753
Selling, delivery, and administration	328,088
Advertising	242,528
Research and development	42,445
Interest expense	18,856
Other (income) expense, net	2,316
Total costs and expenses	1,358,986
Earnings before income taxes	275,185
Income taxes	107,267
Earnings from continuing operations	167,918
Losses from discontinued operations	(867)
Net earnings	$ 167,051
Weighted average shares outstanding	54,698

The Clorox Company
Consolidated Balance Sheet
June 30, 1993

(In thousands)

	1993	1992
Assets		
Current assets:		
Cash and short-term investments	$ 71,164	$ 69,024
Accounts receivable, less allowance	226,675	188,117
Inventories	105,890	93,114
Deferred income taxes	19,360	20,716
Prepaid expenses	16,369	11,136
Other current assets	92,320	-
Total current assets	531,778	382,107
Property, plant, and equipment, net	538,101	508,629
Brands, trademarks, patents and other intangibles - net	463,941	453,195
Investment in affiliates	68,179	90,599
Other assets	47,231	155,463
Total assets	$1,649,230	$1,589,993
Liabilities and Stockholders' Equity		
Current liabilities:		
Accounts payable	$ 84,243	$ 97,767
Accrued liabilities	226,775	212,773
Income taxes payable	20,585	19,236
Commercial paper	39,486	77,410
Current maturity of long-term debt	481	153
Total current liabilities	371,570	407,429
Long-term debt	204,000	203,627
Other obligations	50,663	57,457
Deferred income taxes	143,703	107,739
Stockholders' equity		
Common stock - authorized, 175,000,000 shares, $1 par value; issued: 55,422,297 shares	55,422	55,422
Additional paid-in capital	105,483	105,249
Retained earnings	762,162	690,018
Treasury shares, at cost: 1993, 572,155 shares; 1992, 877,204 shares	(23,357)	(35,025)
Cumulative translation adjustments	(20,416)	(1,923)
Stockholders' equity	879,294	813,741
Total liablilites and stockholders' equity	$1,649,230	$1,589,993

Required

Assume annual dividends of $1.71 and a market price of 52 1/8 per share. Compute the following for 1993:

A)   working capital

B)   current ratio

C)   acid-test (quick) ratio

D)   inventory turnover

E)   accounts receivable turnover

F)   days' sales in receivables

G)   debt ratio

H)   times-interest-earned ratio

I)   rate of return on sales

J)   rate of return on total assets

K)   rate of return on common stockholders' equity

L)   earnings per share

M)   price/earnings ratio

N)   dividend yield

O)   book value per share of common stock

Demonstration Problem #2

SBJ Corporation's balance sheets and income statements are presented below:

SBJ Corporation
Balance Sheet
Years 19X6 and 19X5

	19X6	19X5
Assets		
Current assets:		
Cash	$ 13,300	$ 20,350
Short-term investments	8,200	8,000
Receivables, net	26,000	24,000
Inventories	45,000	40,000
Prepaid expenses	2,500	4,650
Total current assets	95,000	97,000
Property, plant, and equipment, net	185,680	196,500
Land	40,000	35,000
Intangibles and other assets	2,400	2,400
Total assets	$323,080	$330,900
Liabilities and Stockholders' Equity		
Current liabilities:		
Notes payable	$ 10,000	$ 10,500
Current installments of long-term debt	3,550	3,445
Accounts payable - trade	14,447	18,500
Accrued liabilities	3,670	1,605
Total current liabilities	31,667	34,050
Long-term debt, less current installments	95,500	93,330
Capital lease obligations, less current portion	1,100	2,150
Deferred income and deferred income taxes	4,813	4,370
Total common stockholders' equity	190,000	197,000
Total liabilities and stockholders' equity	$323,080	$330,900

SBJ Corporation
Income Statements
Years 19X6 and 19X5

	19X6	19X5
Net sales	$416,500	$406,316
Cost and expenses:		
Cost of goods sold	322,593	315,812
Operating expenses	41,219	43,200
Total costs and expenses	363,812	359,012
Income from operations	52,688	47,304
Interest expense	3,251	3,150
Earnings before income taxes	49,437	44,154
Income taxes	7,437	6,554
Net income	$ 42,000	$ 37,600

Required

1. Prepare a horizontal analysis for 19X6 of the balance sheet, using the 19X5 amounts as the base.

			Amount Increase (Decrease)	% Change
SBJ Corporation				
Balance Sheet				
Years 19X6 and 19X5				
	19X6	**19X5**		
Assets				
Current assets:				
Cash	$ 13,300	$ 20,350		
Short-term investments	8,200	8,000		
Receivables, net	26,000	24,000		
Inventories	45,000	40,000		
Prepaid expenses	2,500	4,650		
Total current assets	95,000	97,000		
Property, plant, and equipment, net	185,680	196,500		
Land	40,000	35,000		
Intangibles and other assets	2,400	2,400		
Total assets	$323,080	$330,900		
Liabilities and stockholders' equity				
Current liabilities:				
Notes payable	$ 10,000	$ 10,500		
Current installments of long-term debt	3,550	3,445		
Accounts payable - trade	14,447	18,500		
Accrued liabilities	3,670	1,605		
Total current liabilities	31,667	34,050		
Long-term debt, less current installments	95,500	93,330		
Capital lease obligations, less current portion	1,100	2,150		
Deferred income and deferred income taxes	4,813	4,370		
Total common stockholders' equity	190,000	197,000		
Total liabilities and stockholders' equity	$323,080	$330,900		

2. Convert the 19X6 and 19X5 Income Statements to common-sized statements, using net sales as the base figures.

SBJ Corporation				
Income Statements				
Years 19X6 and 19X5				
	19X6		19X5	
	Amount	%	Amount	%
Net sales	$416,500		$406,316	
Cost and expenses:				
Cost of goods sold	322,593		315,812	
Operating expenses	41,219		43,200	
Total costs and expenses	363,812		359,012	
Income from operations	52,688		47,304	
Interest expense	3,251		3,150	
Earnings before income taxes	49,437		44,154	
Income taxes	7,437		6,554	
Net income	$ 42,000		$ 37,600	

Solutions

I. Matching

1. Q 2. D 3. E 4. K 5. L 6. G 7. I 8. F 9. A
10. P 11. C 12. O 13. N 14. H 15. M 16. B 17. J

II. Multiple Choice

1.   C   The gross profit percentage is: (Net Sales – Cost of Goods Sold) / Net Sales

2.   D   Debt ratio measures the ability to pay long-term debts. Current ratio measures ability to pay current liabilities. Dividend yield is used in analyzing stock as an investment.

3.   C   Only the most liquid current assets are used to calculate the acid-test ratio.

4.   A   Working capital is current assets less current liabilities. It measure a firm's ability to meet short-term obligations.

5.   B   Times-interest-earned measures how many times greater operating income is than interest expense.

6.   B   Current ratio measures the ability to pay current liabilities. Debt yield ratio has no meaning. Times-interest-earned ratio measures ability to pay interest on debt. The debt ratio is total liabilities/total assets.

7.   A   Let CA = current assets, CL = current liabilities, and X = the amount of cash paid on current liabilities. Then given that CA > CL (or CL < CA), show that:

$$(CA - X) / (CL - X) \quad > \quad CA / CL$$
$$CL(CA - X) \quad > \quad CA(CL - X)$$
$$CL(CA) - CL(X) \quad > \quad CA(CL) - CA(X)$$
$$- CL(X) \quad > \quad - CA(X)$$

dividing by – X: CL   <   CA

Note: In a firm with current assets greater than current liabilities, the current ratio can be improved by using cash to pay current liabilities.

8.   C   Dividend yield compares the amount of dividends per share with the current market price. Therefore it is one way to evaluate a stock as a potential investment.

9.   B   Free cash flow is the excess of cash flows from operations compared to cash flows from investing.

10   D   Book value indicates the value of each share of common stock outstanding. It is one way to analyze a stock investment.

III. Completion

1. horizontal
2. net sales
3. total assets (or total liabilities plus stockholders' equity)
4. current assets minus current liabilities
5. Net sales, total assets
6. increases (Leverage is the practice of increasing the debt financing of an entity with respect to owner financing. Leverage is a two-edged sword, increasing profits [and returns to stockholders] during good times but compounding losses during bad times.)
7. price/earnings
8. (net income plus interest expense)/average total assets
9. earnings per share
10. book value per share of common stock

IV. Exercises

1. Year 2 = $25,000 / $75,000 = 33.33%
   Year 3 = ($20,000) / $100,000 = (20%)

2. A. Cost of goods / Average inventory = [$400,000 / ($30,000 + $60,000) / 2] = 8.89

   B. Net credit sales / Average accounts receivable =
      [$725,000 / ($75,000 + $85,000) / 2] = 9.06

   C. Average accounts receivable / One day's sales =
      [($75,000 + $85,000) / 2] / ($725,000 / 365) = 40.3 days

3. A. Net income / Net sales = $60,000 / $825,000 = .073 = 7.3%

   B. (Net income + Interest expense) / Average total assets =
      ($60,000 + $75,000) / $4,225,000 = .032 = 3.2%

   C. (Net income – Preferred dividends) / Average common stockholders' equity =
      ($60,000 – $20,000) / $3,150,000 = .013 = 1.3%

4. A. Current assets / Current liabilities =
      ($60,000 + $118,000 + $214,000 + $141,000) / ($105,000 + $17,000) = 4.4 (rounded)

   B. (Cash + Short-term investments + Net current receivables) / Current liabilities =
      ($60,000 + $118,000 + $214,000) / ($105,000 + $17,000) = 3.2

   C. Total liabilities / Total assets =
      ($105,000 + $17,000 + $165,000) / $953,000 = .301 = 30.1%

5. A. Market price per share of common stock / Earnings per share = P / $2.57 = 18
      P = $46.26 or $46 1/4.

   B. Dividends per share of com. stock / Market price per share of com. stock
      = $3.00 / $46.26 = .065 = 6.5%

V. Critical Thinking

The operating cycle for Analytic, Inc. is 81 days (rounded). Instruction (C) in the exercis
asked you to calculate the days' sales in average receivables. The correct figure was 40..
days. Another way of characterizing this result is to say that it takes approximately 40 day
to collect an average account receivable. Instruction (A) asked you to calculate inventor
turnover. The correct amount was 8.89—in other words, inventory "turns" slightly les
than 9 times each year. Divide this result into 365 to convert it to days, or 41 days. In othe
words, on average it takes 41 days for an item to sell and 40 days on average to collect
receivable. Therefore, the operating cycle is 81 days.

VI. Demonstration Problems

Demonstration Problem #1 Solved and Explained

A) working capital = current assets – current liabilities
= $531,778 – $371,570 = $160,208

B) current ratio = current assets / current liabilities
= $531,778 / $371,570 = 1.43

C) acid-test (quick) ratio = quick assets / current liabilities
= ($71,164 + $226,675) / $371,570 = 0.80

This means Clorox has 80 cents of quick assets (cash and short-term investment plus net accounts receivable) for every dollar of current liability.

D) inventory turnover = cost of goods sold / average inventory
= $724,753 / [($93,114 + $105,890) / 2] = 7.28 times

Clorox "turns" its inventory 7.28 times each year. Another way of stating this ratio is to convert it to days by dividing the "turn" into 365. For Clorox, the turnover averages 50 days (365 / 7.28).

E) accounts receivable
turnover = net credit sales / average accounts receivable
= $1,634,171 / [($188,117 + $226,675) / 2] = 7.88 times

F) days' sales in
receivables = average net accounts receivable / one day's sales
= $207,396 / ($1,634,171 / 365) = 46.3 days

The numerator for this ratio was the denominator for the previous ratio.

G) debt ratio = total liabilities / total assets = $769,936 / $1,649,230 = 0.467 or 46.7%

This means that 46.7% of the Clorox assets were financed with debt. Notice that the numerator (total liabilities) was not presented on the balance sheet but had to be calculated by adding together total current liabilities, long-term debt, other obligations, and deferred income taxes.

H) times-interest-earned ratio = income from operations / interest expense
= $294,041 / $18,856 = 15.6 times

Note that we used earnings before income taxes plus interest expense as the numerator because interest expense had already been deducted from the earnings before income taxes amount.

I) rate of return on sales = net income / net sales = $167,051 / $1,634,171 = 0.102 or 10.2%

If the figure from "Losses from discontinued operations" had been significant, you would want to calculate this ratio twice—once using "Earnings from continued operations" and a second time using "Net earnings."

J) rate of return on total assets = (net income + interest expense) / average total assets

$$= (\$167,051 + \$18,856) / [(\$1,649,230 + \$1,589,993) / 2]$$
$$= 0.115 \text{ or } 11.5\%$$

This ratio measures the return on assets generated by this year's operations.

K) rate of return on common stockholders' equity = (net income – preferred dividends) / average common stockholders' equity = ($167,051 – 0) / [($813,741 + $879,294) / 2] = 0.197 or 19.7%

Clorox does not have preferred stock, so the numerator is the same as net earnings.

L) earnings per share = (net income – preferred dividends) / weighted average number of common stock outstanding = $167,051 / 54,698 = $3.05 (rounded)

This should be calculated for each "net earnings" amount. For Clorox:

Earnings per share	
Continuing operations	$3.07
Discontinued operations	(0.02)
Net earnings	$3.05

Companies are required to include these per-share amounts on the income statement, not in the footnotes.

M) price/earnings ratio = market price per share of common stock / earnings per share = $52.125 / $3.05 = 17

N) dividend yield = dividend per share of common stock / market price of common stock = $1.71 / $52.125 = 0.033 = 3.3%

O) book value per share of common stock

= (total stockholders' equity – preferred dividends) / number of shares of common stock outstanding

= $879,294,000 / 54,850,142

= $16.03 per share

The dollars are presented "in thousands" so you must add three zeroes to the total stockholders' equity amount. To determine the number of shares outstanding, deduct the treasury shares (572,155) from the issued shares (55,422,297). As emphasized in your text, these ratios would have more meaning if you did them over consecutive years. In addition, to properly evaluate a company, you would also want to compare the ratios with those of competitors (Procter & Gamble and Colgate-Palmolive, for instance) and with the industry as a whole.

Demonstration Problem #2 Solved and Explained

1.

SBJ Corporation				
Balance Sheet				
Years 19X6 and 19X5				
	19X6	19X5	Amount Increase (Decrease)	% Change
Assets				
Current assets:				
Cash	$ 13,300	$ 20,350	$(7,050)	(34.6)
Short-term investments	8,200	8,000	200	2.5
Receivables, net	26,000	24,000	2,000	8.3
Inventories	45,000	40,000	5,000	12.5
Prepaid expenses	2,500	4,650	(2,150)	(46.2)
Total current assets	95,000	97,000	(2,000)	(2.1)
Property, plant, and equipment, net	185,680	196,500	(10,820)	(5.5)
Land	40,000	35,000	5,000	14.3
Intangibles and other assets	2,400	2,400	0	0
Total assets	$323,080	$330,900	$(7,820)	(2.4)
Liabilities and stockholders' equity				
Current liabilities:				
Notes payable	$ 10,000	$10,500	$(500)	(4.8)
Current installments of long-term debt	3,550	3,445	105	3.0
Accounts payable - trade	14,447	18,500	(4,003)	(21.6)
Accrued liabilities	3,670	1,605	2,065	128.7
Total current liabilities	31,667	34,050	(2,383)	(7.0)
Long-term debt, less current installments	95,500	93,330	170	0.2
Capital lease obligations, less current portion	1,100	2,150	(1,050)	(48.9)
Deferred income and deferred income taxes	4,813	4,370	443	10.1
Total common stockholders' equity	190,000	197,000	(7,000)	(3.6)
Total liabilities and stockholders' equity	$323,000	$330,900	$(7,820)	(2.4)

2.

	SBJ Corporation				
	Income Statements				
	Years 19X6 and 19X5				
		19X6		19X5	
	Amount	%	Amount	%
Net sales	$416,500	100.0	$406,316	100.0
Cost and expenses:				
Cost of goods sold	322,593	77.4	315,812	77.7
Operating expenses	41,219	9.9	43,200	10.6
Total costs and expenses	363,812	87.3	359,012	88.3
Income from operations	52,688	12.7	47,304	11.6
Interest expense	3,251	0.8	3,150	.8
Earnings before income taxes	49,437	11.9	44,154	10.8
Income taxes	7,437	1.8	6,554	1.6
Net income	$ 42,000	10.1	$ 37,600	9.2

Points to remember:

1. When you are presenting horizontal analysis, each year's change is divided by the base year amount (in this case, 19X5) and converted to a percentage. While the change in any single item in any single year may not be significant, applying horizontal analysis over a number of years may highlight significant changes.

2. Common-sized statements for a single year are only meaningful when the results are compared to other companies or industry data. However, common-sized statements covering two or more years permit analysis of the particular company being examined. In this case, we see that 19X6 results improved over 19X5 due to lower cost of goods sold and lower operating expenses.

3. Financial ratios are mathematical formulas that quantify the relationship between two or more items reported in the financial statements. Ratios are used to assess and compare a firm's liquidity, profitability, rate of return, and ability to meet debt obligations.

Note: One of the most common mistakes students make is forgetting to use the average amount of inventory, accounts receivable, or shares outstanding in some of the formulas. It is important that an average be used to reduce distortions that might occur if only year-end balances were used.

Chapter 20

Introduction to Management Accounting: Manufacturing Accounting and Job Order Costing

 Chapter Overview

This chapter is the first of eight introducing you to management accounting. Very few of the topics covered in these chapters result in information available to individuals outside the business. Instead, you will learn about techniques businesses use to assist them in planning and controlling activities. In this chapter you are introduced to manufacturing accounting. Unlike service and merchandising businesses, manufacturing companies combine raw materials into a finished product. Accounting for manufacturing businesses is more complex because of the greater variety of "costs" involved. The specific learning objectives for the chapter are:

1. Distinguish between financial accounting and management accounting

2. Prepare the financial statements of a manufacturing company

3. Use cost of goods manufactured to compute cost of goods sold

4. Relate job cost information to inventory and expense accounts

5. Account for direct materials in a job order costing system

6. Account for direct labor in a job order costing system

7. Account for manufacturing overhead in a job order costing system

Chapter Review

OBJECTIVE 1
Distinguish between financial accounting and management accounting.

Financial accounting refers to accounting that reports to parties outside the business. This reporting is summarized in the income statement, balance sheet, and cash flows statement. **Management accounting** provides information to individuals inside a business (called managers). This information helps managers to plan and control the business, allocate resources in the organization, and make strategic decisions. Review Exhibit 20-1 in your textbook for a concise summary of the differences between financial and management accounting.

The **value chain** refers to those business activities that result in value being added to a company's product. Some examples are research and development, manufacturing and marketing (see Exhibit 20-2 in your text). Controlling costs throughout the entire chain is of primary importance to managers. In manufacturing, the term "cost" has a variety of meanings, determined by the context in which it is used. Carefully review Exhibit 20-3 in your text to become familiar with the term "product costs."

OBJECTIVE 2
Prepare the financial statements of a manufacturing company.

Merchandisers have one inventory—the products they sell. Manufacturers have three inventories—**materials, work in process,** and **finished goods.**

Materials inventory is the material used to manufacture the finished goods. **Work in process inventory** tracks the cost of goods that have been put into the manufacturing process but have not yet been completed. **Finished goods inventory** are the final products that are ready to be sold.

Inventory accounts are the only difference between the balance sheet of a merchandiser and that of a manufacturer. Study Exhibit 20-4 in your text to be sure you understand the difference.

Cost of goods manufactured is the manufacturer's counterpart to the merchandisers Purchases account. This is the only difference between a manufacturer's income statement and a merchandiser's income statement. Study Exhibit 20-5 in your text to be sure you understand the difference.

Manufacturing terms:

Direct materials 1) become a physical part of the finished product and 2) are separately and conveniently traceable to finished goods.

Direct labor is the cost of salaries and wages of the employees who physically convert materials into finished goods.

Manufacturing overhead includes all manufacturing costs other than direct materials and direct labor.

Indirect materials are materials used to manufacture a product that are not conveniently traceable to specific finished products. The cost of indirect materials is accounted for as part of manufacturing overhead.

Indirect labor consists of the wages and salaries of all factory workers who are not directly involved in converting material into finished goods. The cost of indirect labor is accounted for as part of manufacturing overhead.

Prime costs are the sum of direct materials plus direct labor.

Conversion costs are the sum of direct labor plus manufacturing overhead.

Computing cost of goods manufactured:

1) Cost of goods manufactured = Beginning work in process inventory + Total manufacturing costs – Ending work in process

2) Total manufacturing costs = Direct materials used + Direct labor + Manufacturing overhead

3) Direct materials used = Beginning materials inventory + Purchases – Ending materials inventory

Familiarize yourself with Exhibit 20-6 to be sure you understand how to compute cost of goods manufactured. Study the diagram below. It will help you to understand the flow of inventory costs through a manufacturing company.

DIRECT MATERIALS	WORK IN PROCESS	FINISHED GOODS
Beginning inventory + Purchases	Beginning inventory + Direct material used Direct labor Manufacturing overhead	Beginning inventory + Cost of goods manufactured
Direct materials available for use – Ending inventory	Total manufacturing costs to account for – Ending inventory	Goods available for sale – Ending inventory
Direct materials used	Cost of goods manufactured	Cost of goods sold

All of the costs that flow through manufacturing inventories are called **inventoriable costs**. **Period costs** are not traced through the inventory accounts. They are accounted for as operating expenses and include selling expenses and general and administrative expenses.

Job order costing accounts for products produced 1) as individual units or 2) distinct batches of products. A job can be a single unit of a product (one airplane) or a distinct batch of similar units of a product (10 sofas).

Costs are recorded and summarized on a **job cost record** (Exhibit 20-9).

A manufacturer acquires materials by sending a purchase order to a supplier. When the materials are received, a receiving report is prepared and a journal entry is recorded:

| Materials Inventory | XX | |
| Accounts Payable | | XX |

A **subsidiary materials ledger** is maintained, which tracks the receipt, usage, and balance of each materials inventory item.

When a job is entered into production, a **materials requisition** is prepared to have materials transferred from inventory storage to the factory floor.

The cost of direct materials is debited to Work in Process Inventory, while the cost of any indirect materials is debited to Manufacturing Overhead:

Work in Process Inventory	XX	
Manufacturing Overhead	XX	
Materials Inventory		XX

OBJECTIVE 6
Account for
direct labor in a
job order costing
system.

This entry records the transfer of materials from inventory to the manufacturing process. At the same time, the cost of the direct materials is entered on the job cost record.

A **labor time ticket** is used to accumulate the time spent on a job and the labor cost associated with the job.

Manufacturing wages are recorded with this entry:

Manufacturing Wages	XX	
Wages Payable		XX

Based on the information from the labor time tickets, the balance in the Manufacturing Wages account is allocated to direct labor and indirect labor, and recorded with this entry:

Work in Process Inventory	XX	
Manufacturing Overhead	XX	
Manufacturing Wages		XX

The direct labor costs associated with each job are posted to the appropriate job cost records.

OBJECTIVE 7
Account for
manufacturing
overhead in a
job order costing
system.

During the year, overhead costs are debited to Manufacturing Overhead as they are incurred:

Manufacturing Overhead	XX	
Various Accounts		XX

At year end, Manufacturing Overhead contains all the actual overhead costs of the period. Our task now is to determine how to apply these overhead costs to the products that were produced. However, applying overhead costs to production cannot wait until the end of each year. Accountants usually compute a **budgeted manufacturing overhead rate** so that overhead can be applied during the year:

$$\text{Budgeted Manufacturing Overhead Rate} = \frac{\text{Total Budgeted Manufacturing Overhead}}{\text{Total Budget Cost Application Base}}$$

The **cost application base** is likely to be 1) budgeted direct labor dollars, 2) budgeted direct labor hours, or 3) budgeted machine hours.

Overhead is applied using the budgeted overhead rate on a uniform basis throughout the year. For example, if overhead is applied at the rate of 70% of direct labor dollars, and actual direct labor dollars are $500, then applied overhead is $500 x 70% or $350.

The entry to record the application of overhead is:

Work in Process Inventory	XX	
Manufacturing Overhead		XX

Once overhead is applied to a job, we can compute unit cost:

$$\text{Unit Cost} = \frac{\text{Direct Materials + Direct Labor + Overhead Applied}}{\text{Number of Units Produced}}$$

As jobs are completed, they are transferred to finished goods:

Finished Goods Inventory	XX	
Work in Process Inventory		XX

When goods are sold, these two entries are recorded:

| Accounts Receivable | XX | |
| Sales Revenue (Retail selling price) | | XX |

| Cost of Goods Sold (Cost) | XX | |
| Finished Goods Inventory | | XX |

Note: The difference in these two entries represents gross profit.

Consider this T-account:

Manufacturing Overhead	
Actual	Applied

If applied overhead is less than actual overhead (a debit balance remains), then overhead is **underapplied.** If applied overhead is greater than actual overhead (a credit balance remains), then overhead is **overapplied.**

Insignificant amounts of over- or underapplied overhead are closed to Cost of Goods Sold at year end. Significant amounts of over- or underapplied overhead are allocated to Work in Process, Finished Goods, and Cost of Goods Sold.

Test Yourself

All the self-testing materials in this chapter focus on information and procedures that your instructor is likely to test in quizzes and examinations.

I. Matching *Match each numbered term with its lettered definition.*

1. Budgeted manufacturing overhead rate

2. Direct labor

3. Direct material

4. Manufacturing overhead

5. Indirect materials

6. Indirect labor

7. Job order cost

8. Job cost record

9. Period costs

10. Inventoriable cost

11. Labor time ticket

12. Materials inventory

13. Materials requisition

14. Overapplied overhead

15. Total manufacturing cost

16. Underapplied overhead

17. Work in process inventory

18. Finished goods inventory

A. A document that identifies the amount of time the employee spent on a particular job.

B. A debit balance remaining in the Manufacturing Overhead account after overhead is applied.

C. A document prepared by manufacturing personnel requesting materials to be used in production.

D. A document used to accumulate and control costs in a job order system.

E. All manufacturing costs other than direct materials and direct labor.

F. An accounting system used by companies that manufacture products as individual units or in batches.

G. Any cost identified with goods manufactured for sale.

H. Budgeted total overhead divided by the budgeted rate base.

I. Completed goods that have not yet been sold.

J. Cost of salaries and wages for the employees who physically convert materials into the company's products.

K. Costs that are never traced through the inventory accounts.

L. Manufacturing labor costs which are difficult to trace to specific products.

M. Goods that are in production but not complete at the end of the period.

N. Manufacturing materials whose costs cannot easily be traced to a particular finished product.

O. Material that becomes a physical part of a finished product and whose cost is separately and conveniently traceable through the manufacturing process to finished goods.

P. Materials on hand to be used in the manufacturing process.

Q. Results when applied overhead exceeds the actual overhead costs.

R. Sum of direct materials used, direct labor, and manufacturing overhead.

II. Multiple Choice *Circle the best answer.*

1. If cost of goods manufactured exceeds total manufacturing costs, which of the following must be true?

   A. finished goods inventory has increased

   B. finished goods inventory has decreased

   C. work in process inventory has decreased

   D. work in process inventory has increased

2. If finished goods inventory has increased, which of the following must be true?

   A. total manufacturing costs are more than cost of goods manufactured

   B. total manufacturing costs are less than cost of goods manufactured

   C. cost of goods sold is less than cost of goods manufactured

   D. cost of goods sold is more than cost of goods manufactured

3. Which of the following manufacturers would be most likely to use process costing?
   A. oil refinery
   B. contractors
   C. aircraft
   D. furniture

4. When indirect materials are used in production:
   A. Work in Process Inventory is debited
   B. Manufacturing Overhead is credited
   C. Manufacturing Overhead is debited
   D. Materials Inventory is debited

5. When direct materials are used in production:
   A. Work in Process Inventory is credited
   B. Manufacturing Overhead is debited
   C. Materials Inventory is debited
   D. Work in Process Inventory is debited

6. When manufacturing wages are allocated, indirect labor is:
   A. Debited to Work in Process Inventory
   B. Debited to Manufacturing Overhead
   C. Credited to Manufacturing Overhead
   D. Credited to Work in Process Inventory

7. The entry to debit Cost of Goods Sold and credit Finished Goods Inventory as sales are made is recorded in:
   A. a periodic inventory system
   B. a perpetual inventory system
   C. both a periodic inventory system and a perpetual inventory system
   D. neither a periodic inventory system or a perpetual inventory system

8. Underapplied overhead implies:
   A. a credit balance in the Manufacturing Overhead account
   B. a debit balance in the Manufacturing Overhead account
   C. too much overhead was applied
   D. Cost of Goods Sold is overstated

9. Which of the following is a period cost?
   A. materials
   B. office salary expense
   C. depreciation expense – manufacturing
   D. manufacturing wages expense

10. A significant amount of under(or over-)applied manufacturing overhead should be:

   A. carried forward to the next accounting period
   B. closed to cost of goods sold
   C. reported as an "Other expenses and revenues" on the income statement
   D. allocated proportionately to Work in Process, Finished Goods, and Cost of Goods Sold

 III. Completion *Complete each of the following statements.*

1. The dual objectives of a cost accounting system are _____ and _____.

2. The inventory accounts of a manufacturing firm will include _____, _____, and _____ inventories.

3. _____ are a physical part of the finished product and their cost is separately and conveniently traceable through the manufacturing process.

4. Indirect materials and indirect labor are part of _____.

5. _____ are also called inventoriable costs.

6. _____ are never traced through the inventory accounts.

7. There are two main types of accounting systems for product costing: _____ and _____.

8. Prime costs include _____ and _____.

9. Conversion costs include _____ and _____.

10. Job order costing is used by companies that manufacture products _____.

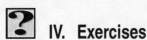 **IV. Exercises**

1. If cost of goods manufactured was $240,000, and beginning and ending Work in Process Inventories were $18,000 and $21,000 respectively, what were total manufacturing costs?

2. Work in Process Inventory increased $4,000 during the year for a manufacturing company. Total manufacturing costs were $305,000. What was Cost of Goods Manufactured?

3. Given the following information, calculate total Manufacturing Overhead:

Factory Building Depreciation	$ 50,000
Sales Office Expense	4,400
Factory Equipment Depreciation	21,900
Advertising Expense	51,000
Administrative Salaries	202,000
Property Taxes - Manufacturing	42,000
Depreciation on Delivery Equipment	17,000
Office Utilities Expense	8,200
Indirect Materials	2,700
Factory Equipment Repair Expense	6,600
Indirect Labor	12,500
Utilities Expense - Manufacturing	9,100

4. The following information pertains to Ace Manufacturing, Inc. for 19X6:

Cost of Goods Sold	$425,000
Direct Materials Purchased	170,000
Direct Materials Used	158,000
Ending Work in Process Inventory	
Less Beginning Work in Process Inventory	18,000

Finished Goods Inventory did not change.
Manufacturing Overhead is twice direct labor cost.
Beginning Work in Process Inventory is 25% of Ending Work in Process Inventory.

A. Compute Beginning and Ending Work in Process Inventories.

B.   Compute Cost of Goods Manufactured.

C.   Compute Total Manufacturing Costs.

D.   Compute Direct Labor and Manufacturing Overhead.

5.   The following information pertains to Bjourn's Company for 19X4:

Actual manufacturing overhead	$72,000
Actual direct labor cost	40,000
Budgeted direct labor cost for the year	42,000
Overapplied overhead	4,000

A.   How much manufacturing overhead was applied in 19X4?

B.   What was the budgeted overhead application rate?

V. Critical Thinking

When would the use of direct labor costs not be an appropriate base for allocating manufacturing overhead?

_____

_____

_____

_____

_____

_____

_____

_____

 ## VI. Demonstration Problems

Demonstration Problem #1

Pat's Pottery had the following inventory balances on January 1, 19X7:

Materials	$28,000
Work in Process	41,250
Finished Goods	62,425

During the month of January 19X7, he completed the following transactions:

A. Pat purchased 900 tons of clay (materials) for $35 per ton.

B. His workers requisitioned $38,000 of direct materials.

C. $4,050 of indirect materials were used.

D. He incurred $9,000 in manufacturing wages (90% was direct labor). (2 entries)

E. He incurred the following additional overhead costs: $1,600 in depreciation on manufacturing equipment and $3,765 in miscellaneous other costs (credit Accounts Payable).

F. Overhead is applied to production at the rate of 30% of direct materials cost.

G. Five orders were completed. The total cost of these orders was $71,215.

H. Pat sold six orders on account. The total cost of these orders was $124,000. The total sales price for the orders was $186,000.

I. The balance in Manufacturing Overhead was considered significant and allocated to Work in Process, Finished Goods, and Cost of Goods Sold.

Required (Use the work space provided on the next two pages.)

1. Record the transactions in the general journal.

2. What were the ending balances in the inventory accounts?

3. Was Manufacturing Overhead overapplied or underapplied?

4. What will be the amount of Cost of Goods Sold on the January income statement?

Requirement 1 (record transactions)

Date	Accounts and Explanation	PR	Debit	Credit

Manufacturing Overhead account:

Manufacturing Overhead

Requirement 2 (inventory balances)

| Materials | Work in Process | Finished Goods |

Requirement 3 (overhead)

Manufacturing overhead is _____.

Requirement 4 (cost of goods sold)

Cost of Goods Sold

Demonstration Problem #2

Review your solution to Demonstration Problem #1 and present a Schedule of Cost of Goods Manufactured for Pat's Pottery for January, 19X7.

Solutions

I. Matching

1. H 2. J 3. O 4. E 5. N 6. L 7. F 8. D 9. K
10. G 11. A 12. P 13. C 14. Q 15. R 16. B 17. M 18. I

II. Multiple Choice

1. C Recall:

> Beginning Work in Process Inventory
> + Total Manufacturing Costs
> – Ending Work in Process Inventory
> = Cost of Goods Manufactured

If cost of goods manufactured exceeds total manufacturing costs, then the effect on WIP inventory must be positive. Accordingly, beginning WIP must be greater than ending WIP inventory. If the ending balance is smaller than the beginning balance, the inventory has decreased.

2. C Recall:

> Beginning Finished Goods Inventory
> + Cost of Goods Manufactured
> = Goods Available for Sale
> – Ending Finished Goods Inventory
> = Cost of Goods Sold

If finished goods inventory has increased, the net effect of finished goods on the above formula is negative. Accordingly, Cost of Goods Sold would be less than Cost of Goods Manufactured. Answers A and B are incorrect because they do not relate to the finished goods account.

3. A Process costing is used by manufacturers producing a continuous flow of the same product. Of the manufacturers listed, the oil refinery is most likely to produce the same product in a continuous flow.

4. C The use of indirect materials requires Materials Inventory to be reduced and Manufacturing Overhead to be increased. The journal entry is:

> Manufacturing Overhead XX
> Materials Inventory XX

5. D The journal entry for the use of Direct Materials is:

> Work in Process Inventory XX
> Materials Inventory XX

6. B Recall that manufacturing wages are cleared through a clearing account so that direct labor and indirect labor can be allocated properly. In recording the payroll allocation, Work in Process Inventory is debited for direct labor and Manufacturing Overhead is debited for indirect labor.

7. B Only a perpetual inventory system has a Cost of Goods Sold account.

8. B   If overhead is underapplied, actual overhead costs were greater than overhead applied to Work in Process Inventory. Accordingly, the debits to Manufacturing Overhead are greater than the credits, and Manufacturing Overhead will have a debit balance.

9. B   Of those listed, only office salaries is a period cost. Materials, manufacturing depreciation, and manufacturing wages are all inventoriable costs.

10. D   When the amount of under(over-)applied overhead is significant, it is allocated to Work in Process, Finished Goods, and Cost of Goods Sold.

II. Completion

1. cost control, product costing
2. materials, work in process, finished goods
3. direct materials
4. manufacturing overhead
5. products costs
6. period costs
7. job order costing, process costing
8. direct materials, direct labor
9. direct labor, manufacturing overhead
10. as individual units or in small batches

IV. Exercises

1.
	Beginning Work in Process	$ 18,000
+	Total Manufacturing Costs	?
–	Ending Work in Process	21,000
=	Cost of Goods Manufactured	$240,000

Total Manufacturing Costs = $243,000

2.
	Beginning Work in Process	$ X
+	Total Manufacturing Costs	305,000
–	Ending Work in Process	X + 4,000
=	Cost of Goods Manufactured	$?

X + $305,000 – (X + $4,000) = $301,000

3.
Factory Building Depreciation	$ 50,000
Factory Equipment Depreciation	21,900
Property Taxes - Manufacturing	42,000
Indirect Materials	2,700
Factory Equipment Repair Expense	6,600
Indirect Labor	12,500
Utilities Expense - Manufacturing	9,100
Total Manufacturing Overhead	$144,800

4. A. Ending Work in Process – Beginning Work in Process = $18,000
        Beginning Work in Process = .25 x Ending Work in Process
        Ending Work in Process – .25 x Ending Work in Process = $18,000
        Ending Work in Process = $24,000
        Beginning Work in Process = .25 x $24,000 = $6,000

    B. Beginning FG + Cost of Goods Manufactured – Ending FG = COGS
        Beginning FG = Ending FG
        Cost of Goods Manufactured = COGS = $425,000

    C. | | Beginning Work in Process | $ 6,000 |
        |---|---|---|
        | + | Total Manufacturing Costs | X |
        | – | Ending Work in Process | 24,000 |
        | = | Cost of Goods Manufactured | $425,000 |

        Total Manufacturing Costs = $443,000

    D. | | Direct Materials Used | $158,000 |
        |---|---|---|
        | + | Direct Labor | X |
        | + | Manufacturing Overhead | 2X |
        | = | Total Manufacturing Costs | $443,000 |

        3X = $285,000
         X = $95,000   (Direct Labor)
        2X = $190,000   (Manufacturing Overhead)

5. A. | Applied Overhead – Actual Overhead | = | Overapplied Overhead |
        |---|---|---|
        | X   – $72,000 | = | $4,000 |
        | X | = | $76,000 |

    B. | Overhead Rate x Actual Direct Labor cost | = | Overhead applied |
        |---|---|---|
        | OH Rate   x $40,000 | = | $76,000 |
        | OH Rate | = | 190% |

V. Critical Thinking

Direct labor costs should not be used to allocate manufacturing overhead when direct labor is not the cost driver for overhead. For instance, with the increasing use of robots in manufacturing, direct labor costs are minor (or non-existent). In this case, machine hours (or the total machine costs) might be a more appropriate base for allocating overhead.

Demonstration Problem #1 Solved and Explained

Requirement 1 (record transactions)

	Accounts and Explanation	PR	Debit	Credit
A.	Materials Inventory		31,500	
	Accounts Payable			31,500
B.	Work in Process		38,000	
	Materials Inventory			38,000
C.	Manufacturing Overhead		4,050	
	Materials Inventory			4,050
D.	Manufacturing Wages		9,000	
	Wages Payable			9,000
	Work in Process (.90 x $9,000)		8,100	
	Manufacturing Overhead (.10 x $9,000)		900	
	Manufacturing Wages			9,000
E.	Manufacturing Overhead		5,365	
	Accumulated Depreciation			1,600
	Accounts Payable			3,765
F.	Work in Process (.30 x $38,000)		11,400	
	Manufacturing Overhead			11,400
G.	Finished Goods Inventory		71,215	
	Work in Process			71,215
H.	Accounts Receivable		186,000	
	Sales Revenue			186,000
	Cost of Goods Sold		124,000	
	Finished Goods Inventory			124,000
I.	Manufacturing Overhead		1,085	
	Work in Process (27,535/161,175 x 1,085)			185
	Finished Goods (9,640/161,175 x 1,085)			65
	Cost of Goods Sold (124,000/161,175 x 1,085)			835

Points to Remember

In transaction D, it is important to distinguish between direct labor and indirect labor. Direct labor is 90% of the total manufacturing wages of $9,000 or $8,100. The remaining is indirect labor.

In transaction F, it is important to note that overhead is applied based on direct materials. The only direct materials in this problem are the $38,000 of direct materials in transaction B.

To prepare the entry for item I, it is necessary to know the balance in the Manufacturing Overhead account:

Manufacturing Overhead			
(C)	4,050		
(D)	900		
(E)	5,365	(F) 11,400	
(I)	1,085	Bal. 1,085	
Bal.	0		

Since the account has a credit balance, we debit it in order to bring its balance to zero, and distribute the balance among Work in Process, Finished Goods, and Cost of Goods Sold. If the balance was not significant, it would be closed to Cost of Goods Sold.

Requirement 2 (inventory balances)

Materials			
Beg. 28,000	(B) 38,000		
(A) 31,500	(C) 4,050		
Bal. 17,450			

Work in Process			
Beg. 41,250			
(B) 38,000	(G)71,215		
(D) 8,100			
(F) 11,400			
Bal. 27,535	(I) 185		
Bal. 27,350			

Finished Goods			
Beg. 62,425			
(G) 71,215			
	(H) 124,000		
Bal. 9,640	(I) 65		
Bal. 9,575			

Requirement 3 (overhead)

A credit balance in the Manufacturing Overhead account indicates that Manufacturing Overhead is overapplied. The T-account in Requirement 1 indicates that Manufacturing Overhead had a credit balance of $1,085 prior to closing the account.

Requirement 4 (cost of goods sold)

Cost of Goods Sold		
(H) 124,000	(I) 835	
Bal. 123,165		

Demonstration Problem #2 Solved and Explained

Pat's Pottery
Schedule of Cost of Goods Manufactured
Month Ended January 31, 19X7

Beginning work in process inventory				$41,250
Direct materials				
Beginning inventory		$28,000		
(A) Purchases of direct materials		27,450		
Materials available for use		55,450		
Less: Ending inventory		17,450		
Direct materials used			$38,000	
Direct labor			8,100	
Manufacturing overhead				
Indirect materials		4,050		
Indirect labor		900		
Depreciation - factory equipment		1,600		
Miscellaneous		3,765		
(B) Total manufacturing overhead			10,315	
Total manufacturing costs incurred				56,415
Total manufacturing costs to account for				97,665
Less: Ending work in process inventory				27,350
(C) Cost of goods manufactured				$70,315

A. Because we only include "direct materials purchased" in this section, the total materials purchased ($31,500) has been reduced by the amount of indirect materials used ($4,050).

B. Total manufacturing overhead includes the actual costs *incurred*, not the actual amount applied.

C. The cost of goods manufactured shown on the schedule ($70,315) differs from the amount recorded in entry (G) ($71,215) for the following reasons:

$71,215 is the amount which includes the *applied* manufacturing overhead, not the actual overhead incurred. After entry (I) is recorded and posted, the three related accounts (work in process, finished goods, cost of goods sold) are reduced proportionately because manufacturing overhead was overapplied (i.e., too much was applied). The ending work in process balance ($27,350) has already been reduced by $185. The remainder ($65 to finished goods and $835 to cost of goods sold for a total of $900) reconciles the $71,215 from entry (G) with the $70,315 reported on the schedule ($71,215 – $70,315 = $900).

Remember, Finished Goods do not appear on this schedule. They are reported on the Income Statement and used to calculate Cost of Goods Sold.

Chapter 21

Process Costing

. . . .

Chapter Overview

*I*n Chapter 20 you were introduced to manufacturing accounting with specific reference to job order costing. In this chapter we turn our attention to a second system found in many manufacturing operations—process costing. Process costing is more complex than job order costing, and both systems assume an understanding of manufacturing accounting. Therefore, it is important that you be familiar with the material in Chapter 20 in order to master these concepts. The specific learning objectives for this chapter are:

1. Distinguish process costing from job order costing
2. Record process costing transactions
3. Compute equivalent units of production
4. Apply total cost to units completed and to units in ending Work in Process Inventory
5. Account for a second processing department by the FIFO method
6. Account for a second processing department by the weighted-average method

Chapter Review

OBJECTIVE 1

Distinguish process costing from job order costing.

Process costing assigns costs to goods produced in a continuous sequence of steps called processes. With process costing, costs are accumulated for a period of time, such as a week or a month. This contrasts with a **job order cost system**, which accounts for costs of specific batches of product.

With process costing, a product typically passes through several departments. For each department, there is a separate Work in Process Inventory account. (In a job order costing system, there is one Work in Process Inventory account supported by job cost records for the various jobs.)

OBJECTIVE 2

Record process costing transactions.

Process costing typically accounts for **direct materials** and **conversion costs**. Recall that conversion costs represent the sum of direct labor plus manufacturing overhead. The journal entries used for process costing are very similar to those used for job order costing.

To record current period costs:

Work in Process Inventory - Dept. 1	XX	
Materials Inventory		XX
Work in Process Inventory - Dept. 1	XX	
Manufacturing Wages		XX
Work in Process Inventory - Dept. 1	XX	
Manufacturing Overhead		XX

To record the transfer to the next department:

Work in Process Inventory - Dept. 2	XX	
Work in Process Inventory - Dept. 1		XX

Additional materials and conversion costs may be added in subsequent departments.

OBJECTIVE 3

Compute equivalent units of production.

The task in process costing is to account for both the cost of goods that have been completed as well as the cost of incomplete units.

Equivalent units of production is a measure of the amount of work done during a production period, expressed in terms of fully complete units of output.

To calculate equivalent units, multiply the number of partially completed units by their percentage of completion. The result is the number of conversion equivalent units. For instance, if 5,000 units are 40% complete, the number of conversion equivalent units is 2,000 (5,000 x 40%).

The **steps in process cost accounting** may be summarized as follows:

Step 1: Summarize the flow of production in physical units.

Total **physical units to account for** = beginning Work in Process + production started during the period.

Total **physical units accounted for** = units completed and transferred out during the period + ending Work in Process

Units to account for must equal units accounted for.

Step 2: Compute output in terms of equivalent units of production.

Compute equivalent units of production separately for direct materials and conversion costs. Remember that this is necessary because the percentage of completion may be different for materials and conversion costs. Exhibit 21-4 in your text reviews Steps 1 and 2.

Step 3: Summarize total costs to account for.

Total costs to account for = cost of Beginning Work in Process + Direct materials + Direct labor + Manufacturing overhead. This is equal to the sum of the debit entries in the Work in Process account for the department. Review Exhibit 21-5.

Step 4: Compute equivalent unit costs.

Compute separate unit costs for direct materials and conversion costs (i.e., make two separate calculations):

$$\text{Unit Costs} = \frac{\text{Costs Added During the Period}}{\text{Equivalent Units}}$$

$$\begin{array}{ccccc} \text{Total Cost} & & \text{Unit Cost} & & \text{Unit Cost} \\ \text{Per} & = & \text{for} & + & \text{for} \\ \text{Unit} & & \text{Direct Materials} & & \text{Conversion Costs} \end{array}$$

Review Exhibit 21-6.

Step 5: Apply total costs to units completed and to units in ending Work in Process Inventory.

OBJECTIVE 4

Apply total cost to units completed and to units in ending Work in Process Inventory.

The unit costs from Step 4 are applied to units completed and to units in ending Work in Process. Cost of units completed and transferred out = units completed and transferred out x total unit costs.

Cost of ending Work in Process = (equivalent units of ending Work in Process for direct materials x unit cost for direct materials) + (equivalent units of ending Work in Process for conversion costs x unit cost for conversion costs).

Review Exhibit 21-7. Note that the total costs accounted for in Step 5 must agree with the total costs from Step 3.

Exhibit 21-8 in your text summarizes these 5 steps. It is important that you understand both the correct order and the meaning of each. (Helpful hint: You may find it helpful to trace through the middle chapter review problem in your text.)

OBJECTIVE 5

Account for a second processing department by the FIFO method.

When working with multiple departments, it is important to distinguish between costs from the prior department and costs in the current department. Remember that the costs follow the units from department to department.

All costs in a department which were incurred in a prior department are called **transferred-in costs**. Only costs in the current department are accounted for as material or conversion costs in that department.

When beginning Work in Process Inventory exists and the FIFO (first-in, first-out) method is used, certain changes occur in the five steps used in the application of process costing:

Step 1: Flow of production in physical units.

With a second department, units started are replaced by units transferred in. This follows the flow of production in physical units.

Total units to account for = beginning Work in Process + units transferred in.

Total units accounted for = units from beginning Work in Process completed and transferred out + units transferred in, completed, and transferred out during the current period + ending Work in Process.

Note that total units to account for must equal total units accounted for. Note also that the FIFO method requires the separation of completed units into units from beginning inventory and units started and completed during the period.

Step 2: Equivalent units of production.

When computing equivalent units, there are three categories: transferred-in equivalent units, direct materials equivalent units, and conversion costs equivalent units. For each category, equivalent units are computed for 1) units from beginning inventory that were completed and transferred out, 2) units started (transferred in) and completed during the period, and 3) units in ending inventory.

Note that equivalent units for units completed from beginning inventory is equal to the percentage of work done during the current month (subtract the percentage completed during the prior month from 100%).

Study Exhibits 21-8 and 21-9 in your text to be sure you understand equivalent unit computations using FIFO in a multiple department process costing system.

Steps 3, 4, and 5.

These steps are similar to what is done for a single department with no beginning inventory. When performing Step 4, remember that costs associated with beginning Work in Process are NOT included in the unit cost calculation.

Review Exhibits 21-10 and 21-11 in your text.

The journal entries to record costs in a second department are:

Work in Process Inventory - Dept. 2	XX	
Materials Inventory		XX
Work in Process Inventory - Dept. 2	XX	
Manufacturing Wages		XX
Work in Process Inventory - Dept. 2	XX	
Manufacturing Overhead		XX

The entry to record the transfer of completed units to Finished Goods Inventory (or to a subsequent department) is:

Finished Goods Inventory (or Work in Process Inventory - Dept. 3)	XX	
Work in Process Inventory - Dept. 2		XX

A production cost report summarizes the operations in a department during the period. Exhibit 21-12 in your text presents a production cost report incorporating all the information contained in the 5 steps outlined above. Study it carefully.

When applying the **weighted-average cost assumption**, consideration is given to both the current period's costs and those from the preceding period. Review each of the 5 steps in process costing and note the differences between weighted-average and FIFO.

Step 1: Summarize the flow of production in physical units.

Same as FIFO! Why? Because the cost flow assumption applied only affects costs, not physical units.

Step 2: Compute output in terms of equivalent units.

With weighted-average, no distinction is made between those units transferred out from beginning Work in Process and those units transferred out that were also transferred in during the period. The key numbers are simply those units transferred out and those units still in process at period's end. For those units transferred out, the equivalent unit is the same as the number transferred out. Those units still in process at the end need to be converted to equivalent units. (Helpful hint: Compare Exhibit 21-9 with 21-14 in your text.)

Step 3: Summarize total costs to account for.

Under weighted-average the total costs to account for include both the beginning work in process costs and those costs added during the current period. This is consistent with the equivalent unit calculation discussed in Step 2.

Step 4: Compute equivalent unit cost.

This step integrates the information from Steps 2 and 3. Using the equivalent unit calculation from Step 2, the equivalent unit costs are quickly determined by dividing the amount from Step 2 into the totals obtained in Step 3. (Helpful hint: Carefully review and compare Exhibit 21-10 with Exhibit 21-15 in your text.)

Step 5: Apply total cost to units completed and to units in ending Work in Process Inventory.

Weighted-average does not distinguish between those units in process at the beginning of the period and those units transferred in and completed during the period. Instead, weighted-average uses the total number of units transferred out, assigning to this total the amounts calculated in Step 4. Thereafter, the ending Work in Process Inventory is calculated, once again using the unit costs determined in Step 4. (Helpful hint: Compare Exhibit 21-11 with 21-16 to clarify this distinction.)

The Production Cost Report is identical in format to the one illustrated with FIFO. Comparing Exhibit 21-12 with 21-17 (the condensed version) or Exhibit 21-13 with 21-18 (the expanded version) demonstrates this. Remember, this report is a summary of the information obtained in the five steps detailed above.

Regardless of cost assumption applied (FIFO or weighted-average), the journal entries are identical; only the amounts differ.

By this point in your study of this chapter you should have the five steps committed to memory:

Step 1: Compute physical units.

Step 2: Compute equivalent units.

Step 3: Summarize total costs.

Step 4: Compute equivalent unit cost.

Step 5: Apply total cost to units completed and units in ending inventory.

Test Yourself

All the self-testing materials in this chapter focus on information and procedures that your instructor is likely to test in quizzes and examinations.

I. Matching *Match each numbered term with its lettered definition.*

1. FIFO
2. equivalent units
3. process costing
4. weighted average

5. conversion cost
6. physical units
7. production cost report
8. equivalent unit costs

A. a costing method that considers both the current and previous period's cost
B. measure of the number of complete units that could have been manufactured from start to finish using the costs incurred during the period
C. a costing method which considers only the current period's costs
D. the actual number of units processed without regard to their percent of completion
E. summary of the activity in a processing department for a period
F. the sum of direct labor and manufacturing overhead
G. used to account for the manufacture of goods that are mass-produced in a continuous sequence of steps
H. the result of dividing equivalent units into total costs

II. Multiple Choice *Circle the best answer.*

1. The journal entry to assign manufacturing overhead in a process costing system would:
   A. debit Work in Process Inventory
   B. debit Manufacturing Overhead
   C. credit Work in Process Inventory
   D. debit Finished Goods

2. All of the following businesses are likely to use a process costing system except:
   A. industrial chemicals
   B. paint
   C. residential construction
   D. soft drinks

3. The journal entry to assign direct labor costs in a process costing system would:
   A. credit Manufacturing Wages
   B. credit Work in Process Inventory
   C. credit Wages Payable
   D. debit Manufacturing Wages

4. The journal entry transferring costs from Department A to Department B in a process costing system would:
   A. debit Work in Process - Department A
   B. credit Work in Process - Department B
   C. debit Work in Process - Department B and credit Work in Process - Department A
   D. debit Work in Process - Department A and credit Work in Process - Department B

5. Which of the following systems will usually have more than one Work in Process Inventory account?
   A. job order costing
   B. process costing
   C. both job order costing and process costing
   D. job order costing and process costing both have only one Work in Process Inventory account

6. Direct materials in the second department refer to:
   A. materials added in the first department
   B. materials added in the second department
   C. materials added in both departments
   D. materials added in departments other than the first or second

7. As manufacturing overhead costs are incurred in a process costing system:
   A. Work in Process Inventory is debited
   B. Work in Process Inventory is credited
   C. Manufacturing Overhead is credited
   D. Manufacturing Overhead is debited

8. The first step in process cost accounting is:
   A. the production cost report
   B. determining physical units
   C. determining equivalent units
   D. determining equivalent unit costs

9. In process cost accounting when the last process is complete and goods are transferred out:
   A. Work in Process Inventory is debited
   B. Finished Goods is credited
   C. Finished Goods is debited
   D. Individual credits are recorded to Materials, Manufacturing Wages, and Manufacturing Overhead

10. The final step in process cost accounting is:
    A. the production cost report
    B. determining physical units
    C. determining equivalent units
    D. determining equivalent unit costs

 III. Completion *Complete each of the following statements.*

1. A manufacturer who produces custom goods uses a _____ cost system.

2. A manufacturer with a continuous mass production of identical units through a sequence of steps uses a _____ cost system.

3. Conversion costs refer to _____ and _____.

4. Ending Work in Process of 5,000 units one-fourth complete would represent _____ equivalent units.

5. If the beginning Work in Process of 8,000 units is one-fifth complete, the amount of work left to complete would represent _____ equivalent units.

6. After the physical units have been determined, the next step in process cost accounting is _____.

7. The "Costs to be accounted for" are on the (debit or credit) _____ side of the Work in Process account.

8. Costs which flow with the goods from one department to another are called _____ _____ cost.

9. Under the _____ cost flow assumption, units transferred out from beginning inventory are treated differently from those units transferred in and out when calculating equivalent units.

10. The last step in process cost accounting is the _____.

 IV. Exercises

1. Using the numbers 1 to 6, place the following steps in correct sequence:
    _____A. Determine equivalent units
    _____B. Determine equivalent unit costs
    _____C. Determine the costs to be accounted for
    _____D. Determine physical units
    _____E. Write the Production Cost Report
    _____F. Apply total cost to units completed and units in ending inventory

2. The following information is for Department 3 of Allied Manufacturing Co. for the month of May:

Beginning Work in Process Inventory (40% complete as to conversion costs)	10,000
Units completed and transferred to Department 4	60,000
Units in ending Work in Process Inventory (20% complete as to conversion costs)	15,000

All materials are added at the beginning of Department 3

A. Assuming FIFO, determine:

   1. The number of units started into production in May.

   2. The number of units started and completed in May.

B. Assuming weighted-average, determine:

   1. The number of units started into production in May.

   2. The number of units started and completed in May.

3. Refer to the information in Exercise 2 and:

A. Assuming FIFO, determine:

1. The number of equivalent units for materials for May.

2. The number of equivalent units for conversion costs for May.

B. Assuming weighted-average, determine:

1. The number of equivalent units for materials for May.

2. The number of equivalent units for conversion costs for May.

4. Martin Manufacturing prepared the following production cost report for Department 1 for November:

	Physical Units	Total Costs
Work in Process Nov. 1 (100% complete as to materials and 20% complete as to conversion)	2,000	$ 11,150
Started into production in November (costs include $102,000 for materials and $82,350 for conversion)	24,000	$184,350
Total to account for	26,000	$195,500
Completed and transferred to Department 2 during November	20,000	?
Work in Process, Nov. 30 (100% complete as to materials and 40% complete as to conversion)	6,000	?
	26,000	$195,500

Assuming FIFO, answer the following:

A. What is the cost per equivalent unit for materials?

B. What is the cost per equivalent unit for conversion costs?

C. What costs are transferred to Department 2 at the end of November?

D.   What costs remain in Ending Work in Process Inventory - Department 1?

5.   Review the information in Exercise 4 for Martin Manufacturing, adding the following assumption: The $11,150 balance in beginning Work in Process consists of $9,540 in materials cost and $1,610 in conversion costs.

A.   Assuming weighted-average, what is the cost per equivalent unit for materials?

B.   What is the cost per equivalent unit for conversion?

V. Critical Thinking

Compare your answers in Exercise 4 (A and B) with your answers in Exercise 5 (A and B). What conclusions can you draw concerning the direction of both materials costs and conversion costs from October to November?

_____
_____
_____
_____
_____
_____
_____
_____
_____
_____

VI. Demonstration Problems

Demonstration Problem #1 (FIFO)

Kitchen Works Corporation produces cooking utensils. The following is a summary of activity and costs for the Enameling Department for the month of June:

Enameling Department
For the Month Ended June 30, 19XX

Units:
Beginning Work in Process Inventory	
(20% complete as to materials; 40% complete	
as to conversion)	22,500
Transferred in from the Fabricating Department	105,000
Total units completed	90,000
Ending Work in Process Inventory	
(40% complete as to materials; 50% complete	
as to conversion)	37,500

Costs:
Beginning Work in Process	$ 54,000
Transferred in costs from the Fabricating Department	157,500
Materials added	14,070
Conversion costs added	205,485

Required

Show the application of total cost to units completed and units in ending Work in Process Inventory for the Enameling Department for the month of June, assuming a first-in, first-out (FIFO) cost flow assumption.

Steps 1 and 2

Flow of Production in Physical Units				
and Equivalent Units of Production				
Enameling Department				
For the Month Ended June 30, 19XX				
		Equivalent Units		
Flow of Production	Flow of Physical Units	Transferred In	Materials	Conversion

Steps 3 and 4

Computation of Unit Cost				
Enameling Department				
For the Month Ended June 30, 19XX				
	Transferred In	Materials	Conversion	Total

Step 5

	Transferred In	Materials	Conversion	Total
Application of Total Cost to Units Completed				
and Units in Ending Work in Process				
Enameling Department				
For the Month Ended June 30, 19XX				

Demonstration Problem #2 (Weighted-Average)

Kitchen Works Corporation produces cooking utensils. The following is a summary of activity and costs for the Enameling Department for the month of June:

Enameling Department
For the Month Ended June 30, 19XX

Units:
Beginning Work in Process Inventory
  (20% complete as to materials; 40% complete
  as to conversion)   22,500
Transferred in from the Fabricating Department   105,000
Total units completed   90,000
Ending Work in Process Inventory
  (40% complete as to materials; 50% complete
  as to conversion)   37,500

Costs:
Beginning Work in Process (Transferred-in cost,
  $34,800; Materials cost, $650; Conversion cost,
  $18,550) $ 54,000
Transferred-in costs from the Fabricating Department   157,500
Materials added   14,070
Conversion costs added   205,485

Required

Show the application of total cost to units completed and units in ending Work in Process Inventory for the Enameling Department for the month of June, assuming a weighted-average cost flow assumption.

Steps 1 and 2

Flow of Production in Physical Units				
and Equivalent Units of Production				
Enameling Department				
For the Month Ended June 30, 19XX				
		Equivalent Units		
Flow of Production	Flow of Physical Units	Transferred In	Materials	Conversion

Steps 3 and 4

	Transferred In	Materials	Conversion	Total
Computation of Unit Cost				
Enameling Department				
For the Month Ended June 30, 19XX				

Step 5

	Transferred In	Materials	Conversion	Total
Application of Total Cost to Units Completed				
and Units in Ending Work in Process				
Enameling Department				
For the Month Ended June 30, 19XX				

Solutions

I. Matching

1. C   2. B   3. G   4. A   5. F   6. D   7. E   8. H

II. Multiple Choice

1.   A   A debit to Work in Process assigns overhead to a department. Manufacturing overhead is debited as overhead is incurred, Work in Process is credited only when goods are transferred out, and Finished Goods is debited only when items are completed and ready for sale.

2.   C   Since residential construction tends to be of identifiable units, job costing would be appropriate for it. Process costing is appropriate for the others listed.

3.   A   The entry to assign direct labor costs in a process costing system would be:

Work in Process Inventory - Dept. C	XX	
Manufacturing Wages		XX

4.   C   The materials, labor, and overhead costs accumulated as Work in Process Inventory in Dept. A would be transferred to Dept. B with the following journal entry:

Work in Process Inventory - Dept. B	XX	
Work in Process Inventory - Dept. A		XX

5.   B   Job order cost systems maintain only one Work in Process Inventory account. The job cost record for each incomplete job in such a system comprises the job cost or Work in Process subsidiary ledger for the control account. In a process cost system, with more than one department, each department has its own Work in Process Inventory account.

6.   B   Materials added in the first department and transferred to the second department are referred to as Transferred-in Costs. Accordingly, only materials added in the current department are called direct materials.

7.   D   Manufacturing overhead is debited as overhead is incurred. Work in Process is debited when costs are added to a department and credited when goods are transferred out. Manufacturing overhead is credited when overhead is assigned to departments.

8.   B   The first of the five steps in process cost accounting is determining physical units.

9.   C   Finished Goods is debited when goods are ready to sell. Work in Process is debited when goods are transferred in and when additional costs are added. Finished Goods is only credited when goods are sold. Materials, Manufacturing Wages, and Manufacturing Overhead are credited as costs are assigned to Work in Process.

10.   A   The last of the five steps in process cost accounting is the production cost report. Choices B, C, and D must be completed before the production cost report can be organized.

III. Completion

1. job order
2. process
3. direct labor, manufacturing overhead
4. 1/4 x 5,000 units =1,250
5. (1 – 1/5) x 8,000 units = 6,400
6. calculating equivalent units
7. debit
8. transferred in
9. FIFO
10. production cost report

IV. Exercises

1. A. 2   B. 4   C. 3   D. 1   E. 6   F. 5

2. The figures for FIFO and weighted-average are the same (remember these assumptions concern the flow of costs, not the actual physical flow).

   A. 1. Units transferred out + Ending inventory   = Units accounted for
            60,000   +   15,000   = 75,000

         Beginning inventory – Units started   = Units to account for
            10,000   –   X   = 75,000
                        Units started   = 65,000

      2. If 65,000 units were started and 15,000 are in process at the end of May, then 50,000 (65,000 -15,000) must have been started and completed. Alternatively, units completed (60,000) less units completed from beginning Work in Process (10,000) equals units started and completed (60,000 - 10,000 = 50,000).

   B. 1. Same as above
      2. Same as above

3. A. 1. Equivalent units for materials = units started = 65,000
      2.

From Beginning Inventory (10,000 x .60)	6,000
+ Started and completed	50,000
+ Ending Inventory (.20 x 15,000)	3,000
Equivalent units for conversion costs	59,000

   B. 1.

Completed and transferred out	60,000
In process, 5/31 (100% complete)	15,000
Equivalent units for materials	75,000

      2.

Completed and transferred out	60,000
In process, 5/31 (20% complete)	3,000
Equivalent units for materials	63,000

4. A. Equivalent units for materials = 24,000
   Cost per equivalent unit for materials = $102,000/24,000 = $4.25

   B. Equivalent units for conversion = (2,000 x .80) + 18,000 + (6,000 x .40) = 22,000
   Cost per equivalent unit = $82,350/22,000 = $3.743 (rounded)

   C.

Cost of beginning Work in Process	$ 11,150
Cost to complete (2,000 x 80% x $3.743)	5,989
Units started and finished	
[18,000 x ($4.25 + $3.743)]	143,877
Cost transferred out	$161,016

   D.

Materials (6,000 x 100% x 4.25)	$ 25,500
Conversion (6,000 x 40% x $3.743)	8,984
Cost of ending Work in Process	$ 34,484

5. A. Equivalent units for materials = 26,000 (20,000 + 6,000)
   Cost per equivalent unit for materials:
   $9,540 + $102,000 = $111,540/26,000 = $4.29

   B. Equivalent units for conversion = 22,400 (20,000 + 2,400)
   Cost per equivalent unit for conversion:
   $1,610 + $82,350 = $83,960/22,400 = $3.748 (rounded)

V. Critical Thinking

The cost of materials appears to be falling whereas the conversion costs (direct labor and overhead) are stable. Since the FIFO assumption only considers current (November) costs while the weighted-average assumption includes both October and November costs, the larger equivalent unit cost for materials under weighted-average ($4.29 vs. $4.25 under FIFO) means that October's material costs were higher than November's. However, the equivalent unit cost for conversion was almost identical under the two assumptions ($3.748 vs. $3.743 under FIFO).

VI. Demonstration Problems

Demonstration Problem #1 Solved and Explained (FIFO)

Steps 1 and 2

Flow of Production in Physical Units
and Equivalent Units of Production
Enameling Department
For the Month Ended June 30, 19XX

Flow of Production	Flow of Physical Units	Transferred In	Materials	Conversion
Units to account for:				
Work in process, May 31	22,500			
Transferred in	105,000			
Total units to account for	127,500			
Units accounted for:				
Completed and transferred out in June:				
From beginning inventory	22,500		18,000[2]	13,500[3]
Transferred in and completed	67,500[1]	67,500	67,500	67,500
Total transferred out	90,000			
Ending inventory	37,500	37,500	15,000[4]	18,750[5]
Total units accounted for	127,500	105,000	100,500	99,750

[1] A total of 90,000 units were transferred out according to the problem. Since 22,500 of those units were from beginning inventory, the balance of 67,500 were transferred in and completed during the period. Since these are completed units, each completed unit equals one equivalent unit, and the completed units are carried across to the equivalent unit computation.

Total transferred out	–	Beginning inventory	=	Transferred in and completed
90,000	–	22,500	=	67,500 units

[2] The Beginning Work in Process Inventory was 20% complete with respect to direct materials. Therefore, 80% of the direct materials were added during June to the physical units in beginning inventory (100% – 20%).

$$.80 \times 22,500 = 18,000 \text{ equivalent units}$$

[3] The Beginning Work in Process Inventory was 40% complete with respect to conversion. Therefore, 60% of the conversion was performed on Beginning Work in Process Inventory during June (100% – 40%).

$$.60 \times 22,500 = 13,500 \text{ equivalent units}$$

[4] The problem states that 40% of the direct materials had been added during June to the physical units remaining in ending inventory.

$$.40 \times 37,500 = 15,000 \text{ equivalent units}$$

[5] The problem states that 50% of the conversion had been performed during June to th physical units remaining in ending inventory.

$$.50 \times 37,500 = 18,750 \text{ equivalent units}$$

Steps 3 and 4

Computation of Unit Cost
Enameling Department
For the Month Ended June 30, 19XX

	Transferred In	Materials	Conversion	Total
Work in Process, May 31 (costs for work done before June)				$ 54,000
Costs added in June	$157,500	$14,070	$205,485	377,055
Divide by equivalent units	105,000	100,500	99,750	
Cost per equivalent unit	$ 1.50	$ 0.14	$ 2.06	
Total cost to account for:				$431,055

Points to Remember:

When computing unit costs, the costs from the prior period are *not included* in the computation of unit costs. The unit cost for each cost category is equal to the costs added to that category during the period divided by the equivalent units for that category, which were computed in Step 2.

Step 5

Application of Total Cost to Units Completed
and Units in Ending Work in Process
Enameling Department
For the Month Ended June 30, 19XX

	Transferred In	Materials	Conversion	Total
Units completed and transferred out to Finished Goods Inventory:				
From Work in Process, May 31				$ 54,000
Costs added during June				
Direct materials		18,000 x $0.14		2,520
Conversion costs			13,500 x $2.06	27,810
Total completed from beginning inventory				84,330
Units transferred in and completed during June	67,500 x ($1.50 + $0.14 + $2.06)			249,750
Total costs transferred out				$334,080
Work in Process, June 30:				
Transferred-in costs	37,500 x $1.50			$ 56,250
Direct materials		15,000 x $0.14		2,100
Conversion costs			18,750 x $2.06	38,625
Total work in process				96,975
Total costs accounted for				$431,055

Points to Remember:

Units Completed and Transferred Out

Units from Work in Process, May 31:

The problem states that $54,000 of cost was associated with the May 31 Work in Process balance. The FIFO process costing method *always* assumes that costs associated with beginning Work in Process are the *first* costs to be transferred out in the next period.

Costs added during June:

Whenever beginning Work in Process exists, it is necessary to compute the balance of costs incurred to complete the work. According to the problem, additional materials and conversion were needed to complete the beginning work in process. The equivalent units were computed in Step 2, and the unit costs for each category were determined in Step 3. The amount of cost to complete beginning Work in Process is the equivalent units times the unit cost. A separate computation is made for (1) direct materials and (2) conversion costs.

Units Transferred In and Completed during June:

Since transferred-in and completed units are 100% complete, separate computations for each of the cost categories are not necessary. The cost associated with units transferred in and completed in the same period will equal the number of units times the sum of the unit costs of 1) transferred-in costs, 2) direct materials, and 3) conversion.

Ending Work in Process, June 30:

To compute the balance of ending Work in Process, it is necessary to make a separate computation for 1) transferred-in costs, 2) direct materials, and 3) conversion. For each of the costs, the balance in ending Work in Process will equal the equivalent units of production from Step 2 times the unit cost from Step 3.

Once the costs have been applied, you should compare the total costs accounted for in Step 5 with the total cost to account for from Step 4. In both cases the amount in this problem is $431,055.

Demonstration Problem #2 Solved and Explained (Weighted-Average)

Steps 1 and 2

Flow of Production in Physical Units
and Equivalent Units of Production
Enameling Department
For the Month Ended June 30, 19XX

Flow of Production	Flow of Physical Units	Equivalent Units		
		Transferred In	Materials	Conversion
Units to account for:				
Work in Process, May 31	22,500			
Transferred in	105,000			
Total units to account for	127,500			
Units accounted for:				
Completed and transferred out in June	90,000[1]	90,000	90,000	90,000
Ending inventory	37,500	37,500	15,000[2]	18,750[3]
Total units accounted for	127,500	127,500	105,000	108,750

[1]   A total of 90,000 units were transferred out according to the problem. Since these are completed units, each completed unit equals one equivalent unit, and the completed units are carried across to the equivalent unit computation.

[2]   The problem states that 40% of the direct materials had been added during June to the physical units remaining in ending inventory.

$$.40 \times 37{,}500 = 15{,}000 \text{ equivalent units}$$

[3]   The problem states that 50% of the conversion had been performed during June to the physical units remaining in ending inventory.

$$.50 \times 37{,}500 = 18{,}750 \text{ equivalent units}$$

Steps 3 and 4

Computation of Unit Cost
Enameling Department
For the Month Ended June 30, 19XX

	Transferred In	Materials	Conversion	Total
Work in Process, May 31	$ 34,800	$ 650	$ 18,550	$ 54,000
Costs added in June	157,500	14,070	205,485	377,055
Total cost	192,300	14,720	224,035	431,055
Divide by equivalent units	127,500	105,000	108,750	
Cost per equivalent unit	$1.508235	$0.14019	$2.06001	
Total cost to account for:				$431,055

Points to Remember:

When computing unit costs using the weighted-average method, the costs from the prior period are included in the computation of unit costs. The unit cost for each cost category is the sum of the current period's cost plus the amounts incurred last period and carried into the current period as beginning inventory.

Step 5

Application of Total Cost to Units Completed
and Units in Ending Work in Process
Enameling Department
For the Month Ended June 30, 19XX

	Transferred In	Materials	Conversion	Total
Units completed and transferred out to				
Finished Goods Inventory: 90,000 x (1.5008235 + 0.14019 + 2.06001)				$333,768[†]
Work in Process, June 30:				
Transferred-in costs	37,500 x $1.508235			56,559
Direct materials		15,000 x $0.14019		2,103
Conversion costs			18,750 x $2.06001	38,625
Total Work in Process				97,287
Total costs accounted for				$431,055

[†]Adjusted for rounding

Points to Remember:

The Step 5 procedure above is less complicated using weighted-average because all 90,000 units transferred out are assigned the unit cost amounts calculated in Step 4. Unlike the FIFO method, there is no need to distinguish between those units in process at the beginning of the period and those units transferred in and completed during the period.

Like the FIFO method, however, the ending Work in Process amounts are determined by multiplying equivalent units (from Step 2) times unit cost (Step 4).

Once the costs have been applied, you should compare total costs accounted for in Step 5 with the total cost to account for from Step 4. In both cases the amount in this problem is $431,055.

Chapter 22

Cost-Volume-Profit Analysis and the Contribution Margin Approach to Decision Making

 Chapter Overview

*I*n Chapters 20 and 21 you learned about a particular type of management accounting concerned with manufacturing businesses wherein direct materials are converted into finished goods. We now turn our attention to a closer examination of "costs" and how costs change relative to changes in output. The interaction of cost and volume results in changes in profits (or losses). The specific learning for this chapter are:

1. Identify different cost behavior patterns
2. Use a contribution margin income statement to make business decisions
3. Compute breakeven sales
4. Compute the sales level needed to earn a target operating income
5. Graph a set of cost-volume-profit relationships
6. Compute a margin of safety
7. Use the sales mix in CVP analysis

Chapter Review

1.
2.
3.

OBJECTIVE 1
Identify different cost behavior patterns.

Cost behavior is the way that costs change in response to changes in business activity. A **cost driver** is any factor that can cause a change in the costs related to it. The three patterns of cost behavior are variable, fixed, and mixed.

Variable costs change in direct proportion to changes in volume or level of activity. Examples of variable costs include direct materials, sales commissions, and delivery expense. Suppose CDs have a cost of $6 per tape when purchased for resale. If a retailer sells 1,000 CDs, cost of goods sold will be $6,000. However, if 2,000 CDs are sold, cost of goods sold will be $12,000. Thus, the more CDs the retailer sells, the higher the cost of goods sold will be, since the $6 variable cost per unit is constant.

Fixed costs do not change as volume changes. Examples of fixed costs include expenses such as rent and depreciation. Suppose the rent for a store is $5,000 per month. The store owner will pay $5,000 per month whether sales increase, decrease, or remain the same.

Mixed costs (also called **semivariable costs**) are part variable and part fixed. The monthly telephone bill, for example, is based both on local service and long distance service. The amount for local (unlimited) service is a fixed cost, while the amount for long distance service is a variable cost. Therefore, the total telephone bill is a mixed cost.

Study the graphs in your text that illustrate cost behavior patterns (Exhibits 22-1, 22-2, and 22-3). The variable cost graph begins at the origin (zero volume, zero cost). Variable cost increases in a straight line whose slope equals the variable cost per unit. As the slope of the line gets steeper, the variable cost per unit increases. The fixed cost graph is a horizontal line that intersects the cost (vertical) axis at the fixed cost level. The mixed cost graph intersects the cost axis at the level of the fixed cost component, and its slope equals the variable cost per unit.

When budgeting costs, companies use the **relevant range concept**. Relevant range is the band of activity or volume of operations within which relationships between costs and volume can be predicted. These relationships will be different in other ranges. See Exhibit 22-4 in your text.

The conventional income statement focuses on the perspective of external users of financial statements. It has the format:

	Sales
−	**Cost of Goods Sold**
=	**Gross Margin**
−	**Operating Expenses**
=	**Income from Operations**

Note that the conventional income statement classifies expenses according to the value chain, such as cost of goods sold or operating expenses.

The **contribution margin income statement** focuses on the **contribution margin**, the excess of sales over variable expenses. It classifies expenses according to cost behavior, which will be either variable or fixed. It has the format:

	Sales
−	**Variable Expenses**
=	**Contribution Margin**
−	**Fixed Expenses**
=	**Income from Operations**

The contribution margin income statement is a useful management tool. Once fixed expenses are covered, the balance of the contribution margin "contributes" to income. Since fixed expenses remain constant, when the contribution margin changes, income will change by the same amount. Remember that, in general, variable expenses will change proportionately with sales. Thus, if sales increase by 10 percent, variable expenses will increase by 10 percent, and the contribution margin will increase by 10 percent.

Using the contribution margin income statement, it is possible to calculate exactly how a change in sales will affect profit. Similar analysis using the conventional income statement is not possible.

Cost-volume-profit analysis is often called **breakeven analysis**. The **breakeven point** is the sales level at which operating income is zero. If sales are below the breakeven point, the result is a loss. If sales are above the breakeven point, the result is a profit.

Decision makers use cost-volume-profit analysis to answer questions such as, "How much do we need to sell to break even?" or "If our sales are some specific amount, what will our profit be?"

Two approaches used in cost-volume-profit (CVP) analysis are the equation approach and the contribution margin approach. With either approach, start by separating total expenses into variable expenses and fixed expenses.

The **equation approach** is:

$$\text{Sales} - \text{Variable Expenses} - \text{Fixed Expenses} = \text{Operating Income}$$

Operating income is zero at breakeven. The equation shows how many units must be sold (and the total dollar amount of the sales) in order to break even.

The **contribution margin approach** is:

$$\text{Contribution Margin} = \text{Sales} - \text{Variable Costs}$$

The contribution margin receives its name because it contributes to the payment of fixed costs and operating income.

The contribution margin may be expressed on a per-unit basis, or as a percentage or ratio:

$$\text{Contribution Margin Per Unit} = \text{Sales Price Per Unit} - \text{Variable Expense Per Unit}$$

$$\text{Contribution Margin Percentage or Ratio} = \frac{\text{Contribution Margin}}{\text{Selling Price}}$$

Breakeven sales in units is computed by dividing fixed expenses by the contribution margin per unit:

$$\text{Breakeven Sales in Units} = \frac{\text{Fixed Expenses in Units}}{\text{Contribution Margin Per Unit}}$$

Breakeven sales in dollars is computed by dividing fixed expenses by the contribution margin ratio:

$$\text{Breakeven Sales in Dollars} = \frac{\text{Fixed Expenses}}{\text{Contribution Margin Ratio}}$$

Review the examples in the text (Exhibit 22-7) so that you know what will happen to the breakeven point if a fixed cost is changed, if the sale price is changed, or if the variable cost per unit is changed. If fixed costs or variable costs increase, breakeven increases. If the sale price increases, breakeven decreases.

OBJECTIVE 4

Compute the sales level needed to earn a target operating income.

The profit that a business wishes to earn is called the target operating income.

$$\text{Target Sales in Units} = \frac{\text{Fixed Expenses} + \text{Target Operating Income}}{\text{Contribution Margin Per Unit}}$$

$$\text{Target Sales in Dollars} = \frac{\text{Fixed Expenses} + \text{Target Operating Income}}{\text{Contribution Margin Ratio}}$$

Notice that the only difference between computing breakeven sales and target sales is that, with target sales, the target operating income amount is added to fixed expenses.

OBJECTIVE 5

Graph a set of cost-volume-profit relationships.

Often, a business is interested in knowing the amount of operating income or operating loss to expect at various levels of sales. One convenient way to provide this information is to prepare a **cost-volume-profit graph**.

In order to familiarize yourself with the components of the CVP graph, study these steps and review Exhibit 22-8 in your text:

Step 1   Draw a sales line from the origin through a preselected sales volume.

Step 2   Draw the fixed expense line.

Step 3   Compute the variable expenses at your preselected sales volume (Step 1), then plot them beginning at your fixed expense line (this is the total expense line).

Step 4   Identify the breakeven point (where sales and total expenses intersect).

Step 5   Identify the operating income and operating loss areas.

OBJECTIVE 6

Compute a margin of safety.

The margin of safety is the excess of expected or actual sales over breakeven sales. It tells a business how much sales can drop before an operating loss is incurred. The margin of safety may be computed in terms of either dollars or units:

Margin of Safety = Expected Sales – Breakeven Sales

The following assumptions underlie CVP analysis:

1.   Expenses can be classified as either variable or fixed.
2.   Cost-volume-profit relationships are linear over a wide range of production and sales.
3.   Sales prices, unit variable costs, and total fixed expenses are constant.
4.   Volume is the only cost driver.
5.   The sales mix of products will not change during the period.

OBJECTIVE 7

Use the sales mix in CVP analysis.

One of the basic assumptions underlying CVP analysis is that the **sales mix**, the combination of products that make up total sales, does not change.

Breakeven questions involving multiple products can be answered using either the contribution margin approach or the equation approach.

Regardless of approach, you begin by establishing the sales mix (for instance, 3 units of one product for every 2 of a second product, or 3:2). The sales mix is then 5 units, the total of 3 and 2. Determine the contribution margin for this mix then divide the result into total fixed expenses. The result is breakeven for the "mix" (3 of one product and 2 of a second). Multiply the breakeven by each component in the mix for the breakeven in sales units.

Income Effects of Alternative Approaches to Product Costing

Carefully review both panels in Exhibit 22-9 in your text, which illustrates the difference between **absorption costing** and **variable costing** within identical income statements. Absorption costing is the traditional approach to the income statement—identical to the assumptions in Chapters 20 and 21, wherein the products absorb all the fixed and variable costs during the period. In contrast, variable costing only assigns variable costs to the product and reclassifies fixed manufacturing costs (usually the fixed overhead expenses) as period costs. This reclassification means the fixed expenses appear on the income statement as incurred rather than later when the output is actually sold.

Test Yourself

All the self-testing materials in this chapter focus on information and procedures that your instructor is likely to test in quizzes and examinations.

I. Matching *Match each numbered term with its lettered definition.*

1. cost behavior
2. variable cost
3. fixed cost
4. mixed cost
5. breakeven point
6. contribution margin
7. target operating income

8. margin of safety
9. relevant range
10. variable costing
11. sales mix
12. CVP analysis
13. absorption costing
14. period costs

A. The amount of unit sales or dollar sales at which revenues equal expenses
B. A costing method that assigns only variable manufacturing costs to products
C. Description of how costs change in response to a shift in volume of business activity
D. The excess of sales price over variable expenses
E. A band of activity or volume in which actual operations are likely to occur
F. A cost that does not change in total as volume changes
G. The excess of expected (or actual) sales over breakeven sales
H. A cost that is part variable and part fixed
I. A cost that changes in total in direct proportion to changes in volume or activity
J. The desired income a business wishes to earn
K. Costs reported on the income statement as incurred
L. The combination of products that make up total sales
M. A costing method that assigns all manufacturing costs to products
N. A part of the budgeting system that helps managers predict the outcome of their decisions by analyzing relationships among costs, volume, and profit or loss

II. Multiple Choice *Circle the best answer.*

Use the following information for questions 1 through 4:

Video Point sells VCR tapes. Last year Video Point sold 5,500 cases at $24 per case. The variable cost per case was $14.40 and fixed costs amounted to $28,800.

1. The breakeven point in cases of tapes was:

    A. 1,200

    B. 2,000

    C. 3,000

    D. 5,500

2. The breakeven point in sales dollars was:

    A. $66,000

    B. $72,000

    C. $24,000

    D. $14,400

3. The margin of safety in dollars was:

    A. $60,000

    B. $48,000

    C. $51,000

    D. $-0-

4. If Video Point wished to earn an operating income of $34,800, how many cases o: tapes would have to be sold?

    A. 3,600

    B. 4,400

    C. 5,500

    D. 6,625

5. Dividing breakeven sales dollars by the unit selling price results in the:

    A. variable cost per unit

    B. breakeven point in dollars

    C. breakeven point in units

    D. variable cost ratio

6. Which of the following will decrease the breakeven point?

   A. decreasing fixed costs

   B. increasing fixed costs

   C. increasing variable costs per unit

   D. decreasing selling price

7. Which of the following will increase the breakeven point?

   A. decreasing fixed costs

   B. increasing fixed costs

   C. decreasing variable cost per unit

   D. decreasing selling price

Use the following graph to answer questions 8 through 10:

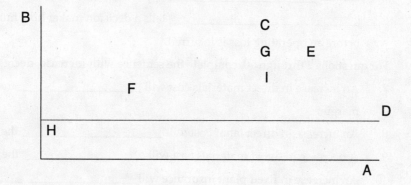

8. Line D must be:

   A. sales line

   B. total expense line

   C. fixed expense line

   D. cannot be determined

9. If E is the total expense line, then I must be:

   A. operating income area

   B. variable expense area

   C. operating loss area

   D. cannot be determined

10. If C is the sales line and E is the total expense line, then F must be:

   A. breakeven point

   B. total units

   C. total dollars

   D. cannot be determined

III. Completion *Complete each of the following statements.*

1. The _____ is equal to the selling price per unit minus the variable expenses per unit.

2. A convenient way to determine operating income or loss at various levels of sales is to prepare a _____.

3. _____ and _____ are examples of costs that change proportionately with sales.

4. The _____ is the combination of products that make up total sales.

5. Two approaches used in CVP analysis are the _____ approach and the _____ approach.

6. _____ tells a decision maker how much sales can drop before an operating loss is incurred.

For questions 7 through 10, complete the sentence with **increase, decrease,** or **not affect.**

7. An increase in direct materials cost will _____ the contribution margin.

8. An increase in direct labor cost will _____ the breakeven point.

9. A decrease in direct materials cost will _____ the breakeven point.

10. An increase in fixed plant insurance will _____ the breakeven point.

11. Absorption costing reports all _____ costs as _____ costs on the income statement.

12. Variable costing reports only _____ costs as _____ costs on the income statement.

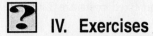

IV. Exercises

1. Classify each of the following costs as fixed, variable, or mixed (assume a relevant range and current period).

Cost	Classification
a) property taxes	
b) direct materials	
c) depreciation on office equipment	
d) advertising expense	
e) office salaries expense	
f) direct labor	
g) manufacturing overhead	
h) rent expense	
i) insurance expense	
j) supplies expense	

2. Baker's Basketry has fixed costs of $420,000. Variable costs are 30% of sales. Assuming each basket sells for $10, what is their breakeven point in unit sales?

3. Ellen's Manufacturing sells a product for $8 per unit. If the variable cost is $4.25 per unit, and breakeven is 48,000 units, what are Ellen's fixed costs?

4. If variable costs are 60% of sales and fixed costs are $230,000, what is the breakeven point in sales dollars?

5. Serene Greetings sells boxes of greeting cards and packages of gift wrap. Boxes sell for $5.00 and packages sell for $1.75. Variable costs are $2.50 for boxes and $1.00 for packages. Serene expects to sell 1,500 boxes of greeting cards and 750 packages of gift wrap. Fixed costs are $2,350. What is the breakeven point?

 V. Critical Thinking

Review Exercise 1. How would your answers change if output remains within the relevant range but the costs listed are classified over a long period?

Cost	Classification
a) property taxes	
b) direct materials	
c) depreciation on office equipment	
d) advertising expense	
e) office salaries expense	
f) direct labor	
g) manufacturing overhead	
h) rent expense	
i) insurance expense	
j) supplies expense	

VI. Demonstration Problems

Demonstration Problem #1

The Norman Novelty Corporation is planning to introduce a new table game. The relevant range of output is between 10,000 and 40,000 units. Within this range, fixed expenses are estimated to be $325,000 and variable expenses are estimated at 35% of the $30 selling price.

Required

1. Using the contribution margin approach, calculate breakeven sales in units and in dollars.

2. If targeted net income (pretax) is $120,000, how many games must be sold?

3. Prepare a graph showing operating income and operating loss areas from 0 to 40,000 games, assuming a selling price of $30. Identify the breakeven sales level and the sales level needed to earn operating income of $120,000.

4. If the corporation increases the selling price to $36, how many games must be sold to earn operating income of $60,000?

Requirement 1 (Breakeven sales in units and dollars)

Requirement 2 (Targeted operating income)

Requirement 3 (Graph)

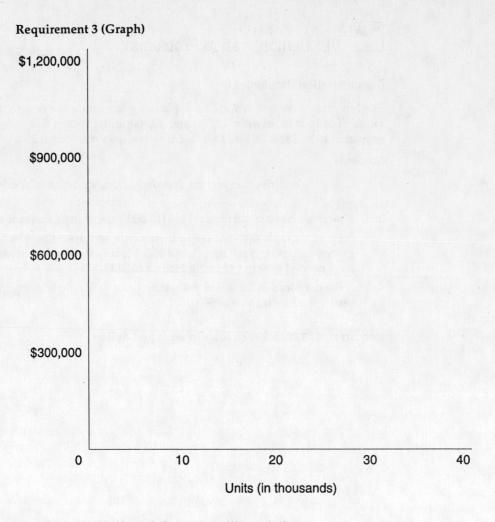

Requirement 4 (Effect of change in selling price)

Demonstration Problem #2

Steve and Scott's Deluxe Ice Cream Company manufactures top-of-the-line premium ice cream. The product, in a variety of styles, is available in pints, quarts, and half-gallons. Past experience has shown that 4 quarts are sold for each half-gallon and 5 pints are sold for each quart. Selling prices and variable costs for the product line are as follows:

	Pints	Quarts	Half-gallons
Selling price	$1.50	$2.75	$5.25
Variable cost	$0.60	$1.15	$2.25

Fixed costs average $900,000 per month. Of this amount, approximately 2/3 is manufacturing overhead and 1/3 is operating expense. Variable costs consist entirely of direct materials (ingredients and packaging) and direct labor.

Part A (Use the space provided on the next page.)

1. Determine the sales mix.
2. Calculate breakeven in units and sales.
3. Assuming the company pays taxes at the rate of 40% of pretax operating income, calculate the sales needed to earn after-tax operating income of $1,200,000 annually.

Part B (Use the space provided on page 539.)

The company is considering an increase in price and, at the same time, eliminating the manufacture of the half-gallon size. Research indicates the elimination of the half gallon would result in a 25% increase in quart sales but have no impact on pint sales. Assuming the decision is made to eliminate the half-gallons and increase the selling price of pints and quarts to $1.75 and $3.00 respectively, answer the following:

1. Which variable and fixed costs are likely to change as a result of this decision?
2. What is the new sales mix?
3. Assuming variable and fixed costs remain the same, what is the new breakeven point in units and sales?
4. Assuming variable costs remain the same but the elimination of half gallons results in a one-time restructuring charge of $750,000 and a 20% reduction in fixed manufacturing costs, what is the effect on operating income?

Part A

1. Determine the sales mix.

2. Calculate breakeven in units and sales.

3. Calculate the sales for the targeted operating income.

Part B

1. Effects on variable and fixed costs

2. New sales mix

3. New breakeven point in units and dollars

4. Effect on operating income

Solutions

I. Matching

| 1. C | 2. I | 3. F | 4. H | 5. A | 6. D | 7. J |
| 8. G | 9. E | 10. B | 11. L | 12. N | 13. M | 14. K |

II. Multiple Choice

1. C $28,800/($24.00 – $14.40) = 3,000

2. B $28,800/[($24.00 – $14.40)/$24.00] = $72,000

3. A   (5,500 boxes – 3,000 boxes) x $24.00 = $60,000

4. D   ($28,800 + $34,800)/[($24.00 – $14.40)/$24.00] = $159,000/$24 = 6,625

5. C   BE$ = Breakeven sales dollars. BEu = Breakeven in units.

    $Pu = unit selling price.

    BE$ = BEu x $Pu

    BE$/$Pu = BEu

6. A   BE$ = Breakeven sales dollars. BEu = Breakeven in units.

    $Pu = unit selling price. FC = Fixed Cost

    VCu = Variable cost per unit.

    Recall that BEu = FC/($Pu – VCu)

    Of the answers listed, only A, "Decreasing fixed costs," will decrease the breakeven point.

7. D   Refer to 6 above. Note that answer D, "Decreasing selling price," will decrease the contribution margin and increase the breakeven point.

    Note: If you had difficulty with questions 5 through 7, consider the formula for the breakeven point in units:

    Fixed Expenses/Contribution Margin Per Unit = Breakeven in Units

    If the numerator increases, or the denominator decreases, the breakeven point increases. If the numerator decreases, or the denominator increases, the breakeven point decreases.

8. C   The sales and total expense lines slope upward; only the fixed expense line is flat.

9. B   The variable expense area is the difference between the total expense line and the fixed expense line.

10. A   Total units and total dollars are the A and B axis. F is the breakeven point where sales intersects total expenses.

III. Completion

1. contribution margin per unit
2. cost-volume-profit graph
3. Cost of goods sold, selling commission (other answers may be acceptable)
4. sales mix
5. equation, contribution margin
6. The margin of safety
7. decrease (An increase in direct materials is an increase in the variable cost per unit. This decreases the contribution margin.)
8. increase (An increase in direct labor cost is an increase in the variable cost per unit. This decreases the contribution margin. As the contribution margin decreases, the breakeven point increases.)
9. decrease (A decrease in direct materials cost is a decrease in variable cost per unit. This increases the contribution margin. As the contribution margin increases, the breakeven point decreases. Contrast with question 9.)
10. increase (An increase in plant insurance is an increase in fixed costs. An increase in fixed costs increases the breakeven point.)
11. manufacturing, product (order important)
12. variable, product (order important)

IV. Exercises

1.

Cost	Classification
a) property taxes	fixed
b) direct materials	variable
c) depreciation on office equipment	fixed
d) advertising expense	fixed
e) office salaries expense	fixed
f) direct labor	variable
g) manufacturing overhead	mixed (because some are fixed, such as rent, depreciation, etc., whereas others are variable, such as indirect materials, utilities, etc.)
h) rent expense	fixed
i) insurance expense	fixed
j) supplies expense	variable

2. If VC = 30% of sales, then CM = 70% of sales, or $7 per unit.

$$\frac{\text{Fixed Expenses}}{\text{Contribution Margin}} = \text{Breakeven Point}$$

$$\frac{\$420,000}{\$7} = 60,000 \text{ units}$$

3.

$$\frac{\text{Fixed Expenses}}{\text{Contribution Margin}} = \text{Breakeven Point}$$

$$\frac{FE}{\$3.75} = 48,000$$

$$FE = \$180,000$$

4. If VC = 60% of sales, then CM = 40% of sales.

$$\frac{\text{Fixed Costs}}{\text{Contribution Margin Ratio}} = \text{Breakeven in Sales}$$

$$\frac{\$230,000}{40\%} = \$575,000$$

5.

	Boxes of Greeting Cards	Packages of Gift Wrap	Total
Sales price per unit	$5.00	$1.75	
Variable expense per unit	$2.50	$1.00	
Contribution margin per unit	$2.50	$0.75	
Estimated sales in units	x 1,500	x 750	2,250
Estimated contribution margin per unit	$3,750 +	$562.50 =	$4,312.50
Weighted-average contribution margin per unit ($4,312.50/2,250)			$1.92 (rounded)

$$\text{Breakeven sales in units} = \frac{\text{Fixed Expenses}}{\text{Weighted-Average Contribution Margin}} = \frac{\$2,350}{\$1.92} = 1,224$$

$$\text{Breakeven sales of boxes of greeting cards} = 1,224 \times \frac{1,500}{2,250} = 816 \text{ boxes}$$

$$\text{Breakeven sales of packages of gift wrap} = 1,224 \times \frac{750}{2,250} = 408 \text{ packages}$$

V. Critical Thinking

a) fixed (While property taxes will probably rise over the long run, they still are a fixed cost.)

b) variable

c) fixed

d) mixed (The business will always advertise, but the amount will vary over the long run.)

e) fixed

f) variable

g) variable

h) mixed

i) possibly mixed (a portion fixed regardless of output with add-ons to reflect changes in output)

j) variable

VI. Demonstration Problems

Demonstration Problem #1 Solved and Explained

Requirement 1 (Breakeven sales in units and dollars)

To compute breakeven in dollars and in units, we need to find the contribution margin per unit and the contribution margin ratio:

$$\text{Contribution Margin Per Unit} = \text{Sales Price Per Unit} - \text{Variable Expense Per Unit}$$

$$\text{Contribution Margin Percentage or Ratio} = \frac{\text{Contribution Margin}}{\text{Sales Price Per Unit}}$$

Since the variable expenses are 35% (0.35) of sales, the contribution margin per unit is:

$$\$30 - (.35 \times 30) = \$30 - \$10.50 = \$19.50$$

The contribution margin ratio is:

$$\$19.50/30 = .65$$

The computation of breakeven sales in units is:

$$\text{Breakeven Sales in Units} = \frac{\text{Fixed Expenses}}{\text{Contribution Margin Per Unit}}$$

$$\$325,000/ \$19.50 = 16,667 \text{ games}$$

The breakeven point in units is 16,667 games.

The computation of breakeven sales in dollars is:

$$\text{Breakeven Sales in Dollars} = \frac{\text{Fixed Expenses}}{\text{Contribution Margin Percentage}}$$

$$\$325,000 / .65 = \$500,000$$

The breakeven point in dollars is $500,000.

Requirement 2 (Targeted operating income)

The target operating income is given as $120,000. The number of games that must be sold to earn a target income of $120,000 is:

$$\text{Target Sales in Units} = \frac{\text{Fixed Expenses} + \text{Target Operating Income}}{\text{Contribution Margin Per Unit}}$$

$$(\$325,000 + \$120,000) / \$19.50 = 22,821 \text{ games}$$

To achieve the target operating income of $120,000, 22,821 games must be sold.

Requirement 3 (Graph)

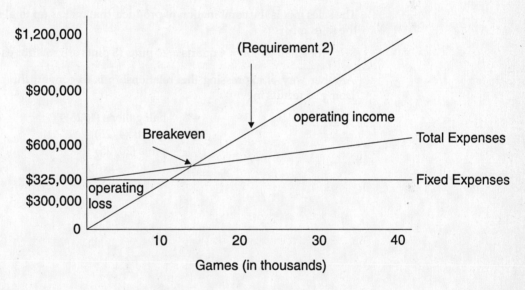

Requirement 4 (Effect of change in selling price)

To find the solution to Requirement 4, you must first determine exactly what items change. No change in fixed expenses is indicated, and the target operating income of $120,000 remains the same. However, the selling price increases from $30 to $36, an increase of $6. Since variable expenses are 35% of the selling price, the new variable cost is $12.60 (35% x $36). Since the selling price of the game has changed, we must find the new contribution margin per unit in order to use the formula for target sales in using in Requirement 2. The new contribution margin per unit is:

$$\$36 - \$12.60 = \$23.40$$

Since the contribution margin per unit has increased to $23.40, the new target sales in units will be:

$$(\$325,000 + \$60,000)/\$23.40 = 16,453 \text{ games}$$

Target sales in units has decreased to 16,453 units. This is due to the increase in the selling price and the resulting increase in the contribution margin per unit.

Demonstration Problem #2 Solved and Explained

Part A

1. Determine the sales mix

    The sales mix is the combination of products that makes up total sales. In this problem the sales mix is:

    one half gallon = 4 quarts = 20 pints (5 pints are sold for each quart)

    Another way of expressing this relationship is to convert the "mix" to percentages. Doing so results in

4%	half gallons (1/25)
16%	quarts (4/25)
80%	pints (20/25)
100%	

2. Calculate breakeven in units and sales.

To do this, we first calculate the weighted-average contribution margin, as follows:

	Half-gallons	Quarts	Pints
Selling price	$5.25	$2.75	$1.50
Less variable cost	2.25	1.15	0.60
Contribution margin	3.00	1.60	0.90
x weight	x 1	x 4	x 20
Weighted-average contribution margin	$3.00 +	$6.40 +	$18.00 = $27.40

$$\text{Breakeven Sales in Units} = \frac{\text{Fixed Expenses}}{\text{Weighted-average Contribution Margin}} = \frac{\$900,000}{\$27.40} = \text{32,847 units}$$

or

Half gallons	Quarts	Pints
32,847	32,847	32,847
x 1	x 4	x 20
32,847	131,388	656,940

Now apply the unit selling price to each result to obtain breakeven sales (or convert the weighted-average contribution margin to a ratio).

Half gallons	Quarts	Pints
32,847	131,388	656,940
x $5.25	x $2.75	x $1.50

Total breakeven sales

$1,519,174 = $172,447 + $361,317 + $985,410

Remember, fixed expenses were given as monthly, so both of the above results are monthly.

3. Targeted operating income

$$\text{Sales} = \frac{\text{Fixed Expenses + Target Operating Income}}{\text{Contribution Margin Ratio}}$$

$$\text{Sales} = \frac{\$10,800,000^* + \$2,000,000^{**}}{59.3\% \text{ (rounded)}}$$

* If fixed expenses are $900,000 monthly, then they are $10,800,000 ($900,000 x 12) annually.

** If the tax rate is 40%, the pretax operating income is $2,000,000 ($1,200,000 / 0.6).

Sales needed to achieve after tax operating income of $1,200,000 are $21,585,160 annually or $1,798,763 monthly.

Part B

1. In the short run, neither variable nor fixed costs will change. In the longer run, variable costs will not change either (the problem states all variable costs are prime costs). However, fixed costs should decrease as facilities (equipment, etc.) needed to produce the half gallons are eliminated (see #4 below).

2. The new sales mix is 5 quarts to 20 pints or 20% quarts and 80% pints.

3.

	Quarts	Pints
Selling price	$3.00	$1.75
Less variable cost	1.15	0.60
Contribution margin	1.85	1.15
x weight	x 5	x 20
Weighted-average contribution margin	$9.25 +	$23.00 = $32.25

$$\frac{\text{Fixed Expenses}}{\text{Contribution Margin}} = \frac{\$900,000}{\$32.25} = 27,907 \text{ units}$$

Quarts	Pints
27,907	27,907
x 5	x 20
139,535 units	558,140 units

In sales:

Quarts	Pints
139,535	558,140
x $3.00	x $1.75
$418,605 +	$976,745 = $1,395,350

Again, these are monthly amounts.

4. Operating income would not be affected by the $750,000 restructuring charge because it is an extraordinary item and is not listed as an operating expense (the $750,000—net of taxes—would be listed after operating income). The problem states that 2/3 of the fixed expenses are manufacturing overhead, or $600,000 (2/3 x $900,000). A 20% reduction would, therefore, result in an increase in operating income of $120,000 (20% x $600,000).

Chapter 23

Cost Behavior Analysis

 Chapter Overview

*I*n Chapter 22 you learned about fixed and variable costs and the effect volume has on those costs. However, things other than volume can affect costs. In this chapter we investigate fixed and variable costs in greater detail and introduce other cost drivers. The specific learning objectives for this chapter are:

1. Identify types of fixed costs

2. Use cost behavior analysis to make business decisions

3. Identify two approaches for controlling operating labor costs

4. Compute the equal-cost volume of two cost behavior patterns

5. Graph the three major types of cost functions

6. Use three methods to estimate mixed-cost functions

7. Evaluate a mixed-cost function

Chapter Review

OBJECTIVE 1
Identify types of fixed costs.

Fixed costs (also called **capacity costs**) are those that remain constant in the short run. Fixed costs can be classified as either committed or discretionary. **Committed fixed costs** result from having property, plant, equipment, and key managerial personnel. For example, property taxes and depreciation are committed fixed costs—they will continue regardless of changes in production and/or sales and cannot be reduced without adversely affecting long-term goals.

OBJECTIVE 2
Use cost behavior analysis to make business decisions.

Discretionary fixed costs (also called **managed fixed costs**) arise from periodic (usually yearly) budget decisions that reflect top-management policies and have no clear relationship between inputs and outputs. Examples of discretionary fixed costs are advertising and training costs. Because the relationship between these costs and production and/or sales is unclear, companies budget amounts for each but have difficulty in determining their effectiveness (unlike the committed fixed costs, where the relationship is clearer). Another distinction between discretionary and committed fixed costs is that discretionary costs are easier to adjust in the short run whereas committed costs are not (e.g., next quarter's advertising budget can be reduced but the property taxes will still have to be paid).

Like fixed costs, **variable costs** can also be classified. Remember that variable costs are those that change in direct proportion to changes in volume. Variable costs may be classified as either engineered or discretionary. **Engineered variable costs** are those that have a direct cause and effect relationship between inputs and outputs. Think of these costs as those inputs that, if not incurred, would result in no production (outputs). For instance, the amount of cream a dairy requires to produce a pound of butter is an engineered variable cost. Another example of engineered variable costs are the direct labor hours required to complete a given task. Most variable costs are engineered.

Discretionary variable costs are those that change with production and/or sales volume (this defines them as variable) because of a decision by management to change the percentage spent (this makes them discretionary). While the relationship between engineered variable costs and production remains the same over time, the relationship between discretionary variable costs and production can change, usually by management decision. Study Exhibit 23-4 in your text.

OBJECTIVE 3
Identify two approaches for controlling operating labor costs.

When budgeting costs, two approaches are available—the discretionary-fixed-cost approach and the engineered-variable-cost approach.

The **discretionary-fixed-cost** approach relies on personal supervision for controlling costs. Because of this reliance, there tends to be little variance between the actual cost and the budgeted cost. A **variance** is simply the difference between amounts.

The **engineered-variable-cost approach** relies on work measurement to determine a budgeted cost. **Work measurement** is the careful analysis of a task, with the task measured in terms of cost drivers. Review Exhibit 23-5 in your text for a comparison between these two approaches.

When managers have the option of selecting a cost, they frequently choose between a discretionary and a variable cost. Exhibit 23-6 in your text illustrates graphically the differences between these classifications. To determine the point where one option is more favorable than the other in minimizing costs and thereby maximizing profits, the following formula is used:

Plan A Mixed Cost = Plan B Variable Cost
Fixed Cost + Variable Cost = Variable Cost

Reconciling the variable-cost portion of Plan A with Plan B (which is all variable cost) results in an amount more favorable to one plan.

Managers need to know the relationship between cost drivers and costs in order to plan effectively. Mathematical functions are used to predict costs on the basis of the cost drivers.

A **cost function** is a mathematical statement of the relationship between a cost and one or more cost drivers. The cost is the dependent variable (y) and the cost driver is the independent variable (x). Once a cost function has been estimated, it can be used to predict answers to specific questions about estimated total costs given some level of cost driver activity.

Cost estimations are based on two assumptions: 1) One cost driver (rather than two or more) adequately explains most cost behavior, and 2) within the relevant range, the relationship between the two variables (the costs and the cost driver) is linear (i.e., it appears as a straight line when graphed).

Under these assumptions, the **cost behavior pattern** is:

$$E(y) = A + Bx$$

Cost analysts use this cost behavior pattern to predict or estimate total cost (y') given a particular cost driver (x) using the following formula:

$$y' = a + bx$$

where a is the total fixed cost and b is the unit variable cost. For instance, assume total fixed cost is $65,000 and variable cost is $28. If the cost driver is direct hours, then the total cost for 7,500 direct labor hours is $65,000 + ($28 x 7,500 hours) = $65,000 + $210,000 = $275,000.

Carefully review the three panels in Exhibit 23-8 in your text. In this exhibit, fixed, variable, and mixed costs are presented graphically, using the basic cost estimation formula described above.

Mixed costs are those that contain variable and fixed components. A company's water bill is frequently an example of mixed costs because most water bills begin with a set minimum charge, regardless of consumption. Thereafter, increased usage is charged on a per unit basis.

To estimate a linear mixed-cost function, the following steps should be followed:

1. Choose the cost driver.

2. Collect a sample of data on the cost and the cost driver.

3. Plot the data.

4. Estimate the cost function.

Review Exhibit 23-9, which lists some examples of cost drivers in various industries.

Three **methods for estimating mixed-cost functions** are 1) the **high-low method**, the **visual-fit method**, and the **least-squares-regression method**. It is important to remember that a linear relationship is assumed for each method.

The **high-low method** estimates the cost function using only the highest and lowest volume points within the relevant range. These two points are connected, with the line extended back to the vertical axis. The point where the line intercepts the vertical axis is the fixed cost portion of the total cost (identified as *a* in the cost estimation formula described above). The slope of the line becomes the variable cost per unit of cost driver (identified as *b* in the formula). This variable rate is computed as follows:

$$\text{Variable Rate} = \frac{\text{Change in Costs}}{\text{Change in Volume}}$$

This result is then used to determine the fixed portion, as follows:

Fixed Portion = Total Cost – Variable Portion (from above)

While the high-low method is quick and easy, it only uses two data observations. With the **visual-fit method**, all data is used. The data observations are plotted and a line drawn through them with an approximately equal number of observations falling on either side. The intercept of the line with the axis sets the fixed cost portion (this is identical to the high-low method described above). Once this intercept is determined, variable cost is calculated as follows:

$$\text{Variable Rate} = \frac{\text{Change in Costs}}{\text{Change in Volume}}$$

Again, this is identical to the high-low method. However, with the visual-fit method, all points are considered, while the high-low method uses only the highest and lowest values. The disadvantage of the visual-fit method is its subjectivity—i.e., drawing the line between all the data observations is subjective.

The most accurate way to determine cost behavior of a mixed-cost function (again, assuming a linear relationship) is to use **regression analysis**. This method calculates a line that results in the best fit among all the observation data.

Exhibit 23-13 illustrates these three methods. Study it carefully! Each method results in different figures. Regression analysis provides the best result because it uses all the available information and is the most objective.

OBJECTIVE 7
Evaluate a mixed-cost function.

When evaluating a cost function, **economic plausibility** and **goodness of fit** need to be considered. Economic plausibility simply means that the result must make sense. When the results seem irrational, one needs to rethink the problem. Remember, the analysis described above is based on assumptions and sample observations. Perhaps the sample is too small or a flaw exists in one of the assumptions.

Goodness of fit refers to the extent to which the two variables are related (y being total cost and x being the cost driver). The **coefficient of determination** is a goodness of fit statistic. The coefficient of determination is identified as r^2. Expressed as a percent, r^2 indicates the extent to which there is confidence in the results. The greater the r^2, the more confident the analyst can be in the result.

Test Yourself

All the self-testing materials in this chapter focus on information and procedures that your instructor is likely to test in quizzes and examinations.

I. Matching *Match each numbered term with its lettered definition.*

1. work measurement
2. variance
3. least-squares regression method
4. high-low method
5. engineered variable cost
6. discretionary fixed costs
7. cost function
8. committed fixed costs
9. visual-fit method
10. step-function variable cost
11. independent variable
12. goodness of fit
13. discretionary variable cost
14. dependent variable
15. cost estimation
16. coefficient of determination

A. the statistic that tells the percentage of variation in a cost that is explained by changes in the cost driver

B. fixed costs that result from having property, plant, equipment, and key managerial personnel

C. determination of the underlying relationship between a cost and its cost driver over a specified relevant range of the cost driver

D. a mathematical statement of the relationship between a cost and one or more cost drivers

E. the cost to be predicted in a cost function

F. fixed costs arising from periodic budget decisions that reflect top management policies and that have no clear relationship between inputs and outputs

G. variable costs that change with sales or production volume because management has decided to spend a certain percentage of each sales dollar or a certain dollar amount for each unit sold

H. variable costs that result from measurable, often observable, cause-and-effect relationships between inputs and outputs

I. a cost function evaluation criterion that means that the relationship between the cost and the cost driver must explain past costs well

J. a way of estimating a cost function that uses only the highest volume and lowest volume points within the relevant range of a sample

K. the cost driver in a cost function

L. a formal model that measures the average amount of change in the dependent variable that is associated with a one-unit change in the independent variable

M. a variable cost that is purchased in whole quantities but used in fractional quantities

N. the difference between an actual and the corresponding budgeted amount

O. a cost function estimation method in which the analyst visually fits a line to the plot of all sample data points

P. the careful analysis of a task—its size, the methods used and its efficiency

II. Multiple Choice *Circle the best answer.*

1. Work measurement is associated with:

    A. committed fixed costs

    B. discretionary fixed costs

    C. discretionary variable costs

    D. engineered variable costs

2. Costs and cost drivers are most closely associated with:

    A. fixed costs

    B. variable costs

    C. mixed costs

    D. both B and C

3. Goodness of fit is measured by:

    A. r^2

    B. coefficient of determination

    C. economic plausibility

    D. high-low method

4. Among the following r^2s, which is the most desirable?

    A. 0.95

    B. 0.50

    C. 0.10

    D. none of the choices

5. If the cost of operating a machine is $5,000 for one eight-hour shift and $7,000 for five eight-hour shifts, the fixed cost associated with using the machine must be:

   A. $500

   B. $4,500

   C. $5,000

   D. $7,000

6. Assumptions underlying cost approximations are:

   A. a linear relationship

   B. a relevant range

   C. one cost driver

   D. all of the above

7. Over the short run, which of the following statements best describes the relationship between committed fixed costs and discretionary fixed costs?

   A. Committed fixed costs decline while discretionary fixed costs remain constant.

   B. Committed fixed costs increase while discretionary fixed costs remain constant.

   C. Committed fixed costs remain constant while discretionary fixed costs vary.

   D. Committed fixed costs decline while discretionary fixed costs increase.

8. Direct materials and direct labor are examples of:

   A. engineered variable costs

   B. discretionary variable costs

   C. committed fixed costs

   D. discretionary fixed costs

9. A car rental company offers cars at $25 a day plus $0.20 a mile. From the rental company's perspective, this arrangement is an example of:

   A. a discretionary fixed cost

   B. a discretionary variable cost

   C. a mixed cost

   D. none of the above

10. In the cost estimation formula $y' = a + bx$, x represents:

    A. the dependent variable

    B. total cost

    C. the cost driver

    D. the independent variable

III. Completion *Complete each of the following statements.*

1. _____ fixed costs are ones that cannot be reduced without hurting the company's ability to meet long-term goals.

2. The lower the fixed costs, the _____ the breakeven point and the _____ the margin of safety.

3. Discretionary fixed costs have a _____ planning horizon compared with committed fixed costs.

4. The three methods for estimating mixed-cost functions are _____, _____, and _____.

5. Mixed-costs are so named because _____ _____.

6. In a cost function, cost is the _____ variable while the cost driver is the _____ variable.

7. Costs that are purchased in whole quantities but used in fractional quantities are called _____.

8. Over the relevant range, a cost function is linear when _____ _____.

9. The basic cost estimation formula is _____.

10. Direct materials and direct labor are examples of _____ variable costs.

? IV. Exercises

1. Soto and Ng manufacture T-shirts and sweatshirts for special events. Classify each of the following costs as discretionary fixed, committed fixed, engineered variable, discretionary variable, or mixed cost.

   a. Monthly rent for the administrative support personnel office covered by a 5-year lease

   b. Salary for the chief accountant

   c. Depreciation on the equipment used to silk-screen the shirts

   d. Wages for a college student called in on a part-time, as-needed basis to help with packing and shipping

   e. Cost of dyes and paints used in silk-screening

   f. Royalties paid to promoters based on sales at each event

   g. Wages paid to operator of silk-screening equipment

   h. Health insurance premiums for all employees

   i. Cost of packing and shipping material

   j. Miscellaneous manufacturing overhead costs incurred

2. Lee Tran is negotiating with a vehicle leasing company for a delivery van. Tran is offered the following options:

a. $450 per month

b. $300 per month plus $0.15 per mile

c. $0.40 per mile

All options require Tran to pay for operating costs, routine maintenance, and insurance.

Classify each plan by type of cost:

a. _____

b. _____

c. _____

Classify each of the following by type of cost:

operating costs _____

routine maintenance _____

insurance _____

Graph each of the options on a single graph.

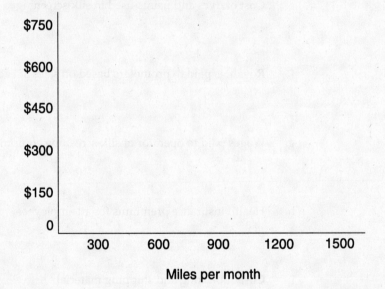

3. Refer to the information in Exercise 2 above. Tran decided to lease the van for a flat $450 per month. During the first six months of operation, the van was driven as follows:

1st month	625 miles
2nd month	470 miles
3rd month	720 miles
4th month	1,020 miles
5th month	1,415 miles
6th month	1,680 miles

Tran's original contract allowed the lessee (Tran) to switch to a different option at the end of six months. Should Tran switch? If so, to which option?

4. The following cost and usage information was collected for a robot used to weld joints on a metal frame:

Month	Total Cost	Hours Used
1	$1,360	300
2	1,576	480
3	1,324	270
4	1,732	610
5	1,792	660
6	1,852	710

Using the high-low method, estimate the monthly fixed cost and the monthly variable cost per hour used.

V. Critical Thinking

Review the information in Exercises 2 and 3, assuming the following additional information. Monthly insurance on Tran's vehicle is $200, routine maintenance costs averaged $150 a month, and operating costs averaged $0.075 per mile. What impact does this additional information have on your decision in Exercise 3?

_____

_____

_____

_____

_____

_____

_____

_____

_____

_____

_____

_____

_____

_____

_____

_____

_____

_____

_____

VI. Demonstration Problems

Demonstration Problem #1

You have been asked to estimate the cost behavior of a particular machine used to produce special orders. Data gathered over ten equal time periods are presented below. The cost driver is number of units produced.

Observations	Total Costs	Units Produced
1.	$6,385	394
2.	4,505	260
3.	6,460	488
4.	6,570	585
5.	4,910	305
6.	3,915	175
7.	9,230	625
8.	5,245	450
9.	5,035	215
10.	5,665	340

Requirement 1

Use the high-low method to estimate the cost function for total costs.

Requirement 2

Plot the observations on the graph and visually fit a line on the graph. Estimate the cost function for total costs using this information and compare your answer with the one you obtained in Requirement 1.

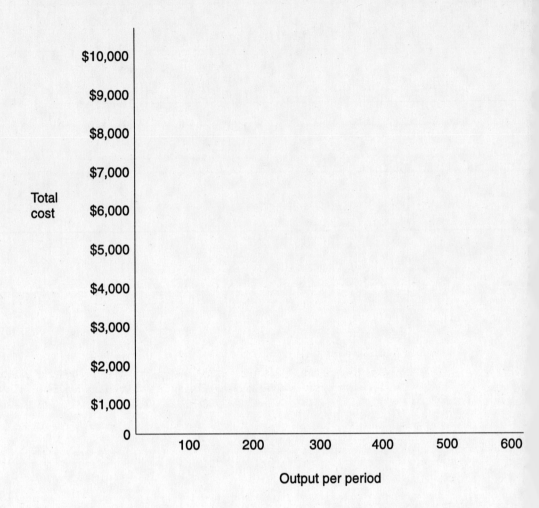

Requirement 3

Given your results in Requirement 2, re-estimate the cost function using the high-low method after eliminating any outlier points, and compare the result with your answer in Requirement 2.

Requirement 4

Given your results in Requirements 2 and 3, which is the better estimate of cost behavior? Why? What could you do to arrive at a more accurate cost function?

Demonstration Problem #2

Warren Brown owns and operates a wholesale video business employing six telemarketing representatives. At present, each telemarketer is paid $2,000 a month plus a 5% commission on each video sold. Brown is considering an alternate compensation plan that would eliminate the base salary entirely and pay a 15% commission on each video sold. Last year the business sold 185,000 videos at an average selling price of $12 each. Variable expenses including the sales commissions averaged 65% of the selling price, while fixed expenses were $600,000 for the year. Brown estimates that by employing two additional telemarketing representatives the video sales could increase 40%. The change would cause committed fixed costs to increase an additional $50,000.

Requirement 1

Graph the current and proposed salary plans.

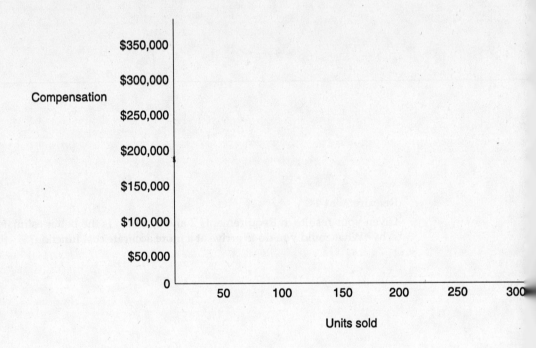

Requirement 2

Using the graph in Requirement 1, determine the number of videos that would need to be sold for the compensation of both plans to be equal. Prove the accuracy of your answer using an equation.

Requirement 3

Using a contribution margin income statement, compute last year's operating income under the existing compensation plan and under the alternative.

Requirement 4

Assuming Brown's estimates for next year are accurate and the additional telemarketing representatives are hired, which compensation plan should Brown adopt?

Solutions

I. Matching

1. P   2. N   3. L   4. J   5. H   6. F   7. D   8. B

9. O   10. M   11. K   12. I   13. G   14. E   15. C   16. A

II. Multiple Choice

1. **D**   Work measurement is a scientific approach to determining the number of employees needed to perform a given task. It is used in the engineered-variable-cost approach.

2. **D**   Costs and cost drivers refer to variable, not fixed costs. Mixed costs contain both fixed and variable costs.

3. **A & B** r^2 is the symbol for the coefficient of determination, which measures goodness of fit. Economic plausibility refers to a credible relationship between a cost and a cost driver. The high-low method is one way to estimate a cost function.

4. **A**   Since r^2 is a measure of the confidence one has in the results of estimating a cost function using regression analysis, the higher the r^2, the greater the confidence in the result.

5. **B**   The difference between one shift and five is $2,000, or $500 per shift ($2,000/4). Therefore, $500 is the variable cost and $4,500 ($5,000 – $500) is the fixed cost.

6. **D**   Cost approximations are based on a linear relation within the relevant range where cost behavior is adequately explained by one cost driver instead of two or more.

7. **C**   Committed fixed costs are those that management can change over the long run, but not the short run, while discretionary fixed costs are reviewed periodically and adjusted as needed—therefore they can vary over the short run.

8. **A**   Direct materials and direct labor are costs that change in direct proportion to changes in output; therefore they are variable costs. They are engineered variable costs because their efficiency can be measured by relating the quantity of inputs with the quantity of outputs achieved.

9. **D**   From the company's perspective, this is revenue, not cost!

10. **C & D** y' is total cost, which is the dependent variable. x is the cost driver, the dependent variable.

III. Completion

1. Committed
2. lower, higher
3. shorter
4. high-low, visual-fit, least squares regression (order not important)
5. they contain both fixed and variable costs
6. dependent, independent
7. step-function variable costs
8. it can be graphed as a straight line
9. $y' = a + bx$
10. engineered

IV. Exercises

1.
   a. committed fixed cost
   b   committed fixed cost
   c. committed fixed cost
   d. discretionary variable cost
   e. engineered variable cost
   f. discretionary variable cost
   g. engineered variable cost
   h. discretionary variable cost
   i. discretionary variable cost
   j. mixed cost

2.

    a.   discretionary fixed cost

    b.   mixed cost

    c.   discretionary variable

operating costs: variable

routine maintenance: mixed (because some are based on use and some are needed regardless of use)

insurance: committed fixed

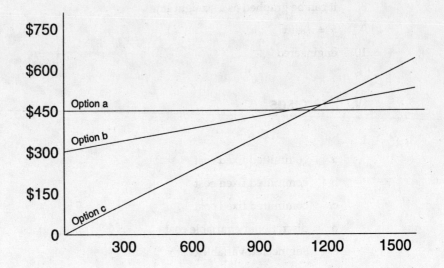

3.   To analyze the situation, we need to calculate the total cost for each option:

Month	Option A	Option B	Option C
1	$450	$394	$250
2	450	371	188
3	450	408	288
4	450	453	408
5	450	512	566
6	450	552	672
Total cost	$2,700	$2,690	$2,372

From the above it is clear that Option C ($0.40 per mile) would have been the least costly given the three options. However, it is also clear that Option A was the least costly for the most recent months. How much use can be expected in the coming months? If wide fluctuations are anticipated, then Option C should be selected. However, if the most recent use is indicative of future use, then Option A should be selected.

4.   The dependent variable (y) is cost; the independent variable (x) is hours. The high-low method uses the highest and lowest values in the sample, as follows:

	Cost	Hours
High	$1,852	710
Low	1,324	270
Difference	528	440

Now we can solve for (b) the variable cost per hour:

Variable rate = change in cost/change in volume = $528/440 = $1.20 per hour

Once the variable cost per hour is known, we can solve for the fixed component.

Fixed component	=	Total cost – variable cost
At high	=	$1,852 – (710 x $1.20) = $1,000
At low	=	$1,324 – (270 x $1.20) = $1,000

The monthly fixed cost is $1,000. The variable cost is $1.20 per hour.

V. Critical Thinking

The additional information provided in the question is irrelevant information. (You will be introduced to this concept in Chapter 27.) This simply means that it should not be used in your analysis because it does not change given the three options available. Regardless of which option is selected, Tran will still pay these costs. Therefore, these costs should be ignored in making the decision.

VI. Demonstration Problems

Demonstration Problem #1 Solved and Explained

Requirement 1

The high-low method uses only two observations to estimate cost behavior—the highest and lowest points. These two points are Observations 6 and 7. The formula is:

Variable Rate = Change in Costs ÷ Change in Volume

	Units	Cost
High	625	$9,230
Low	175	3,915
Difference	450	5,315

$$\text{Variable Rate} = \text{Change in Costs} \div \text{Change in Volume} = \frac{\$9,230 - \$3,915}{625 - 175} = \frac{\$5,315}{450}$$

Variable Rate = $11.811 (rounded) per unit

To find the fixed portion of total cost, substitute the variable rate (calculated above) for x in the following formula:

$$y' = a + bx$$

and solve for a :

At the high point	$9,230 = a + (625 \times \$11.811)$
	$9,230 = a + \$7,382$
	$a = \$1,848$
At the low point	$3,915 = a + (175 \times \$11.811)$
	$3,915 = a + \$2,067$
	$a = \$1,848$

Therefore, using the high-low method, the cost behavior is estimated as $1,848 + $11.811 per unit produced.

Requirement 2

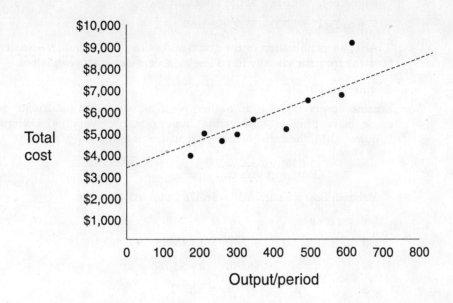

The points you plotted should approximate those shown on the graph because the points are based on objective information. However, the fitted line (identified as - - - -) is somewhat subjective because two people can visualize the same information differently.

The visual-fit line intercepts the total cost axis at $3,500. Next select any point on the line and note the point on both the vertical and the horizontal axis. For instance, the visual line passes through $5,000 at approximately 300 units/period.

We can now calculate the variable cost per unit, as follows:

Change in Costs   = $5,000 – $3,500   = $1,500

Change in Volume =   300 – 0   =   300

Variable Cost   = $1,500/300   = $5.00 per unit

Using the visual-fit method, we estimate the cost behavior as:

$3,500 + $5.00 per unit produced

A comparison between this estimate and the one obtained in Requirement 1 shows radically different results, as follows:

High-Low $1,848 + $11.811 per unit

Visual-Fit $3,500 + $5.00 per unit

Also, an examination of the graph shows there is an outlier—an observation that is too far away from the visually fitted line to be considered representative.

Requirement 3

Because observation 7 is an outlier, we eliminate it and recalculate the high-low method using the next highest observation (in our case, observation 4). Using the same formula in Requirement 1, the variable cost is calculated as follows:

$$\frac{\text{Change in Costs}}{\text{Change in Volume}} = \frac{\$6,570 - \$3,915}{585 - 175} = \frac{\$2,655}{410}$$

Variable Cost = $2,655/410 = $6.476 (rounded) per unit

Solving for a :

At the high point $6,570 $= a + (585 \times \$6.476)$

$6,570 $= a + \$3,788$

a $= \$2,782$

At the low point $3,915 $= a + (175 \times \$6.476)$

$3,915 $= a + \$1,133$

a $= \$2,782$

Requirement 4

The visual fit method is the better estimator because it is based on 10 observations compared with only two observations using the high-low method.

To arrive at a more accurate cost function (one in which you would have greater confidence), you could (1) increase the number of observations or (2) apply regression analysis.

Demonstration Problem #2 Solved and Explained

Requirement 1 (graph the compensation plans)

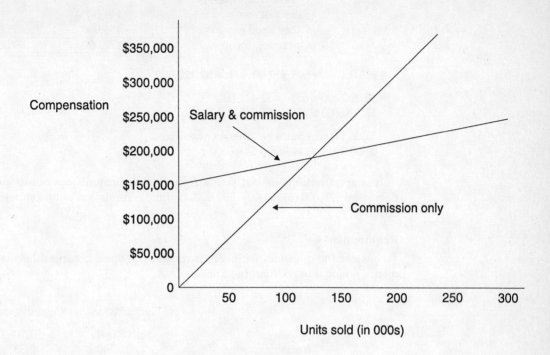

Requirement 2

Visually the graph indicates that approximately 120,000 videos sold is the point where both compensation plans are equal. To determine the exact number, use an equation to compare the two plans, as follows:

Salary + Commission = Commission only

$24,000 x 6 + ($0.60 x number of videos sold) = $1.80 x number of videos sold

$144,000 = ($1.80 - $0.60) x number of videos sold

$144,000 = $1.20 x number of videos sold

number of videos sold = 125,000

Requirement 3

Sales[1]	$2,220,000	$2,220,000
Variable expenses[2]	1,443,000	1,665,000
Contribution margin	777,000	555,000
Sales salaries	144,000	–
Other fixed expenses[3]	456,000	456,000
Operating income	$177,000	$99,000

[1] 185,000 videos x $12.00 each = $2,220,000

[2] $2,220,000 x 65% = $1,443,000
$2,220,000 x 75% = $1,665,000

[3] Total Fixed – Sales Salaries = Other Fixed
$600,000 – $144,000 = $456,000

It is apparent, given last year's figures, that Brown's operating income would have decreased $78,000 ($177,000 – $99,000) had the commission-only compensation plan been in effect.

Requirement 4

To answer the question, we need to construct revised contribution margin income statements, taking into account the estimates.

	Salary & Commission	Commission Only
Sales[1]	$3,108,000	$3,108,000
Variable expenses[2]	2,020,200	2,331,000
Contribution margin	1,087,800	777,000
Sales salaries[3]	192,000	–
Other fixed expenses[4]	506,000	506,000
Operating income	$389,800	$271,000

[1] $2,220,000 + (40% x $2,220,000) = $3,108,000

[2] $3,108,000 x 65% = $2,020,200
$3,108,000 x 75% = $2,331,000

[3] 8 x $2,000 per month x 12 = $192,000

[4] $456,000 + 50,000 = $506,000

Brown should keep the existing salary plus commission plan.

Chapter 24

The Master Budget and
Responsibility Accounting

 ## Chapter Overview

I n the last two chapters you learned more about costs—specifically how CVP analysis is used to predict outcomes (Chapter 22) and how to analyze cost behavior and make decisions based on that analysis (Chapter 23). We now turn our attention to some of the ways managers plan and control their organization's activities. The specific learning objectives for this chapter are:

1. Identify the benefits of budgeting
2. Prepare an operating budget for a company
3. Prepare the components of a financial budget
4. Use sensitivity analysis in budgeting
5. Distinguish among different types of responsibility centers
6. Prepare a performance report for management by exception
7. Allocate service department costs to production departments

Chapter Review

OBJECTIVE 1

Identify the benefits of budgeting.

A **budget** is a quantitative expression of a plan of action that helps managers to coordinate and implement the plan. The benefits of budgeting are:

1. Compels planning – budgets require managers to make plans, set goals, and design strategies for achieving those goals.

2. Promotes coordination and communications – since the master budget is an overall company plan, it requires managers to work with other departments to achieve organization goals.

3. Aids performance evaluation – the budget can be used to evaluate performance by comparing actual results with the budgeted ones.

4. Motivates employees – when employees participate in the budgeting process and/or accept the goals as fair, they are more likely to work towards achieving the goals.

The **performance report** compares actual figures with budgeted figures in order to identify areas that need corrective action. The performance report also serves as a guide for the next period's budget.

The **master budget** has three components: 1) the **operating budget**, 2) the **financial budget**, and 3) the **capital expenditures budget**.

You should study Exhibit 24-4 to understand the flow of information in preparation of the master budget.

OBJECTIVE 2

Prepare an operating budget for a company.

The **operating budget** starts with preparation of the sales or revenue budget, the purchases budget, the cost of goods sold budget, the inventory budget, and the operating expenses budget and culminates with the budgeted income statement. The budgeted income statement contains budgeted amounts rather than actual amounts.

Preparing the Budgeted Income Statement:

Step 1. Prepare the **sales budget** (Schedule A in your text). Remember that there is no way to accurately plan for inventory purchases or inventory levels without a sales budget. The sales budget will generally schedule sales for each month, and present a total for the entire budget period.

Step 2. Prepare a schedule of the **purchases**, **cost of goods sold**, and **inventory budgets** (Schedule B in your text). Remember that you need to buy enough to meet both expected sales levels and the desired ending inventory levels. If there is a beginning inventory, it reduces the amount of inventory you need to purchase.

Purchases = Cost of Goods Sold + Ending Inventory – Beginning Inventory

Step 3. Calculate **budgeted operating expenses** (Schedule C in your text). Remember that some expenses vary with sales, such as sales commissions, while other expenses, such as rent, are fixed amounts from month to month.

The schedules prepared for the operating budget are now used to prepare **the budgeted income statement**. Budgeted sales on the income statement were determined by preparation of the sales budget. Budgeted cost of goods sold was determined by the preparation of the purchases, cost of goods sold, and inventory budgets. The gross margin is equal to sales minus cost of goods sold. Operating expenses were scheduled on the operating expense budget. Operating income is equal to the gross margin minus the operating expenses. The one remaining part of the budgeted income statement is interest expense, which is determined from the cash budget. Remember, all of these are budgeted amounts. (Review Exhibit 24-6 in your text.)

OBJECTIVE 3

Prepare the components of a financial budget.

Once the operating budget is complete, the second part of the master budget is the **financial budget**. The financial budget includes two parts: the **cash budget** (also called the **statement of budgeted cash receipts and disbursements**) and the **budgeted balance sheet**.

Budgeted cash collections from customers (Schedule D in your text) requires that you estimate 1) cash sales and 2) cash collections from credit sales. These amounts should be determined for each period contained in the budget. **Budgeted cash disbursements** are generally divided into budgeted cash disbursements for purchases (Schedule E) and budgeted cash disbursements for operating expenses (Schedule F).

The budgeted acquisition of long-term assets appears in the **capital budget**, which is discussed in more detail in Chapter 27.

Carefully study the statement of budgeted cash receipts and disbursements, Exhibit 24-7 in your text. To prepare a **cash budget**, perform these steps for each budget period:

1. Add cash receipts from customers (Schedule D) to the beginning cash balance to determine cash available before financing.
2. Calculate total cash disbursements. Subtract this total from the total you calculated in step 1 above. This equals the ending cash balance before financing.
3. Subtract the minimum cash balance desired to obtain the cash excess or deficiency.
4. If a cash deficiency exists, then borrowing will occur to cover the deficiency. If a cash excess exists and there was prior borrowing, there will be repayments of principal and interest expense applicable to the prior borrowing. Obtain the total effects of financing by adding cash borrowed or subtracting principal and interest payments.
5. Calculate the ending cash balance: ending cash available before financing (from step 2 above) plus the total effects of financing (from step 4 above).

The **budgeted balance sheet** is prepared using the budgeted income statement, cash budget, and schedules we have reviewed. The ending balance of some items, such as cash, is carried to the balance sheet directly from a budget or schedule. Other items, such as owner's equity, are carried from the previous balance sheet and adjusted for the activity specified in the budget. Study Exhibit 24-8 in your text.

OBJECTIVE 4

Use sensitivity analysis in budgeting.

Remember that the master budget is a plan. What happens if actual results differ from the plan? **Sensitivity analysis** is a technique that addresses this dilemma. Specifically, what will happen if predicted outcomes are not achieved or if there is a change in one of the assumptions underlying the budgeting?

Computer spreadsheets are particularly useful in answering many of the questions which arise when there is a difference in an assumption or an actual result because their speed permits managers to react and adjust more quickly.

Responsibility accounting is a system used to evaluate the performance of managers based on the activities they supervise.

A **responsibility center** can be any unit or subunit of an organization which management wishes to evaluate. Three common types of responsibility centers are: 1) **cost centers**, 2) **profit centers**, and 3) **investment centers**.

A **cost center** generates no revenue and is evaluated on cost control.

A **profit center** such as a sales department is evaluated on its revenues, expenses, and income. An **investment center** such as a single department store in a chain is evaluated on its revenues, expenses, income, and investment needed to finance its operations. Review Exhibit 24-9 and 24-10 in your text.

Management by exception is a strategy in which management investigates important deviations from budgeted amounts. Responsibility and authority are delegated to lower-level employees; management does not become involved unless necessary. Exhibit 24-11 in your text illustrates a **performance report** which stresses variances. The format of a performance report is a matter of personal preference of the users. Basically, the report compares actual and budgeted performance at different levels of the organization.

The most common responsibility center is a department. Calculating departmental operating income can be difficult because of indirect costs. **Direct costs** can be traced to a department, but **indirect costs** are not traceable to a single department.

Cost allocations assign various indirect costs to departments. An allocation base is a logical common denominator used to assign a specific cost to two or more departments. For example, heating cost allocation may be based on a department's cubic footage. Exhibit 24-12 lists typical allocation bases for various types of costs.

The general method to allocate costs is:

1. Determine the allocation base.
2. Obtain the proportion of the allocation base assigned to each department.
3. Multiply the cost by the proportion assigned to each department to obtain the cost assigned to each department.

Two methods for **allocating service department costs** to production departments are:

1. **Direct method** – where all service department costs are allocated directly to production departments, ignoring any benefits received by other service departments from the one whose costs are being allocated (called reciprocal services).
2. **Step-down method** – where reciprocal services are recognized, frequently allocating first the service department rendering the greatest amount of service to other service departments, then proceeding through the other service departments in a descending order. After the last service department costs have been allocated, the sum total of all the service department costs should equal the amount absorbed by the production departments.

Test Yourself

All the self-testing materials in this chapter focus on information and procedures that your instructor is likely to test in quizzes and examinations.

I. Matching *Match each numbered term with its lettered definition.*

1. master budget
2. responsibility center
3. indirect costs
4. cash budget
5. sensitivity analysis
6. operating budget
7. financial budget
8. capital expenditures budget

9. service department
10. production department
11. direct method
12. step-down method
13. reciprocal services
14. management by exception
15. direct costs

A. A company's plan for purchases of property, plant, equipment, and other long-term assets.

B. Details how the business expects to go from the beginning cash balance to the desired ending balance.

C. Costs that are conveniently identified with and traceable to a particular department.

D. A method of service department cost allocation that ignores all services provided by one service department to another.

E. Projects cash inflows and outflows and the period ending balance sheet.

F. Costs that cannot be traced to a single department.

G. The practice of directing management attention to important deviations from budgeted amounts.

H. Sets the target revenues and expenses for the period.

I. A department whose main function is to add value to products or services sold to customers.

J. Mutual services provided among service departments.

K. A part, segment, or subunit of an organization whose manager is accountable for specified activities.

L. A "what if" technique that asks what a result will be if a predicted amount is not achieved or if an underlying assumption changes.

M. A department whose primary function is to provide services to other departments.

N. A method of service department cost allocation that recognizes some, but not all, reciprocal services.

O. The comprehensive budget that includes the operating budget, the capital expenditures budget, and the financial budget.

II. Multiple Choice *Circle the best answer.*

1. A variance occurs when:
   A. actual results exceed budgeted amounts
   B. actual result is less than budgeted amounts
   C. actual results differ from budgeted amounts
   D. none of the above

2. Which of the following is a cost center:
   A. the men's department in a retail store
   B. the West coast division of a large oil refinery
   C. the administrative division of a corporation
   D. the local branch of a statewide chain store

3. When preparing the master budget, the first step is the:
   A. financial budget
   B. operating budget
   C. cash budget
   D. capital expenditures budget

4. When preparing the operating budget, the first step is:
   A. the purchase budget
   B. the sales budget
   C. the operating expense budget
   D. the inventory budget

5. An example of a profit center is:
   A. the housewares department in a department store
   B. the accounting department in a hardware store
   C. both of these
   D. neither of these

6. An example of an investment center is:
   A. a department store in a chain of stores
   B. the delivery department of an auto parts store
   C. the shipping department of a manufacturer
   D. both B and C

7. Which factor is important in an effective responsibility accounting system?
   A. control over operations
   B. access to information
   C. both of these
   D. neither of these

8. Responsibility accounting systems are used for:
   A. finding fault
   B. placing blame
   C. both finding fault and placing blame
   D. determining who can explain specific variances

9. Indirect costs are:
   A. all costs other than direct costs
   B. traceable to a single department
   C. costs which cannot be allocated
   D. direct material and direct labor

10. The most logical way of allocating payroll department costs would be:
    A. square feet of space
    B. cubic feet of space
    C. number of orders in each department
    D. number of employees in each department

III. Completion *Complete each of the following statements.*

1.   The benefits of budgeting are

   1) _____

   2) _____

   3) _____

   4) _____

2.   The budgeted income statement can be prepared after the _____
   has been completed.

3.   _____ costs are traceable to specific departments.

4.   The three components of the master budget are _____,
   _____, and _____.

5.   To determine what might happen if predicted outcomes are not achieved or underlying assumptions change, managers use _____.

6.   _____ are evaluated on their ability to control costs.

7.   The process for assigning indirect costs to departments is called _____.

8.   The financial budget consists of the _____ and the
   _____.

9.   A _____ results when actual results differ from projected
   results.

10. The _____ compares actual results with budgeted
   figures.

? IV. Exercises

1.

    A.   Assuming Inventory decreased by $13,000 during the period and Cost of Goods Sold was $141,000, what was purchases?

    B.   If ending Cash is 50% greater than beginning Cash, cash receipts are $400,000 and cash disbursements are 75% of cash receipts, calculate the beginning and ending cash balances.

2. Jim and Larry's Appliance Store sells family entertainment appliances. Monthly rent is $40,000. Data for three departments for April, 19X4 , follow:

Department	Sales	Square Feet Occupied
Televisions	$425,000	7,000
VCRs	225,000	1,600
CD players	150,000	1,400

A. Allocate rent to each department based on sales.

B. Allocate rent to each department based on square feet occupied.

3. Fanny's Fashion has three locations in Anytown, USA. The owner received the following data for the third quarter of the current year:

	Revenues		Expenses	
	Budget	Actual	Budget	Actual
North Store	$220,000	$250,000	$210,000	$198,000
City Store	187,000	175,000	146,000	150,000
South Store	713,000	874,000	706,000	696,000

Arrange the data in a performance report, showing third-quarter results in thousands of dollars.

4. Conor's Cameras sells disposable, recyclable cameras for use underwater. The units cost $3 each and are sold for $6 a piece. At the end of the first quarter, 200 cameras were on hand. Projected sales for the next four months are 700 units, 900 units, 1,200 units, and 1,000 units, respectively. Conor wants to maintain inventory equal to 40% of the next months sales.

Prepare a sales budget, purchases budget, cost of goods sold, and inventory budget for the next quarter.

Sales Budget - 2nd Quarter			
1st month	2nd month	3rd month	Total

Purchases, Cost of Goods Sold, and Inventory Budget				
	1st month	2nd month	3rd month	Total

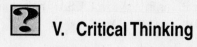

V. Critical Thinking

Review the information in Exercise 2 above. How would your answers change given the following two additional assumptions:

A. In addition to the three departments, there is an administrative office using 1,000 square feet of space.

B. In addition to the three departments and the office, there is an appliance repair department using 1,500 square feet of space.

VI. Demonstration Problems

Demonstration Problem #1

Business System's cash budget for the first three quarters of 19X6 is given below (note that some of the data is missing and must be calculated). The company requires a minimum cash balance of at least $40,000, and owes $4,000 on a note payable from a previous quarter. (Ignore interest.)

Business Systems
Quarterly Cash Budget
19X6

	1	2	3
Beginning cash balance	$ 64,000	$ D	$ 52,000
Add collections from customers	A	280,000	268,000
Cash available	$ B	$ E	$320,000
Deduct disbursements			
Inventory purchases	$124,000	$ F	$ 92,000
Operating expenses	100,000	88,000	120,000
Equipment purchases	40,000	44,000	116,000
Dividends	0	24,000	J
Total disbursements	$264,000	$ G	$ K
Excess (deficiency) in cash	$ 28,000	$ 68,000	($ 8,000)
Financing			
Add borrowing	$ C	–	$ 48,000
Deduct repayments	–	H	0
Ending cash balance	$ 40,000	$ I	$ 40,000

Required

Find the missing value represented by each letter. (Hint: It may not be possible to solve this problem in sequence, A first, B second, and so on.)

A.

B.

C.

D.

E.

F.

G.

H.

I.

J.

K.

Demonstration Problem #2

Elite Shoes has two departments, casual shoes and dress shoes. The company's income statement for 19X8 appears as follows:

Net Sales		$1,130,000
Cost of Goods Sold		548,000
Gross Margin		582,000
Operating expenses:		
Salaries	$310,000	
Depreciation	45,000	
Advertising	18,000	
Other	30,000	403,000
Operating income		$ 179,000

Cost of goods sold is distributed $226,000 for casual shoes and $322,000 for dress shoes. Salaries are allocated to departments based on sales: casual shoes, $472,000; dress shoes $658,000. Advertising is evenly allocated to the two departments. Depreciation is allocated based on square footage: casual shoes, 4,000 square feet; dress shoes, 6,000 square feet. Other expenses are allocated based on sales.

Prepare a departmental income statement showing revenue, expenses, and operating income for two departments.

Elite Shoes			
Departmental Income Statement			
For the Year Ended December 31, 19X8			
		Department	
	Total	Casual Shoes	Dress Shoes
Net sales	$1,130,000		
Cost of goods sold	548,000		
Gross margin	582,000		
Operating expenses:			
Salaries	310,000		
Depreciation	45,000		
Advertising	18,000		
Other	30,000		
Total operating expenses	403,000		
Operating income	$ 179,000	$	$

Solutions

I. Matching

1. O	2. K	3. F	4. B	5. L	6. H	7. E	8. A
9. M	10. I	11. D	12. N	13. J	14. G	15. C	

II. Multiple Choice

1. C A variance does not imply direction, only a difference.

2. C The men's department is a profit center, while choices B and D are investment centers.

3. B The order is operating budget, financial budget (which includes the cash budget), and the capital expenditures budget.

4. B The operating budget always begins with the sales budget — the others are prepared after the sales budget is completed.

5. A The accounting department is a cost center.

6. A Both choices B and C are cost centers.

7. C Both the control over operations and access to information are important factors in an effective responsibility accounting system.

8. D Responsibility accounting systems are not intended to find fault or place blame.

9. A Costs are either direct or indirect. Direct costs are those traceable to a single department (choice B), examples of which are direct materials and direct labor (choice D). Choice C is not appropriate because any cost can be allocated.

10. D Since payroll costs are directly related to the number of employees, choice D is the most appropriate way of allocating the cost.

III. Completion

1. compels planning; promotes coordination and communication; aids performance evaluation; motivates employees (order not important)
2. operating budget
3. direct
4. operating budget, financial budget, capital expenditures budget
5. sensitivity analysis
6. cost centers
7. cost allocation
8. cash budget, budgeted balance sheet
9. variance
10. performance report

IV. Exercises

1. A. Beginning inventory + Purchases – Ending inventory = Cost of goods sold
   X + Purchases – (X – $13,000) = $141,000
   X + Purchases – (X + $13,000) = $141,000
   Purchases = $128,000

   B. Beginning cash = X
   Ending cash = 150%X
   Cash disbursements = 75% x $400,000 = $300,000

   Beginning cash + Receipts – Disbursements = Ending cash
   X + $400,000 – $300,000 = 150%X
   Beginning cash = $200,000
   Ending cash = 150% x $200,000 = $300,000

2. A. Based on sales:

   Total sales = $425,000 + $225,000 + $150,000 = $800,000
   Television department rent = ($425,000/$800,000) x $40,000 = $21,250
   VCR department rent = ($225,000/$800,000) x $40,000 = $11,250
   CD player department rent = ($150,000/$800,000) x $40,000 = $7,500

   B. Based on space occupied:

   Total square feet = 7,000 + 1,600 + 1,400 = 10,000
   Television department rent = (7,000/10,000) x $40,000 = $28,000
   VCR department rent = (1,600/10,000) x $40,000 = $6,400
   CD player department rent = (1,400/10,000) x $40,000 = $5,600

3.

Operating income by location	Budget	Actual	Variance Favorable (Unfavorable)
North Store			
(220 – 210)	10		
(250 – 198)		52	42
City Store			
(187 – 146)	41		
(175 – 150)		25	(16)
South Store			
(713 – 706)	7		
(874 – 696)		178	171
	$58	$255	$197

4.

Sales Budget - 2nd Quarter			
1st month	2nd month	3rd month	Total
$4,200	$5,400	$7,200	$16,800

Multiply number of units by unit cost.

Purchases, Cost of Goods Sold, and Inventory Budget

	1st month	2nd month	3rd month	Total
Cost of Goods Sold[1]	$2,100	$2,700	$3,600	$8,400
+ Desired Ending Inventory[2]	1,080	1,440	1,200[5]	1,200
Subtotal	3,180	4,140	4,800	9,600
− Beginning Inventory[3]	600[4]	1,080	1,440	600
= Purchases	$2,580	$3,060	$2,360	$9,000

[1] Cost of Goods Sold is 50% of budgeted sales: $3/$6 = 50%

[2] Desired Ending Inventory is 40% of the following month's Cost of Goods Sold

[3] Beginning Inventory is 40% of current month's Cost of Goods Sold (or simply last month's Ending Inventory!)

[4] Beginning Inventory is 200 units x $3 ea = $600

[5] The next month's projected Cost of Goods Sold = 1,000 units x $3 ea = $3,000; Ending Inventory = 40% x $3,000 = $1,200

V. Critical Thinking

A. Because the office is a cost center and not a profit center, whatever amount of monthly rent is allocated to the office would later have to be allocated to the three departments (along with the other expenses allocated to the office). Therefore, assuming these costs are allocated using either sales or square feet, the end result would be the same as the amounts calculated in the exercise.

B. Assuming the repair department is a profit center (i.e., it generates revenue) then the amount of rent expense allocated to the three departments in the exercise will decrease by the amount allocated to the repair department. However, if the repair department is a cost center (for instance, it may only do repairs covered by warranties) then the amounts ultimately allocated to the three departments would remain unchanged.

VI. Demonstration Problems

Demonstration Problem #1 Solved and Explained

The solution is given in the order in which the exercise may be worked.

B. Cash available – Total disbursements = Excess (deficiency)
    B – $264,000 = $28,000
    B = $292,000

A. Beginning cash balance + Cash collections = Cash available
    $64,000 + A = $292,000
    A = $228,000

C. Excess + Borrowing = Ending cash balance
    $28,000 + C = $40,000
    C = $12,000

D. $40,000; the beginning cash balance for any quarter is the ending cash balance from the previous quarter.

E. Beginning cash balance + Cash collections = Cash available
    $40,000 + $280,000 = E
    E = $320,000

I. $52,000; the ending cash balance for any quarter is the beginning cash balance for the next quarter.

H. Excess – Repayments = Ending cash balance
    $68,000 – H = $52,000
    H = $16,000

G. Cash available – Total disbursements = Excess
    $320,000 – G = $68,000
    G = $252,000

F. Inventory purchases + Operating expenses + Equipment purchases + Dividends = Total disbursements
    F + $88,000 + $44,000 + $24,000 = $252,000
    F = $96,000

K. Cash available – Total disbursements = (deficiency)
    $320,000 – L = ($8,000)
    $320,000 + $8,000 = L
    L = $328,000

J. Inventory purchases + Operating expenses + Equipment purchases + Dividends = Total disbursements
    $92,000 + $120,000 + $116,000 + K = $328,000
    $328,000 + K = $328,000
    K = $0

Demonstration Problem #2 Solved and Explained

Elite Shoes
Departmental Income Statement
For the Year Ended December 31, 19X8

		Department	
	Total	Casual shoes	Dress shoes
Net sales	$1,130,000	$472,000	$658,000
Cost of goods sold	548,000	226,000	322,000
Gross margin	582,000	246,000	336,000
Operating expenses:			
Salaries	310,000	129,487	180,513
Depreciation	45,000	18,000	27,000
Advertising	18,000	9,000	9,000
Other	30,000	12,531	17,469
Total operating expenses	403,000	169,018	233,982
Operating income	$ 179,000	$ 76,982	$102,018

Calculations:

Salaries:
Casual shoes   [($472,000 ÷ $1,130,000)] x $310,000 = $129,487
Dress shoes   [($658,000 ÷ $1,130,000)] x $310,000 = $180,513

Depreciation:
Casual shoes   [4,000 ÷ (4,000 + 6,000)] x $45,000 = $18,000
Dress shoes   [6,000 ÷ (4,000 + 6,000)] x $45,000 = $27,000

Advertising:
Casual shoes $18,000 ÷ 2 = $9,000
Dress shoes $18,000 ÷ 2 = $9,000

Other:
Casual shoes   ($129,487 ÷ $310,000) x $30,000 = $12,531
Dress shoes   ($180,513 ÷ $310,000) x $30,000 = $17,469

Chapter 25

Flexible Budgets
and Standard Costs

Chapter Overview

*I*n Chapter 24 you were introduced to the master budget and its components. In addition, you learned how budgeted amounts can be compared with actual results as one means of evaluating performance. The topics in the previous chapter provide a foundation for those covered in this chapter—flexible budgets and standard costs. The specific learning objectives for this chapter are:

1. Prepare a flexible budget for the income statement
2. Prepare an income statement performance report
3. Identify the benefits of standard costs
4. Compute standard cost variances for direct materials and direct labor
5. Analyze overhead in a standard cost system
6. Record transactions at standard cost
7. Prepare a standard cost income statement for management

Chapter Review

OBJECTIVE 1

Prepare a
flexible budget
for the income
statement.

Cost behavior may be fixed or variable. Mixed costs have both variable and fixed components. Cost behaviors are valid only for a relevant range of activity.

A **static budget** is prepared for only one level of activity. The static budget is used to budget unit costs and overhead rates. A **performance report** compares actual with budgeted results to show the **variance** (difference) and whether the variance is favorable or unfavorable.

A **flexible (or variable) budget** is a set of budgets covering a range of different sales volumes. Generally, the flexible budget is prepared for actual volume achieved (that is, when actual volume is known). Review Exhibit 25-2 in your text.

To prepare a flexible budget, we use the **budget formula** to compute the budget amounts:

Revenues – Variable Expenses – Fixed Expenses = Operating Income (Loss)

Units Sold x Unit Sale Price	–	Units Sold x Variable Cost Per Unit	–	Fixed Expenses	=	Operating Income (or Loss)

Note that fixed expenses remain constant. They do not change while the firm operates within the relevant range.

Study Exhibit 25-3 in your text to understand the preparation of a flexible budget income statement.

Graphing the expense formula provides a budget for any level of volume. The vertical axis of the budget expense graph shows total expenses and the horizontal axis shows the level of volume. Both budgeted and actual results can be graphed. Remember that the only valid portion of the graph is the area within the relevant range. Refer to Exhibit 25-4 and 25-5 in your text for a graph of a flexible expense budget and a graph of actual and budgeted total expenses.

OBJECTIVE 2

Prepare an
income
statement
performance
report.

An **income statement performance report** is a five-column report:

Column 1   contains actual results at actual prices.

Column 3   contains the flexible budget for actual volume achieved (prepared using the budget formula).

Column 5   contains the static (master) budget.

Column 2   contains flexible budget variances. Flexible budget variances are differences between actual results (Column 1) and the flexible budget (Column 3).

Column 4   contains sales volume variances. Sales volume variances are the difference between the flexible budget (Column 3) and the static budget (Column 5).

See Exhibit 25-6 in your text for an income statement performance report.

OBJECTIVE 3

Identify the
benefits of
standard costs.

A **standard cost** is a predetermined cost that management expects to attain. The benefits to an organization of standard costs are:

1. Providing the unit amounts needed for budgeting
2. Assisting management control by calling attention to significant variations
3. Motivating employees by setting goals against which performance will be evaluated
4. Providing a unit cost basis for establishing selling prices
5. Reducing clerical costs

OBJECTIVE 4

Compute
standard cost
variances for
direct materials
and direct labor.

Variances between actual and standard costs are separated into **price variances** and **efficiency variances** for direct materials and direct labor.

Direct Materials:

The total flexible budget variance for direct materials is separated into the price variance and the efficiency variance. The **direct materials price variance** measures the difference between the actual and the budgeted price of materials for the amount of materials used.

$$\text{Price Variance} = \begin{array}{c}\text{Difference Between}\\\text{Actual and Budgeted}\\\text{Unit Prices of Inputs}\end{array} \quad \times \quad \text{Actual Inputs Used}$$

If the actual unit price is less than the budgeted unit price, the variance is favorable. If the actual unit price is greater than the budgeted unit price, the variance is unfavorable.

$$\begin{array}{c}\text{Efficiency}\\\text{Variance}\end{array} = \left[\begin{array}{c}\text{Inputs}\\\text{Actually}\\\text{Used}\end{array} - \begin{array}{c}\text{Inputs That Should}\\\text{Have Been Used}\\\text{For Actual Output}\end{array}\right] \times \begin{array}{c}\text{Standard}\\\text{Unit Price}\\\text{of Input}\end{array}$$

The **direct materials efficiency** (quantity or usage) **variance** measures the difference between the quantity of inputs actually used and the inputs that should have been used for the actual output achieved.

Note that INPUTS THAT SHOULD HAVE BEEN USED FOR ACTUAL OUTPUT is equal to standard input per unit times actual units produced.

If inputs actually used are less than inputs that should have been used, the variance is favorable. If inputs actually used are greater than inputs that should have been used, the variance is unfavorable.

Exhibit 25-9 in your text summarizes the direct materials variance computations.

Direct Labor:

The **direct labor price** (rate) **variance** measures the difference between the actual rate per labor hour and the budgeted rate per labor hour.

$$\text{Price Variance} = \left[\begin{array}{c}\text{Difference Between}\\\text{Actual and Budgeted}\\\text{Unit Prices of Inputs}\end{array}\right] \times \text{Actual Inputs Used}$$

The **direct labor efficiency variance** measures the difference between hours actually used and hours that should have been used for the output achieved.

$$
\begin{array}{ccc}
\begin{array}{c} \text{Efficiency} \\ \text{Variance} \end{array} = &
\left[\begin{array}{ccc} \text{Inputs} & & \text{Inputs That Should} \\ \text{Actually} & - & \text{Have Been Used} \\ \text{Used} & & \text{For Actual Output} \end{array} \right] \times &
\begin{array}{c} \text{Standard} \\ \text{Unit Price} \\ \text{of Input} \end{array}
\end{array}
$$

Note that these equations are identical to the direct materials variance equations. Exhibit 25-10 in your text summarizes direct labor variance computations.

The advantage to the company of calculating these variances is that management can investigate when the variances are significant.

In addition to direct materials and direct labor, variances are also calculated for manufacturing overhead as one means of evaluating performance. Some companies group individual overhead cost into a single cost pool, distinguishing between the variable and fixed amounts.

<table>
<tr><td>

OBJECTIVE 5

Analyze overhead in a standard cost system.

</td><td>

Overhead variances are computed differently from material and labor variances. Production overhead variances are commonly separated into an **overhead flexible budget variance** and a **production volume variance**.

The **overhead flexible budget variance** (also called the **overhead controllable variance**) is the difference between total overhead incurred and the flexible budget amount for actual production. The **production volume variance** is the difference between the flexible budget for actual production and standard overhead applied to production.

Exhibit 25-13 in your text summarizes this two-variance approach.

A **three-variance overhead analysis** further refines the overhead flexible budget variance by splitting it into an **overhead efficiency variance** and an **overhead spending variance**. The efficiency variance measures the difference between the flexible budget for actual production and the flexible budget for the actual units of the overhead cost application base (the cost driver). The spending variance measures the difference between the flexible budget for the actual units of the cost application base (the cost driver) and the total actual overhead cost. The spending variance is the difference between the flexible budget variance and the efficiency variance. Exhibit 25-16 in your text illustrates the efficiency and spending variances.

</td></tr>
<tr><td>

OBJECTIVE 6

Record transactions at standard cost.

</td><td>

To record purchases of direct materials:

Materials Inventory	XX		
Direct Materials Price Variance	X	or	X
Accounts Payable			XX

To record direct materials used:

Work in Process	XX		
Direct Materials Efficiency Variance	X	or	X
Materials Inventory			XX

To record direct labor costs incurred:

Manufacturing Wages	XX		
Direct Labor Price Variance	X	or	X
Wages Payable			XX

</td></tr>
</table>

To apply direct labor to production:

Work in Process	XX		
Direct Labor Efficiency Variance	X	or	X
Manufacturing Wages			XX

To record overhead incurred:

Manufacturing Overhead	XX	
A/P, Accum. Dep., etc.		XX

To apply Overhead:

Work in Process	XX	
Manufacturing Overhead		XX

The overhead variance is recorded when the Overhead account is reduced to zero.

In all of these entries, credit variances are favorable, debits are unfavorable. At year end all variance accounts are closed with a reconciling net debit (or credit) to Income Summary.

OBJECTIVE 7
Prepare a standard cost income statement for management.

A **standard cost income statement** lists cost of goods sold at standard cost followed by the specific variances for direct materials, direct labor, and overhead. Remember, debit variances are unfavorable (and therefore added to the cost of goods sold amount) while credit variances are favorable (and therefore deducted from the cost of goods sold amount). This format shows management what needs to be improved or corrected. See Exhibit 25-17 in your text.

Test Yourself

All the self-testing materials in this chapter focus on information and procedures that your instructor is likely to test in quizzes and examinations.

I. Matching *Match each numbered term with its lettered definition.*

1. Price variance
2. Standard cost
3. Cost pool
4. Efficiency variance
5. Overhead efficiency variance
6. Production volume variance

7. Overhead spending variance
8. Sales volume variance
9. Static budget
10. Flexible budget
11. Flexible budget variance
12. Overhead flexible budget variance

A. A budget prepared for only one level of activity
B. Any group of individual cost items
C. The difference between the actual quantity and the standard quantity of input allowed for actual output, multiplied by the standard unit price of input
D. Difference between an amount in the flexible budget and the actual results
E. Difference between a revenue, expense, or operating income in the flexible budget and the revenue, expense, or income amount in the master budget
F. Difference between total actual overhead (fixed and variable) and the flexible budget amount for actual production volume
G. Difference between the actual unit price of an input (materials and labor) and a standard unit price, multiplied by the actual quantity of inputs used
H. Difference between the flexible budget for actual production and standard overhead applied to production
I. Predetermined cost that management believes the business should incur in producing an item
J. Set of budgets covering a range of volume rather than a single level of volume
K. The difference between the flexible budget for actual production and the flexible budget for the actual units of the overhead cost application base
L. The difference between the flexible budget for the actual units of the cost application base and the total actual overhead cost

II. Multiple Choice *Circle the best answer.*

1. As volume decreases, which of the following is true?
   A. total variable costs decrease
   B. variable cost per unit decreases
   C. fixed cost per unit decreases
   D. total fixed costs increase

2. A budget covering a range of activity levels is a:
   A. flexible budget
   B. static budget
   C. conversion budget
   D. pliable budget

3. Flexible budgets can be used as a:
   A. planning tool
   B. control device
   C. both a planning tool and a control device
   D. neither a planning tool nor a control device

4. One possible explanation for a favorable sales volume variance and an unfavorable flexible budget variance is:
   A. higher than expected sales and costs
   B. higher than expected sales and lower than expected costs
   C. lower than expected sales and higher than expected costs
   D. lower than expected sales and costs

5. The term standard cost usually refers to ___ cost. The term budgeted cost usually refers to ___ cost.
   A. unit, unit
   B. unit, total
   C. total, unit
   D. total, total

6. Price variances relate to:
    A. direct materials only
    B. direct labor only
    C. manufacturing overhead only
    D. both direct materials and direct labor

7. A spending variance relates to:
    A. direct materials only
    B. direct labor only
    C. manufacturing overhead only
    D. both direct materials and direct labor

8. In a standard cost income statement, gross margin equals:
    A. net sales – cost of goods sold at standard cost
    B. net sales – operating expenses
    C. net sales – cost of goods sold at standard cost + unfavorable variances – favorable variances
    D. net sales – cost of goods sold at standard cost – unfavorable variances + favorable variances

9. At the end of the accounting period, variance account balances are:
    A. carried forward to the next accounting period
    B. closed to cost of goods sold
    C. closed to Income Summary
    D. none of the above

10. An overhead controllable variance is another term for:
    A. production volume variance
    B. overhead spending variance
    C. overhead efficiency variance
    D. overhead flexible budget variance

III. Completion *Complete each of the following statements.*

1. _____ are resources given up to achieve a specific objective.

2. Total _____ costs change proportionately with changes in volume or activity.

3. Total _____ costs do not change during a given time period over a wide range of volume.

4. A _____ cost has both variable and fixed components.

5. If rent expense is fixed at $1,000 per month and sales increase from 2,500 units to 10,000 units, the rent per unit is _____ as much as it originally was.

6. A(n) _____ variance for materials or labor measures whether the quantity of inputs used to make a product is within the budget.

7. A(n) _____ variance for materials or labor measures how well a business keeps unit prices of materials and labor within standards.

8. A budget prepared for only one level of volume is called a _____ budget.

9. A _____ refers to any group of individual items.

10. _____ measures the amount of inputs used to achieve a given level of output.

? IV. Exercises

1. If variable costs are $5.00 per unit, the relevant range is 6,000 to 15,000 units, and total costs were $60,000 for 8,000 units:

A. How much were fixed costs?

B. What is the flexible budget formula for costs?

C. At the 10,000 unit level, what are total budgeted costs?

2. Actual production   3,300 units

    Actual cost (6,700 feet of direct materials) $33,701

    Standard price $4.75 per foot

    Materials efficiency variance $2,660 F

    A.   Compute the materials price variance.

    B.   Compute standard feet per unit.

3. Assuming 2,400 hours of direct labor were budgeted for actual output at a standard rate of $12.00 per hour and 2,500 hours were worked at a rate of $11.75 per hour,

    A.   Compute the labor price variance.

    B.   Compute the labor efficiency variance.

4. The Edwards Manufacturing Company hopes to produce 360,000 units of product during the next calendar year. Monthly production can range between 20,000 and 40,000 units. Per unit variable manufacturing costs have been budgeted as follows: direct materials, $2; direct labor, $2.50; and overhead, $1.25. Prepare a flexible budget for 20,000, 30,000, and 40,000 units of output.

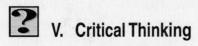 **V. Critical Thinking**

Refer to the information (and solution) for Exercise 4 above. During June, 30,000 units were manufactured. Costs incurred were as follows: $59,000 for direct materials, $77,250 for direct labor, and $37,300 for overhead. Were the costs controlled?

_____

_____

_____

_____

_____

_____

_____

_____

_____

_____

_____

_____

_____

_____

_____

_____

_____

VI. Demonstration Problems

Demonstration Problem #1

A flexible budget for Mendoza Manufacturing is presented below:

Mendoza Manufacturing
Flexible Budget
For the Year 19X2

	Budget Formula per unit	Various Levels of Volume		
Units	–	40,000	48,000	56,000
Sales	$4.75	$190,000	$228,000	$266,000
Variable expenses	$2.20	88,000	105,600	123,200
Fixed expenses		56,000	56,000	56,000
Total expenses		144,000	161,600	179,200
Operating income		$ 46,000	$ 66,400	$ 86,800

The static (master) budget is based on volume of 48,000 units. Actual operating results for 19X2 are as follows:

Sales (49,500 units) $227,700
Variable expenses   106,920
Fixed expenses   57,570

Required (Use the work space provided on the next page.)

1. Prepare an income statement performance report for 19X2.

2. Show that the total variances in operating income account for the net difference between actual operating income and the static (master) budget income.

Requirement 1 (income statement performance report)

Mendoza Manufacturing
Income Statement Performance Report
For the Year Ended December 31, 19X2

	(1) Actual Results at Actual Prices	(2) (1) – (3) Flexible Budget Variances	(3) Flexible Budget for Actual Volume Achieved	(4) (3) – (5) Sales Volume Variances	(5) Static (Master) Budget
Units					
Sales	$_____	$_____	$_____	$_____	$_____
Variable expenses					
Fixed expenses					
Total expenses					
Operating income	$_____	$_____	$_____	$_____	$_____

Requirement 2 (reconciling variances)

$_____

_____

$_____

$_____

_____

$_____

Demonstration Problem #2

Feng Fabricators uses a standard cost system. They produce specially manufactured goods in large batches for catalogue companies featuring unusual household decorative items. They have just received an order for 10,000 units of a decorative wall hanging. Their standard cost for one wall hanging is:

Direct materials: 2.5 feet $2/ft	$ 5.00
Direct labor: 1.5 hours $8/hr	12.00
Overhead: 1.5 hours $6/hr	9.00
Standard cost/unit	$26.00

The normal capacity for the factory this period is 16,000 direct labor hours. Overhead costs are equally divided between variable and fixed expenses and are applied on the basis of direct labor hours. Lily Feng, the company president, has promised to have the wall hangings ready for shipment by the end of the month. The customer has agreed to pay $40 each.

During the month, the following events occurred:

1. Purchased 27,500 feet of raw materials at $1.90/ft.
2. Received and placed into production 27,500 feet of raw materials.
3. Direct manufacturing wages incurred, 14,700 hours at $8.25/hr.
4. Assigned 14,700 direct labor hours to the job.
5. Recorded $91,600 of overhead costs.
6. Applied manufacturing overhead to the job.
7. The wall hangings were completed.
8. Shipped 10,000 units to the customer and billed the customer $400,000.

Required (Use the work space provided on the following three pages.)

1. Journalize the transactions.
2. Post your transactions to the appropriate T-accounts.
3. Record the overhead variances.
4. Prepare a standard cost income statement.

Requirement 1 (journal entries)

	Explanation	Debit	Credit

Requirement 2 (post to T-accounts)

Materials Inventory		Direct Materials Price Variance		Direct Materials Efficiency Variance

Manufacturing Wages		Direct Labor Price Variance		Direct Labor Efficiency Variance

Manufacturing Overhead

Work in Process		Finished Goods		Cost of Goods Sold

Requirement 3 (record overhead variances)

Explanation	Debit	Credit

Requirement 4

Feng Fabricators
Standard Cost Income Statement

Solutions

I. Matching

1. G	2. I	3. B	4. C	5. K	6. H
7. L	8. E	9. A	10. J	11. D	12. F

II. Multiple Choice

1. A Variable costs on a per unit basis are not affected by changes in volume (B). Fixed cost per unit increases as volume decreases (C). Fixed costs do not change as a result of volume changes in the relevant range of production (D).

2. A A static budget is prepared for only one level of activity (B). Answers C and D have no meaning.

3. C All budgets are used for planning. Since the flexible budget is prepared for the actual level of activity achieved, it provides for precise control.

4. A The sales volume variance measures differences between the static budget and the flexible budget for actual volume achieved. The flexible budget variance measures differences between actual results and the flexible budget for actual volume achieved. Accordingly, higher than expected sales could be expected to give a favorable sales volume variance, and actual costs above flexible budget costs could be expected to give an unfavorable flexible budget variance.

5. B A standard cost is a carefully predetermined cost that is usually expressed on a per-unit basis. It is a target cost, a cost that should be attained. Budgeted costs are total costs. Think of a standard variable cost as a budget for a single unit.

6. D Price variances relate to materials and labor. Efficiency, spending, and volume variances relate to overhead.

7. C Spending variances relate to overhead. The variances relating to direct materials and direct labor are the price and efficiency variances.

8. C Unfavorable variances are added to cost of goods sold and favorable variances are deducted.

9. C Because the variances relate to only the current period, they are closed out to Income Summary at the end.

10. D The production volume variance is different from the overhead controllable variance, whereas the spending and efficiency variances are subdivisions of the overhead flexible budget variance.

III. Completion

1. Costs
2. variable
3. fixed
4. mixed
5. one-fourth (2,500 units / 10,000 units)
6. efficiency
7. price
8. static
9. cost pool
10. Efficiency

IV. Exercises

1. A. Total costs = Fixed costs + Variable costs
   $60,000 = X + ($5 x 8,000)
   $60,000 = X + $40,000
   $20,000 = X

   Fixed costs were $20,000

   B. Total budgeted costs = ($5 x # of units produced) + $20,000

   C. Total budgeted costs = ($5 x 10,000) + $20,000 = $70,000

2. A.

Actual cost	$33,701
Less: Budgeted unit cost x actual usage	
($4.75 x 6,700)	31,825
Materials price variance	$ 1,876 U

   B. $2,660 F = (6,700 feet – X) x $4.75
   X = 7,260 feet = inputs that should have been used
   7,260 feet / 3,300 units = 2.2 standard feet

3. A.

Actual cost (2,500 hours @ $11.75)	$29,375
Less: Budgeted unit cost x actual usage	
(2,500 x $12.00)	30,000
Labor price variance	$ 675 F

   B.

Budgeted costs for actual hours (see above)	$30,000
Less: Standard cost for actual production	
(2,400 x $12.00)	28,800
Labor efficiency variance	$ 1,200 U

4.

Edwards Manufacturing Company
Monthly Flexible Budget Report

Output	20,000	30,000	40,000
Variable costs			
Direct materials ($2)	$ 40,000	$ 60,000	$ 80,000
Direct labor ($2.50)	50,000	75,000	100,000
Overhead ($1.25)	25,000	37,500	50,000
	$115,000	$172,500	$230,000

V. Critical Thinking

To answer the question we need to compare actual results with the budget.

Edwards Manufacturing Company
Budget Report
June 19XX

	Actual	Budget	Variance
Units	30,000	30,000	0
Variable costs			
Direct materials	$ 59,000	$ 60,000	$1,000 F
Direct labor	77,250	75,000	2,250 U
Overhead	37,300	37,500	200 F
Totals	$173,550	$172,500	$1,050 U

Overall, costs were controlled. The unfavorable variance was less than 1% of the budgeted amount (1,050 / 172,500). However, this overall result has been adversely affected by a 3% (2,250 / 75,000) unfavorable variance in direct labor costs while both direct materials and overhead show favorable variances.

VI. Demonstration Problems

Demonstration Problem #1 Solved And Explained

Requirement 1 (income statement performance report)

Mendoza Manufacturing
Income Statement Performance Report
For the Year Ended December 31, 19X2

	(1) Actual Results at Actual Prices	(2) (1) – (3) Flexible Budget Variances	(3) (1) – (3) Flexible Budget for Actual Volume Achieved	(4) (3) – (5) Sales Volume Variances	(5) Static (Master) Budget
Units	49,500	0	49,500	1,500 F	48,000
Sales	$227,700	$7,425 U	$235,125	$7,125 F	$228,000
Variable expenses	106,920	1,980 F	108,900	3,300 U	105,600
Fixed expenses	57,570	1,570 U	56,000	—	56,000
Total expenses	164,490	410 F	164,900	3,300 U	161,600
Operating income	$ 63,210	$7,015 U	$ 70,225	$3,825 F	$ 66,400

Explanations:

Column 1

Column 1 contains actual results that were presented in the problem statement.

Column 3

Column 3 contains the flexible budget for the volume actually sold. Actual sales were 49,500 units. Budgeted revenue is $235,125 ($4.75 per unit x 49,500). Budgeted variable expenses are $108,900 ($2.20 per unit x 49,500). Budgeted revenue and budgeted variable expenses may be calculated by multiplying units actually sold by the budget formula amounts in the flexible budget. Note that fixed expenses of $56,000 are constant at all the production levels presented in the flexible budget.

Column 5

The amounts in column 5 are the static, or master budget amounts. The problem notes that the static budget is based on 48,000 units, a volume level also found in the flexible budget.

Column 2

The flexible budget variances are the differences between actual results (column 1) and flexible budget amounts (column 3). When actual revenue or income is greater than budgeted, the variance is *favorable*. When revenue or income is *less* than budgeted, the variance is *unfavorable*. For example, the flexible budget variance for sales is $7,425 U (actual sales were less than the flexible budget amount). When expenses are *greater* than budgeted, the variance is unfavorable. When expenses are less than budgeted, the variance is *favorable*. For example, the flexible budget variance for variable expenses is $1,980 F (actual variable expenses were less than the flexible budget amount). It may help to remember that spending less than planned is favorable, while spending more is unfavorable.

Column 4

Sales volume variances are the differences between flexible budget amounts for actual sales and static budget amounts. Note that no sales volume variance exists for fixed expenses, since fixed are constant within the relevant range. The criteria to determine whether the variances are favorable or unfavorable are the same as detailed in the explanation for column 2.

Requirement 2 (reconciling variances)

Static (master) budget operating income	$66,400
Actual operating income at actual prices	63,210
Total difference to account for	$ 3,190 U

Note that when actual operating income is less than static budget operating income, the variance is unfavorable.

Sales volume variance	$ 3,825 F
Flexible budget variance	7,015 U
Total net variance	$ 3,190 U

Since the unfavorable flexible budget variance is greater than the favorable sales volume variance, the overall net variance is unfavorable.

Demonstration Problem #2 Solved And Explained

Requirement 1 (journal entries)

		Explanation	Debit	Credit
1)		Materials Inventory (27,500 x $2)	55,000	
		Direct Materials Price Variance (27,500 x $.20)		2,750
		Accounts Payable (27,500 x $1.90)		52,250
2)		Work in Process (25,000 x $2)	50,000	
		Materials Efficiency Variance (2,500 x $2)	5,000	
		Materials Inventory		55,000
3)		Manufacturing Wages (14,700 x $8)	117,600	
		Direct Labor Price Variance (14,700 x $.25)	3,675	
		Wages Payable (14,700 x $8.25)		121,275
4)		Work in Process (15,000 x $8)	120,000	
		Direct Labor Efficiency Variance (300 x $8)		2,400
		Manufacturing Wages		117,600
5)		Manufacturing Overhead	91,600	
		Various accounts		91,600
6)		Work in Process (15,000 x $6)	90,000	
		Manufacturing Overhead		90,000
7)		Finished Goods (10,000 x $26)	260,000	
		Work in Process		260,000
8)		Cost of Goods Sold	260,000	
		Finished Goods		260,000
		Accounts Receivable	400,000	
		Sales		400,000

Requirement 2 (post to T-accounts)

Materials Inventory	
(1) 55,000	(2) 55,000

Direct Materials Price Variance	
	(1) 2,750

Direct Materials Efficiency Variance	
(2) 5,000	

Manufacturing Wages	
(3) 117,600	(4) 117,600

Direct Labor Price Variance	
(3) 3,675	

Direct Labor Efficiency Variance	
	(4) 2,400

Manufacturing Overhead	
(5) 91,600	(6) 91,600

Work in Process	
(2) 50,000	(7) 260,000
(4) 120,000	
(6) 90,000	

Finished Goods	
(7) 260,000	(8) 260,000

Cost of Goods Sold	
(8) 260,000	

Requirement 3 (record overhead variances)

Explanation	Debit	Credit
Production Volume Variance (1)	3,000	
Overhead Flexible Budget Variance (2)		1,400
Manufacturing Overhead (3)		1,600

(1) the fixed portion of overhead costs ($3) times the difference between normal capacity and budgeted or, $3 x 1,000 hour = $3,000

(2) the difference between actual overhead ($91,600) and the sum of the budgeted variable ($3 x 15,000) and normal fixed ($3 x 16,000) or, $45,000 + $48,000 = $93,000 – $91,600 = $1,400

(3) the balance in the manufacturing overhead account

Requirement 4

Feng Fabricators
Standard Cost Income Statement

Sales revenue		$400,000
Cost of goods sold at standard cost	$260,000	
Manufacturing cost variances:		
Direct materials price variance	(2,750)	
Direct materials efficiency variance	5,000	
Direct labor price variance	3,675	
Direct labor efficiency variance	(2,400)	
Overhead flexible budget variance	(1,400)	
Production volume variance	3,000	
Cost of goods sold at actual cost		265,125
Gross margin		$134,875

Points to remember:

The standard cost income statement reports cost of goods sold at standard cost, then modifies this amount by the variances for direct materials, direct labor and overhead.

Debit variances reflect additions to cost of goods sold while credit variances are deductions.

The standard cost income statement is for internal purposes only.

Chapter 26

Strategy, Cost Management, and Continuous Improvement

Chapter Overview

*A*s businesses attempt to remain competitive in an international environment, they strive for competitive advantages. Some of these efforts involve better management of costs, research to deliver higher quality products to the customer, and the introduction of systems that allow management to effectively plan for future operations. While we have been investigating a variety of topics concerning "costs" in recent chapters, we now turn our attention to some of the issues at the forefront of cost management. The specific learning objectives for this chapter are:

1. Describe the distinctive features of activity-based costing (ABC)
2. Use activity-based costs to make management decisions
3. Compare the major features of a traditional production system and a just-in-time (JIT) production system
4. Record manufacturing costs for a backflush costing system
5. Prepare a life-cycle budget for a product
6. Relate target costing and kaizen costing to continuous improvement
7. Contrast the four types of quality costs

Chapter Review

OBJECTIVE 1

Describe the distinctive features of activity-based costing (ABC).

Activity-based costing (ABC) is the primary source of information for **activity-based management. Activity-based costing** is a system that focuses on activities as cost objects and uses the costs of those activities as building blocks for compiling the costs of products and other **cost objects.** A cost object is anything (specific task, particular product, function) for which it is worthwhile to compile cost information. Activity-based costing can be implemented by any business—it is not associated only with manufacturing.

When ABC Is in Use

ABC is the result of the need by companies for more accurate information concerning product costs, thereby allowing managers to make decisions based on accurate information. ABC recognizes that frequently multiple cost drivers exist. When this occurs, applying manufacturing overhead costs on the basis of a single cost driver results in distorted product costs. Applying ABC to products requires these steps:

1. Identify manufacturing activities.
2. Budget the total cost of each activity.
3. Identify the primary cost driver as the application base for each activity.
4. Budget the total units of each application base.
5. Divide the budgeted costs in Step 2 above by the budgeted application base (Step 4) to compute the cost application.
6. Apply activity costs to products by multiplying the application base units that pertain to the products by the cost application rates computed in Step 5.

Organizing cost information by activity provides detailed information not available using a single application rate. When ABC is applied to upstream activities (those that precede manufacturing) and downstream (those activities that follow manufacture), a product's total cost can be determined.

OBJECTIVE 2

Use activity-based costs to make management decisions.

With ABC in place, managers are able to make more accurate decisions because they are based on more precise product cost information. Once the product pricing has been determined, other decisions based on product pricing can be made with accuracy. For instance deciding whether to produce something or simply purchase it from a supplier can now be more accurately determined.

OBJECTIVE 3

Compare the major features of a traditional production system and a just-in-time (JIT) production system.

In a **traditional production system** large inventories are maintained. However, maintaining large inventories consumes cash that could be used for other purposes. In addition, problems caused by inferior quality, obsolescence, and production bottlenecks might be overlooked with large amounts of inventory.

The actual manufacturing processes in a traditional production system can also result in inefficiencies. The actual physical movement of goods in process can be quite long, resulting in further inefficiencies. **Throughput time** is a term used to describe the time between the receipt of raw materials and the completion of a finished good. As an equation, it is expressed as follows:

$$\text{Throughput time} = \begin{array}{l} \text{Processing time} \\ + \text{ waiting time} \\ + \text{ moving time} \\ + \text{ inspection time} \\ + \text{ reworking time} \end{array}$$

Whereas processing time adds value to a product, the other elements in the equation are non-value-added activities and considered waste.

Just-in-time (JIT) production systems are designed to eliminate the waste found in a traditional system. Underlying JIT systems are the following four concepts:

1. **arrangement of production activities** — Processes are arranged so production is continuous without interruption.

2. **setup times** — The greater the amount of setup time, the greater the amount of non-value-added activity. JIT minimizes the amount of time required for setup.

3. **production scheduling** — Under JIT, products are produced in smaller batches, frequently the amount needed to fill a specific order. In addition, production is not begun until an order is received. This is referred to as a "demand-pull" system because the customer's order (the demand) "pulls" the product through the manufacturing process. In turn, the product acts as a "demand" to "pull" raw materials into the manufacturing process. All of which results in less inventory and activities, and an early detection of production problems.

4. **employee roles** — In a traditional system, employees are trained to complete a specific task. Under JIT, employees are cross-trained to perform different tasks. This means greater flexibility and lower costs.

Review Exhibit 26-3 in your text for a comparison of a traditional system with a JIT system.

OBJECTIVE 4
Record manufacturing costs for a backflush costing system.

In Chapter 25, you learned about the traditional standard cost system in which costs are tracked through the manufacturing process from raw materials to finished goods. Under JIT, a backflush costing system is used. **Backflush costing** is a standard costing system that starts with output completed and works backward to apply manufacturing costs to units sold and to inventories. Backflush costing takes less time and is less expensive to use than the traditional standard costing.

In a backflush system, no distinction is made between Raw Materials Inventory and Work in Process. Instead they are combined into one account, Raw and In Process (RIP).

When materials are acquired:

RIP Inventory	XX	
Accounts Payable		XX
Recorded at standard amounts		

As conversion costs are incurred:

Conversion Costs	XX	
Various Accounts		XX
Recorded at actual costs		

When the number of units of finished product is known:

Finished Goods	XX	
RIP Inventory		XX
Conversion Costs		XX

The amount for each account above is based on standard costs.

When goods are sold:

Cost of Goods Sold	XX	
Finished Goods		XX
Recorded at standard amounts		

Price variances are recorded at the time materials are acquired, while efficiency variances are not recorded until goods have been completed. Over/under applied conversion costs are transferred to Cost of Goods Sold.

OBJECTIVE 5

Prepare a life-cycle budget for a product.

To remain competitive, companies must continuously strive to improve their activities. The reduction of costs over a product's life cycle is one means of doing so. When a new product is planned, a life-cycle budget is prepared. A **life-cycle budget** lists projected revenues and costs before any reduction efforts are made. Based on this budget, managers decide whether or not the new product is worth pursuing. See Exhibit 26-5 in your text as an example of a life-cycle budget.

OBJECTIVE 6

Relate target costing and kaizen costing to continuous improvement.

Target costing is a cost management technique that helps managers set goals for cost reductions through product design. First, cost reduction goals are set. **Value-engineering** (VE) is then used to meet these goals. Value-engineering refers to the process of designing products that achieve cost targets and meet specified standards of quality and performance. Careful analysis may highlight processes where costs can be saved while maintaining quality. Once identified, these amounts are used to reduce budgeted costs to a target cost. Coordination among functional areas is necessary for target costing to work.

Once manufacturing has begun, **kaizen costing** techniques are employed to further reduce costs. If the techniques succeed, standard costs will continually drop over the product's life cycle.

OBJECTIVE 7

Contrast the four types of quality costs.

Quality is the conformance of the attributes of a product or service to a specific set of standards. **Total quality management** (TQM) refers to formal efforts to improve quality throughout an organization's value chain. An important feature of TQM is employee education and training. TQM is based on the theme that superior work benefits the whole organization and inferior work hurts the whole organization.

Four types of **quality costs** are prevention costs, appraisal costs, internal failure costs and external failure costs. **Prevention costs** are those a company incurs to avoid poor quality goods and services. **Appraisal costs** occur when a company wants to detect poor quality goods and services. **Internal failure costs** result when inferior goods or services are detected before delivery to the customer. **External failure costs** are those incurred after the customer has received the good or service. See Exhibit 26-8 in your text for examples of quality costs.

Benchmarking, the comparison of current performance with some standard, is used as nonfinancial performance measure. Benchmarking recognizes that not all performance measures are financial, and that these nonfinancial measures do, nevertheless, affect profitability. See Exhibit 26-9 for some examples of benchmarking.

Test Yourself

All the self-testing materials in this chapter focus on information and procedures that your instructor is likely to test in quizzes and examinations.

I. Matching

Match each numbered term with its lettered definition.

1. product life cycle
2. throughput time
3. kaizen costing
4. appraisal costs
5. life-cycle budget
6. backflush costing
7. just-in-time production systems
8. strategy

9. target costing
10. benchmarking
11. value-engineering
12. total quality management
13. activity-based costing
14. prevention costs
15. trigger points
16. internal failure costs

A. the process of designing products that achieve cost targets and meet specified standards of quality and performance

B. points in operations that prompt entries in the accounting records

C. a formal effort to improve quality throughout an organization's value chain

D. the time between receipt of purchased materials and completion of finished products

E. a cost management technique that helps managers set goals for cost reductions through product design

F. a set of business goals and the tactics to achieve them

G. the time from original research and development to the end of a product's sales and customer service

H. costs incurred to avoid poor quality goods or services

I. a budget that compiles predicted revenues and costs of a product over its entire life cycle

J. the relentless pursuit of cost reduction in the manufacturing stage of a product's life cycle, achieved by planned reductions in cost drivers

K. systems designed to eliminate waste by such means as sequentially arranged production scheduling, and a high level of employee training and commitment

L. cost incurred when poor quality goods or services are detected before delivery to customers

M. comparison of current performance with some standard. The standard often is the performance level of a leading outside organization.

N. a standard costing system that starts with output completed and works backward to apply manufacturing costs to units sold and to inventories

O. costs incurred in detecting poor quality goods or services

P. a system that focuses on activities as the fundamental cost objects and uses the costs of those activities as building blocks for compiling the costs of products and other cost objects

II. Multiple Choice *Circle the best answer.*

1. In manufacturing, all the following are non-value-added activities except:
    A. inspection time
    B. moving time
    C. processing time
    D. reworking time

2. Relative to actual production, all the following are downstream activities except:
    A. customer service
    B. distribution
    C. advertising
    D. product design

3. High-commitment, high-performance team training is a feature of:
    A. total quality management
    B. value-engineering
    C. activity-based costing
    D. a backflush costing system

4. All of the following are characteristics of quality costs except:
    A. use of benchmarking for evaluation
    B. difficult to measure
    C. difficult to identify individual components
    D. types of financial performance measures

5. Which of the following are likely to use an activity-based costing system?
    A. financial institutions
    B. retailer
    C. textile manufacturer
    D. all of the above

6. Which of the following is an example of an external failure cost?
    A. reworking time
    B. cost to honor warranties
    C. training program costs
    D. inspection costs

7.   All of the following are nonfinancial measures of quality except:
     A.   amount of machine "down" time
     B.   return on sales
     C.   unit failure
     D.   training hours per employee per month

8.   Value-engineering is most closely associated with:
     A.   total quality management
     B.   activity-based management
     C.   target costing
     D.   none of the above

9.   Benchmarking is most closely associated with:
     A.   kaizen costing
     B.   nonfinancial measures of quality
     C.   value-engineering
     D.   activity-based costing

10. Kaizen costing concerns the _____ phase whereas target costing concerns the _____ phase.
     A.   testing, product design
     B.   manufacturing, distribution
     C.   manufacturing, product design
     D.   distribution, product design

III. Completion *Complete each of the following statements.*

1. The key to successful business management is _____.

2. The key distinction between the traditional product costing system and activity-based costing when applying overhead costs is _____.

3. Processing time, waiting time, moving time, inspection time, and reworking time are all features of _____.

4. Four characteristics common to the just-in-time inventory are:

   1._____

   2._____

   3._____

   4._____

5. Combining Raw Materials and Work in Process inventories is a feature of a _____ system.

6. Identify the following acronyms:

   VE _____

   ABC _____

   TQM _____

   JIT _____

7. Quality costs are features of _____.

8. The four types of quality costs are:

   1._____

   2._____

   3._____

   4._____

9. Demand-pull refers to a production process where _____ triggers the manufacturing process.

10. Of the four types of quality costs, the one that is potentially the most devastating to company is _____.

IV. Exercises

1. Sea Container Manufacturing Co. uses activity-based costing to account for its manufacturing process. The direct materials in each container cost $1,500. Each container includes 80 parts, and finishing requires 20 hours of direct labor time. Each container requires 125 welds. The manufacture of 10 containers requires two machine setups.

Manufacturing Activity	Cost Driver Chosen as Application Base	Conversion Cost per Unit of Application Base
Materials handling	Number of parts	$ 4.00
Machine setup	Number of setups	$ 800.00
Welding of parts	Number of welds	$ 2.00
Finishing	Direct labor hours	$ 28.00

Compute the cost of each container.

2. Classify each of the following quality costs as a prevention cost, an internal failure cost, an appraisal cost, or an external failure cost.

    a. direct materials and direct labor costs incurred to repair defective products returned by customers

    b. a training class for customer service representatives to teach them techniques for completing customer orders quickly, efficiently, and correctly

    c. salary of a technician who randomly selects goods from the warehouse and tests them for conformance to company specifications

    d. time and materials costs incurred to rework those items determined by the testing technician as below standard

    e. $28,000 balance in Sales Returns for the return of defective products

    f. fee paid to pickup and dispose of rejected products

    a. _____

    b. _____

    c. _____

    d. _____

    e. _____

    f. _____

3. Carol's Clothing Company uses a backflush costing system, with trigger points at the time of direct materials purchase and the transfer of completed goods to finished goods. The company has received an order for 20,000 sweaters at $15 each. The standard direct materials cost is $6.50 per sweater and the standard conversion cost is $5.50 per sweater. Direct materials were purchased for $129,000 and conversion costs totaling $110,400 were incurred. 20,000 sweaters were produced and shipped to the customer.

Prepare journal entries for the above transactions.

Date	Accounts	Debit	Credit

4.   Micro Manufacturing is designing a new lightweight, portable microwave oven. The budgeted sales price is $550.00 with a desired manufacturing contribution of $120.00 per oven. Assuming kaizen cost reductions during the product's life cycle will be $25.00 per oven and the value-engineering cost reduction goal has been established at $40 per oven, determine the initial budgeted unit manufacturing cost in the life-cycle budget.

 V. Critical Thinking

Clothing manufacturers typically produce 5% more units than called for in a contract. Called "overruns," these excess units are deemed necessary because of anticipated defects in some of the units produced. Usually, these defects are the result of faulty direct materials and/or workmanship. Part of the overrun cannot be reworked and is scrapped. Other parts can be reworked but are not needed to fill the order. A third part is simply excess. Many times, the excess that is not scrapped is sold to a factor, who then resells the merchandise to an outlet store where it is sold as "seconds."

Analyze a typical 5% overrun with respect to quality costs—prevention, appraisal, internal failure, and external failure.

_____

_____

_____

_____

_____

_____

_____

_____

_____

_____

_____

_____

VI. Demonstration Problems

Demonstration Problem #1

Fit-N-Trim hopes to manufacture a new multi-purpose piece of exercise equipment for in-home use. Demand over an estimated 3-year life cycle totals 80,000 units, selling for $500 each. Research indicates the following per-unit manufacturing costs:

Direct materials	$123.00
Purchased parts	155.00
Direct labor	80.00
Indirect materials	4.50
Indirect labor	17.50
Other variable conversion costs	8.15

Fixed conversion costs for 80,000 units are:

Indirect labor	$148,000
Machinery depreciation	720,000
Other fixed conversion costs	97,200

Upstream and downstream fixed costs are estimated as:

Product development, design	$210,000
Engineering, testing	106,000
Marketing	1,750,000
Other downstream fixed costs	490,000

The exercise equipment will be sold through exclusive dealers who receive a 10% commission on each unit sold.

Required (Use the work space provided on the next page.)

Present an initial life-cycle budget based on sales of 80,000 units.

Fit-N-Trim Exerciser
Initial Life-Cycle Budget
80,000 units

Demonstration Problem #2

De Castro Cup Company manufactures environmentally friendly cups in two sizes for coffee bars offering carryout service. The company uses a traditional system for allocating manufacturing overhead costs. Last year, the following results were reported:

	8 oz. cups	12 oz. cups	Total
Direct materials	$1,350,000	$1,800,000	3,150,000
Direct labor	400,000	600,000	1,000,000
Overhead	2,400,000	3,600,000	6,000,000
Total	$4,150,000	$6,000,000	$10,150,000

Overhead costs were allocated on the basis of direct labor costs. Last year 510,000 cases of 8 oz. cups were manufactured (each case contains 500 cups), and 800,000 cases (each containing 300 cups) of 12 oz. cups were manufactured.

You have been asked by the company controller to analyze the allocation of overhead costs to the two products using an activity-based costing system. You begin by analyzing the specific components of the $6,000,000 in overhead costs assigned last year. Your investigation determines the following:

Components	Cost
Indirect materials	$300,000
Supervisors' salaries	450,000
Equipment depreciation	3,150,000
Equipment conversion costs	1,500,000
Miscellaneous overhead costs	600,000
Total	$6,000,000

In consultation with the controller, the following decisions were made regarding costs and cost drivers:

Cost	Cost Driver
Indirect materials	Direct materials
Supervisors' salaries	Direct labor cost
Equipment depreciation	Hours of equipment use
Equipment conversion costs	Number of conversions
Miscellaneous overhead	Cases of output

Further investigation disclosed the following:

The equipment was used 70% for the 12 oz. cups and 30% for the 8 oz. cups. The equipment was converted a total of 120 times during the year: 90 times for the 12 oz. cups and 30 times for the 8 oz. cups.

Required (Use the work space below and on the next page.)

1. Calculate the per-cup cost of each size using the traditional system of overhead allocation.

2. Apply activity-based costing using the results of your investigation to allocate overhead.

3. Calculate the per-cup cost given your results in Requirement 2.

Requirement 1

Requirement 2

Requirement 3

Solutions

I. Matching

1. G	2. D	3. J	4. O	5. I	6. N	7. K	8. F
9. E	10. M	11. A	12. C	13. P	14. H	15. B	16. L

II. Multiple Choice

1. **C** Non-value-added activities are those that do not add value to the product. Inspecting, moving, and reworking are examples of non-value-added activities. Processing costs are value-added activities.

2. **D** If production is the point of reference, downstream activities are those that occur after production is completed. Of the four choices listed, only product design would occur before production begins.

3. **A** High-commitment, high-performance team training is a key feature of total quality management.

4. **D** Because quality costs are difficult to identify and measure, benchmarking is one way to evaluate them. Quality costs are nonfinancial performance items.

5. **D** Activity-based costing is a concept of accumulating costs using multiple cost drivers and is not specific to particular businesses or industries—it can be used by any organization.

6. **B** External failures are those that occur after the product or service has been received by the customer. Of the four options, the only one that would involve a customer is the cost of warranties.

7. **B** Return on sales is the only choice listed that can be expressed in financial terms.

8. **C** Value-engineering refers to techniques used to reduce the cost of a product while maintaining its satisfaction to the customer. Value-engineering is one way to achieve target costing.

9. **B** Kaizen costing, value-engineering, and activity-based costing all relate to either cost measurement (ABC) or cost reduction (kaizen and VE). Benchmarking is a way to evaluate nonfinancial measures of quality.

10. **C** Kaizen costing is concerned solely with manufacturing activities, while target costing sets goals for cost reduction during the product design phase.

III. Completion

1. intelligent decision making
2. the use of multiple cost drivers in the ABC system
3. throughput time
4. arrangement of production activities, setup times, production scheduling, employee roles (order not important)
5. backflush costing
6. VE = value-engineering; ABC = activity-based costing; TQM = total quality management; JIT = just-in-time
7. total quality management
8. prevention costs, appraisal costs, internal failure costs, external failure costs
9. the receipt of a customer order
10. external failure costs

IV. Exercises

1.

Direct materials	$1,500
Materials handling (80 parts @ $4.00)	320
Machine setup ($800 x 2 / 10)	160
Welding (125 x $2.00)	250
Finishing (20 x $28.00)	560
Total cost	$2,790

2. a. external failure cost
    b. prevention cost
    c. appraisal cost
    d. internal failure cost
    e. external failure cost
    f. internal failure cost

3.

RIP Inventory	130,000	
Direct materials price variance		1,000
Accounts Payable		129,000
Conversion costs	110,400	
Various accounts		110,400
Finished Goods	240,000	
RIP Inventory		130,000
Conversion costs		110,000
($6.50 + $5.50 x 20,000)		
Cost of Goods Sold	240,000	
Finished Goods		240,000
Accounts Receivable	300,000	
Sales		300,000
Cost of Goods Sold	400	
Conversion costs		400
(to transfer underapplied overhead)		

4. The relevant formulas are:

Sales price – desired manufacturing contribution = life-cycle cost

Budgeted cost – value-engineering reductions = target cost

Target cost – kaizen cost reductions = life-cycle cost

If life-cycle sales price is $550 and desired manufacturing contribution is $120, then the allowable life-cycle cost is $430 ($550 – $120).

If life-cycle cost = $430, and kaizen cost reductions equal $25, the target cost = $430 + $25 = $455.

If target cost = $455 and value-engineering reductions equal $40, then budgeted cost = $455 + $40 = $495.

The initial budgeted unit manufacturing cost in the life-cycle budget was $495.00.

V. Critical Thinking

Ideally, a manufacturer should strive for zero defects. However, this is not always possible. To obtain defect-free material, the manufacturer needs to work closely with the suppliers. This is a prevention cost. During the manufacturing process, appraisal costs are involved as a result of inspection costs. In addition, internal failure costs are incurred to both rework (when possible) and to dispose of units that can neither be reworked nor sold as seconds. If you analyze the situation carefully you will see that there are no external failure costs. The clothing manufacturer ships only goods that conform to the order. Any excess goods that can be sold are factored to an outlet store. As long as the costs associated with the excess are considered when they are sold, no external failure costs are involved. As stated above, zero defects is the ideal and something companies should strive to achieve. However, given the 5% excess, clothing manufacturers seem to have adjusted well enough to cover the costs incurred with the excess (one of the fastest-growing segments in retailing is the "outlet store").

VI. Demonstration Problems

Demonstration Problem #1 Solved and Explained

Fit-N-Trim Exerciser
Initial Life-Cycle Budget
80,000 units

Sales @ $500 per unit		$40,000,000
Direct materials @ $123 per unit	$ 9,840,000	
Purchased parts @ $155 per unit	12,400,000	22,240,000
Materials contribution margin		17,760,000
Other costs direct to product:		
Variable conversion costs $110.15 per unit		
Direct labor $80 per unit	$6,400,000	
Indirect materials $4.50 per unit	360,000	
Indirect labor $17.50 per unit	1,400,000	
Other $8.15 per unit	652,000	8,812,000
Product contribution margin		8,948,000
Fixed conversion costs:		
Indirect labor	$ 140,000	
Depreciation	720,000	
Other fixed	97,200	957,200
Life-cycle manufacturing contribution		7,990,800
Other fixed costs:		
Product development, design	$ 210,000	
Engineering, testing	106,000	
Marketing	1,750,000	
Sales commission	4,000,000	
Other downstream fixed	490,000	6,556,000
Life-cycle operating contribution		$1,434,800

The initial life-cycle budget is organized into four parts: the materials contribution margin, product contribution margin, life-cycle manufacturing contribution, and life-cycle operating contribution. As the name implies, the initial life-cycle budget is the starting point. It shows all the costs (not just manufacturing) that can be traced to the product. After the budget is prepared, managers need to determine whether or not to proceed with the project. It is at this point that target costing techniques are applied to attempt further cost reductions, if needed.

Demonstration Problem #2 Solved and Explained

Requirement 1

8 oz. cups:

Total cost	$4,150,000
Total cups (500,000 cases x 500 ea)	250,000,000
Cost per cup ($4,150,000/250,000,000)	$0.017

12 oz. cups:

Total cost	$6,000,000
Total cups (800,000 cases x 300 ea)	240,000,000
Cost per cup ($6,000,000/240,000,000)	$0.025

Requirement 2

Component	Cost	8 oz.	Calculations	12 oz.	Calculations
Indirect material	$300,000	$128,571	$\frac{\$1,350,000}{\$3,150,000}$ x $300,000	$171,429	$\frac{\$1,800,000}{\$3,150,000}$ x $300,000
Supervisors' salaries	450,000	180,000	$\frac{\$400,000}{\$1,000,000}$ x $450,000	270,000	$\frac{\$600,000}{\$1,000,000}$ x $450,000
Equipment depreciation	3,150,000	945,000	30% x $3,150,000	2,205,000	70% x $3,150,000
Conversion costs	1,500,000	375,000	30/120 x $1,500,000	1,125,000	90/120 x $1,500,000
Miscellaneous	600,000	233,588	$\frac{\$510,000}{\$1,310,000}$ x $600,000	366,412	$\frac{\$800,000}{\$1,310,000}$ x $600,000
Total		$1,862,159		$4,137,841	

Requirement 3

8 oz. cups

	$1,350,000	(Direct materials)
	400,000	(Direct labor)
	1,862,159	(Overhead from Requirement 2)
Total cost	$3,612,159	

or $3,162,159/250,000,000 = $0.014 per cup

12 oz. cups

	$1,800,000	(Direct materials)
	600,000	(Direct labor)
	4,137,841	(Overhead from Requirement 2)
Total cost	$6,537,841	

or $6,537,841/240,000,000 = $0.027 per cup

Chapter 27

Special Business Decisions and Capital Budgeting

 Chapter Overview

*I*n recent chapters you have learned about a variety of issues all related to the topic of "costs." Most of these issues looked at costs (and behavior) in the short run. When costs are correctly recorded and carefully analyzed, a business is in a better position to plan for future operations. We now turn our attention to some special decisions that businesses frequently must make and to issues concerning the acquisition of long-term (capital) assets. The specific learning objectives for this chapter are:

1. Identify the relevant information for a special business decision

2. Make seven types of special business decisions

3. Explain the difference between correct analysis and incorrect analysis of a particular business decision

4. Allocate joint processing costs to joint products

5. Use opportunity cost in decision making

6. Use four capital budgeting models to make investment decisions

7. Compare and contrast popular capital budgeting models

Chapter Review

OBJECTIVE 1

Identify the relevant information for a special business decision.

To achieve business goals, managers must develop tactics by choosing among different courses of action. To do this, the manager must gather information and distinguish between the relevant information and that which is not relevant. This approach to decision making is called the **relevant information approach.**

Relevant information is expected future data or information that differs for the alternative courses of action. Information that does not differ is irrelevant and will not change a business decision. See Exhibit 27-1 in your text.

OBJECTIVE 2

Make seven types of special business decisions.

Special sales orders are evaluated by comparing the expected increase in revenues and the expected increase in expenses. If fixed expenses do not change, they are not relevant and should be ignored.

A quick summary analysis (Exhibit 27-3 in your text) subtracts the expected increase in expenses from the expected increase in revenues to arrive at the expected increase in operating income. An income statement analysis with and without the special order (Exhibit 27-4) compares total revenues, expenses, and operating income for both courses of action. (Both analyses should give the same result.)

OBJECTIVE 3

Explain the difference between correct analysis and incorrect analysis of a particular business decision.

Correctly analyzing a business decision requires you to ignore **irrelevant costs**. A cost that is the same for all decision alternatives is *not* relevant and must be ignored. You should consider only those costs and revenues that change between alternatives.

The oil filter illustration in your text is an excellent example of this difference. Using the conventional income statement as the basis for the decision is not the correct analysis because of the nature of fixed costs. However, when the question is analyzed using the contribution margin format, the irrelevant costs (fixed expenses) are ignored and a better decision results.

When considering **the deletion of products, departments, or territories, with no change in fixed costs**, the only relevant information is the expected decreases in revenues and variable expenses, which together show the contribution margin and change in operating income. Study Exhibit 27-5 in your text.

When considering the **deletion of products, departments, or territories with a change in fixed costs**, the analysis must include the change in fixed expenses as well as changes in variable expenses and revenues. Refer to Exhibit 27-6 for an example.

When deciding **which product to emphasize**, it is necessary to determine whether a constraint or limiting factor exists. A **constraint** restricts production or sales. Constraints may be stated in terms of labor hours, machine hours, materials, or storage space.

The way to **maximize profits for a given capacity** is to maximize the contribution margin per unit of the limiting factor. Exhibit 27-7 in your text presents an example of how to maximize the contribution margin per labor hour.

The **make or buy decision** determines how best to use available facilities. The relevant information for the make analysis includes: 1) direct materials, 2) direct labor, 3) variable overhead, and 4) fixed overhead. The relevant information for the buy analysis is: 1) the fixed overhead that will continue whether the part is made or bought and 2) the purchase price to buy the part. This analysis shows whether it is cheaper to make the part or to buy the part. Review Exhibit 27-8 in your text.

Sometimes facilities can be used to make other products if the product currently produced is purchased from an outside supplier. In the make or buy decision, the alternatives become: 1) make, 2) buy and leave the facilities idle, and 3) buy and use the facilities for other products. As indicated in Exhibit 27-9, the alternative with the lowest net cost is the **best use of the facilities.**

Businesses are continually faced with decisions concerning the **replacement of equipment**. As with the other types of decisions mentioned above, the first issue is to separate relevant information from irrelevant information. Concerning equipment replacement, the relevant information is: 1) expected future cash operating costs of the equipment, 2) disposal value of the old equipment, and 3) acquisition cost of the new equipment. The book value of the old equipment is not relevant because it is a **sunk cost**—a past cost that is unavoidable because it cannot be changed. The gain or loss on disposal of the old equipment is also irrelevant because it is based on the book value of the old equipment. Review exhibits 27-10 and 27-11 in your text, which illustrate a comparison of the relevant items.

OBJECTIVE 4
Allocate joint processing costs to joint products.

Joint products are separated into identifiable individual products at the **split-off point**. To be called a joint product, the item must have a significant sales value in relation to the other item produced. Costs incurred before split-off are **joint processing costs**. They are allocated using the **relative sales value method.**

$$
\begin{array}{ccc}
\text{Allocated} & & \text{Joint} \\
\text{Cost of a} & = & \text{Processing} \\
\text{Product} & & \text{Cost}
\end{array}
\quad \times \quad
\left[
\begin{array}{c}
\textbf{Sales Value of Product A} \\
\textbf{Total Sales Value of} \\
\textbf{All Joint Products}
\end{array}
\right]
$$

Study Exhibits 27-12 and 27-13 in your text.

The **sell as is or process further** decision compares the expected net revenue (revenue minus costs) of processing further with selling inventory as-is. Exhibit 27-14 illustrates the sell as-is or process further decision. Note that past historical costs of inventory are sunk costs—they cannot make a difference to the decision; the sunk costs are irrelevant because they are present under both alternatives.

The costs to consider are the **separable costs**—those after split-off that can be associated with each product.

OBJECTIVE 5
Use opportunity cost in decision making.

An **opportunity cost** is the benefit that can be obtained from the next best course of action in a decision. An opportunity cost is not associated with a transaction and is therefore not recorded although it must be considered in decision making. Outlay costs are recorded. Suppose Alternative A will generate $5,000 income and Alternative B will generate $6,000 income. The opportunity cost of Alternative B is the $5,000 of income from Alternative A that you have given up.

Capital budgeting is a long-range investment plan for purchasing, using, and disposing of capital assets such as land, buildings, and machinery. Four **capital budgeting decision models** are presented; they help managers evaluate and choose among alternatives. Capital budgeting focuses on cash and all four models use net cash inflow from operations to analyze alternatives.

1) **Payback** is the length of time it takes to recover the dollars invested in a capital outlay. If annual cash inflows are identical each year, then:

$$\text{Payback Period} \quad = \quad \frac{\text{Amount Invested}}{\text{Expected Annual Net Cash Inflows}}$$

If annual cash inflows are not equal, you might construct a table, as in Exhibit 27-18, to determine the payback period. Payback highlights cash inflows, but ignores profitability which is a major weakness of this model. However, it can be useful in eliminating some unwise alternatives.

2) The **accounting rate of return** measures the average rate of return from using an asset over its entire life:

$$\text{Accounting Rate of Return} \quad = \quad \frac{\text{Average Annual Operating Income from Investment}}{\text{Average Amount Invested}}$$

$$\text{Average Annual Operating Income from Invested} \quad = \quad \text{Average Annual Net Cash Inflow from Operations} \quad - \quad \text{Annual Depreciation}$$

$$\text{Average Amount Invested} \quad = \quad \frac{\text{Amount Invested} + \text{Residual Value}}{2}$$

See Exhibit 27-19 for an example of this calculation.

Although the accounting rate of return measures profitability, it ignores the time value of money, a topic you were introduced to in Chapter 16.

The following two models consider the timing of the cash outlay for the investment and the timing of the net cash inflows which result. These models are the most commonly used in capital budgeting.

3) **Net present value** is a method used to compute expected net monetary gains or losses from a project by discounting expected future cash flows to their present values using a minimum desired rate of return. The **minimum desired rate of return** used to calculate present value is called the **discount rate**. Exhibit 27-21 in your text illustrates present value analysis in which: 1) the annual cash inflows are equal (an annuity) and 2) the annual cash inflows are different. Note that when the annual cash inflows are equal, you use Exhibit 27-20, Present Value of an Annuity of $1, to find the present value factor. When the cash inflows are not equal, you use Exhibit 27-22, Present Value of $1, to find the present value factor for each year of the analysis. Exhibit 27-23 in your text includes in the analysis the residual value of an asset (an inflow of cash) that is expected to be recovered at the end of the assets useful life.

The steps to determine the net present value of a project are:

1. Find the present value of annual cash inflows.

2. Find the present value of the residual, if any.

3. Add (1) and (2) to obtain the present value of the net cash inflows.

4. Subtract the investment (which is already in present value terms) from the present value of the net cash inflows (3) to obtain the net present value of the project.

   The net present value method is based on cash flows and considers both profitability and the time value of money. A company should only consider those investments that produce at least zero net present value or a positive net present value in this calculation.

4) **Internal rate of return** is another discounted cash flow model. The internal rate of return (IRR) is the rate of return that makes the net present value of an investment project equal to zero. There are three steps in calculating the internal rate of return:

1. Identify the expected net cash inflows.

2. Find the interest rate that equates the present value of the cash inflows to the present value of the cash outflows. For a single investment of cash followed by a series of equal cash inflows, use the following equation:

   Investment   =   Expected Annual   x   Annuity Present Value Factor
   Net Cash Inflow

   Solve this equation for the annuity present value factor. Scan the row in Exhibit 27-20 that represents the life of the project for the present value factor closest to your calculation. The percent for that column is the approximate IRR.

3. Compare the IRR with the minimum desired rate of return. Projects should be accepted if the IRR is greater that the minimum desired rate.

OBJECTIVE 7

Compare and contrast popular capital budgeting models.

Exhibit 27-25 summarizes some of the strengths and weaknesses of the four capital budgeting models described above. The two discounted cash flow models (net present value and internal rate of return) are favored because they consider both profitability and the time value of money whereas the payback model ignores both while the accounting rate of return considers only profitability.

Test Yourself

All the self-testing materials in this chapter focus on information and procedures that your instructor is likely to test in quizzes and examinations.

I. Matching *Match each numbered term with its lettered definition.*

1. accounting rate of return
2. capital budgeting
3. decision model
4. time value of money
5. opportunity cost
6. relevant information
7. annuity
8. constraint
9. discount rate
10. net present value
11. payback
12. sunk cost
13. internal rate of return
14. joint products
15. separable cost

A. a method or technique for evaluating and choosing among alternative courses of action

B. actual outlay incurred in the past and present under all alternative courses of action; irrelevant because it makes no difference in a current decision

C. expected future data that differs between alternative courses of action

D. formal means of making long-range decisions for investments such as plant locations, equipment purchases, additions of product lines, and territorial expansions

E. item that restricts production or sales

F. calculated as average annual net cash inflow from operations minus annual depreciation, divided by average amount invested

G. length of time it will take to recover, in net cash inflows from operations, the dollars of a capital outlay

H. management's minimum desired rate of return on an investment, used in a present value computation

I. the benefit that can be obtained from the next best course of action in a decision

J. method of computing the expected net monetary gain or loss from a project by discounting all expected cash flows to their present value, using a desired rate of return

K.   stream of equal periodic amounts

L.   the fact that one can earn income by investing money for a period of time

M.   the rate of return on a project that makes the net present value equal to zero

N.   costs which attach exclusively to an individual product after the split-off point

O.   goods identified as individual products after the split-off point

 II. Multiple Choice *Circle the best answer.*

1.   Relevant information:

    A.   is expected future data

    B.   differs among alternative courses of action

    C.   does not include sunk costs

    D.   all of the above

2.   The standard income statement categorizes expenses:

    A.   into cost of goods sold and selling and administrative expenses

    B.   into variable and fixed expenses

    C.   both A and B

    D.   neither A nor B

3.   The contribution margin income statement categorizes expenses:

    A.   into cost of goods sold and selling and administrative expenses

    B.   into variable expenses and fixed expenses

    C.   both A and B

    D.   neither A nor B

4.   Select the correct statement concerning the payback period.

    A.   the longer the payback period, the less attractive the asset.

    B.   the shorter the payback period, the less attractive the asset.

    C.   the longer the payback period, the more attractive the asset.

    D.   both B and C are correct.

5.   The accounting rate of return considers:

    A.   the timing of cash flows

    B.   the time value of money

    C.   profitability

    D.   all of the above

6. The net present value method of capital budgeting considers:

    A. only cash flows

    B. only the time value of money

    C. both cash flows and the time value of money

    D. the length of time to recoup the initial investment

7. If a potential investment has a negative net present value:

    A. it should be accepted in all situations

    B. it should be rejected in all situations

    C. it should be accepted if payback is less than five years

    D. it should be rejected if the accounting rate of return is less than 16%

8. The internal rate of return (IRR) model, while similar to the net present value (NPV) method, is different in which of the following respects:

    A. IRR identifies expected future cash flows.

    B. IRR identifies the excess of the project's present value over its investment cost.

    C. IRR identifies a specific rate of return for the investment.

    D. all of the above.

9. The relative sales value method is used to:

    A. analyze a capital investment

    B. make a best-use-of-facilities decision

    C. allocate joint costs at split-off

    D. make a special sales order decision

10. In deciding whether to take a year off from college and work full-time or continue in school and work part-time, the opportunity cost is:

    A. the amount of money already invested in your education

    B. the amount saved from college expenses by working full-time

    C. the amount of earnings foregone by selecting one option over the other

    D. the difference between the projected total income of the two options

III. Completion *Complete each of the following statements.*

1. A(n) _____ income statement is more useful for special decision analysis than the standard income statement.

2. The item that restricts production or sales is called the _____ or _____.

3. Fixed costs are only relevant to a special decision if _____.

4. A(n) _____ is the cost of the forsaken next best alternative, or profit given up, by selecting one alternative over another one.

5. _____ costs are not formally recorded in the accounting records.

6. The major weakness of the payback is that it _____.

7. An investment should be rejected if its net present value is _____ _____.

8. A projects internal rate of return (IRR) is that rate of interest that makes the present value of the project's cash inflows and cash outflows _____ _____.

9. _____ costs are those that attach exclusively to a product after the split-off point.

10. _____ costs are those which attach to a product up to the split-off point.

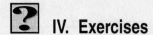 **IV. Exercises**

1. A clothing wholesaler has offered to pay $20.00 per unit for 2,500 hats. This offer would put idle manufacturing capacity in use and not affect regular sales. Total fixed costs will not change. There will be only half the normal variable selling and administrative costs on this special order.

Normal selling price per hat	$25.00
Variable costs per hat:	
Manufacturing	14.00
Selling and Administrative	3.00
Fixed costs per hat:	
Manufacturing	2.00
Selling and Administrative	2.50

    A. What is the relevant information associated with this special order?

    B. What difference would accepting this special order have on company profits?

2. Alfonse, a bright young CPA, has provided you with the following information:

Salary at current position	$40,000
Revenues expected by opening his own office	125,000
Expenses expected for the new office	100,000

    A. What is the opportunity cost associated with working at his current position?

    B. What is the opportunity cost associated with starting his own business?

    C. From a purely quantitative standpoint, what should he do?

3. Eric's Nursery is concerned that operating income is low, and is considering dropping its gardening tools department. The following information is available:

	Total	Plants & Fertilizers	Gardening Tools
Sales	$425,000	$225,000	$200,000
Variable expenses	239,500	91,500	148,000
Contribution margin	185,500	133,500	52,000
Fixed expenses	153,000	81,000	72,000
Operating income (loss)	$32,500	$52,500	($20,000)

Eric can avoid $48,000 of Gardening Tools expenses by dropping the Gardening Tools division.

Determine whether Eric should drop the Gardening Tools department.

4. Gilbert's Garlic Company has processing costs for marinated chopped garlic totaling $80,000. Garlic cloves can be sold for $240,000, while chopped garlic pieces can be sold for $160,000. Using the relative sales value method, what cost should be assigned to the whole cloves and the pieces?

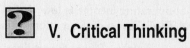 **V. Critical Thinking**

Review the information in Exercise 2 and list additional considerations (both quantitative and qualitative) that might influence Alfonse's decision.

_____

_____

_____

_____

_____

_____

_____

_____

_____

VI. Demonstration Problems

Demonstration Problem #1

A.   S&L Inc. produces two products, S and L, with the following per unit data:

	Product S	L
Selling price	$50	$24
Variable expenses	30	15
Units that can be produced each hour	4	8

The company has 8,000 hours of capacity available. Which product should the company emphasize?

B. Body Works, Inc. has the following manufacturing costs for 4,000 of its natural bath sponges:

Direct materials	$6,000
Direct labor	3,000
Variable overhead	2,000
Fixed overhead	5,000
Total	$16,000

Another manufacturer has offered to sell similar sponges to Body Works for $3.25 each. By purchasing the sponges from an outside source, Body Works can save $2,000 of fixed overhead cost. The released facilities can be devoted to the manufacture of other products that will contribute $2,000 to profits. What is Body Works' best decision?

	Alternatives		
	Make	Buy and leave facilities idle	Buy and use facilities for other products

Decision:

Demonstration Problem #2

The data for some equipment follows:

Cost	$40,000
Estimated annual net cash flows:	
Year 1	12,000
Year 2	12,000
Year 3	12,000
Year 4	12,000
Residual value	8,000
Estimated useful life	4 years
Annual rate of return required	12%

The present value of an amount of $1 at 12% is:

Year	1	2	3	4
Interest factor	0.893	0.797	0.712	0.636

The present value of an annuity of $1 at 12% is:

Year	1	2	3	4
Interest factor	0.893	1.690	2.402	3.037

Required (Use the work space below and on the next page.)

1. What is the payback period for the equipment?
2. What is the accounting rate of return for the equipment?
3. What is the net present value of the equipment?
4. Indicate whether each decision model leads to purchase or rejection of this investment. Would you decide to buy the equipment? Explain your reason.

Requirement 1 (payback period)

Requirement 2 (accounting rate of return)

Requirement 3 (net present value analysis)

Requirement 4 (decision)

Solutions

I. Matching

1. F	2. D	3. A	4. L	5. I	6. C	7. K	8. E
9. H	10. J	11. G	12. B	13. M	14. O	15. N	

II. Multiple Choice

1. **D** Relevant information is the expected future data that differ between alternative courses of action. A sunk cost is an actual outlay that has been incurred in the past and is present under all alternatives. Sunk costs are irrelevant.

2. **A** Answer B describes the contribution margin format income statement.

3. **B** Answer A describes the "standard" income statement format.

4. **A** Payback is the length of time it will take to recover, in net cash flow from operations, the dollars of a capital outlay. The shorter the payback, the better. The longer it is, the less attractive.

5. **C** The accounting rate of return is calculated by:
   Average Annual Operating Income ÷ Average amount invested.
   By looking at the numerator, answer C can be seen to be the best.

6. **C** The net present value method computes the present value of expected future net cash flows and compares the present value to the initial investment. Answer C covers this approach.

7. **B** The initial investment is subtracted from the present value of the investment's expected future cash flows. If negative, the investment does not recover its cost. If positive, the investment generates a return above the minimum required. Only projects with zero or positive net present value should be considered.

8. **C** Both the NPV and IRR methods make use of expected future cash flows (answer A). Answer B is not correct because it describes only NPV. Only the IRR method (and not NPV) generates a specific rate of return for the project.

9. **C** The relative sales value method is the preferred means for allocating joint costs to individual products at the split-off point.

10. **C** The opportunity cost is the benefit obtained from the next best course of action, so if the decision is to remain in school, the opportunity cost is the full-time wages not earned, whereas if the decision is to work full-time, the opportunity cost is the foregone part-time income.

III. Completion

1. contribution margin (The contribution margin format highlights how costs and income are affected by decisions.)

2. limiting factor, constraint (Factors such as the size of the factory labor force, available storage space, availability of raw materials, available machine time, or market share can act as constraints.)

3. fixed cost differs among alternatives (Recall: a cost is relevant only if it differs between alternatives. A cost can differ between alternatives and still be fixed for each alternative.)

4. opportunity cost (It is not the usual outlay (cash disbursement) cost. If you quit your job to start your own business, the salary from the job you gave up is the opportunity cost of starting your own business.)

5. Opportunity (Since these costs do not involve giving up an asset or incurring a liability, they are not recorded.)

6. ignores profitability and the time value of money (Because of these shortcomings, the payback period can lead to unwise decisions.)

7. negative (If negative, the investment does not recover its cost. If positive, the investment generates an acceptable rate of return. Only projects with zero or positive net present value should be considered.)

8. equal

9. Separable

10. Joint

IV. Exercises

1. A. The relevant information is the special order price of $20.00 per unit, the variable manufacturing cost of $14.00 per unit, and one-half the normal variable selling and administrative expenses which amount to $1.50 per unit ($3 x 1/2).

   B.
Additional revenues from special orders (2,500 x $20)	$50,000
Less: Variable manufacturing cost (2,500 x $14)	(35,000)
Less: Variable selling and admin. cost (2,500 x $1.50)	(3,750)
Increase in profits	$11,250

2. A. The opportunity cost is the net revenue given up by keeping the existing position: $125,000 revenue – $100,000 expense = $25,000.

   B. The opportunity cost is the cost of giving up the existing position: $40,000.

   C. The current position pays $40,000. Going into business will net $25,000. Keeping the present position makes Alfonse better off by $15,000.

3. The relevant information is the contribution margin that would be lost if the gardening tools department were eliminated and the fixed costs were eliminated. The nursery would lose the $52,000 contribution margin if the department is closed and would reduce fixed costs by $48,000. The lost contribution margin is $4,000 greater than the reduction in fixed costs ($52,000 contribution margin lost – $48,000 fixed costs eliminated), so the department should not be closed. The nursery is $4,000 better off by keeping it.

4. $$\text{Cloves} = \left[240,000 \div (240,000 + 160,000) \right] \times \$80,000 = \$48,000$$
$$\text{Pieces} = \left[160,000 \div (240,000 + 160,000) \right] \times \$80,000 = \$32,000$$

V. Critical Thinking

Probably the most significant quantitative consideration is the potential increase in salary compared with the potential increase in income from the business. For instance, if salary increases are likely to average 10% over the foreseeable future while the business growth potential is 20% annually, in a few years the income from the business will surpass the salary. An important qualitative consideration is being an employee versus your own boss. Frequently, it is the intangible costs and benefits that cloud the issue and make decision making so complex.

VI. Demonstration Problems

Demonstration Problem #1 Solved and Explained

A.   Product to Emphasize

	Product	
	S	L
(1) Units that can be produced each hour	4	8
(2) Contribution margin per unit*	$20	$9
(3) Contribution margin per hour (1) X (2)	80	72
Capacity: Number of hours	x 8,000	x 8,000
Total contribution margin for capacity	$640,000	$576,000

* Contribution margins: S: $50 – $30 = $20; L: $24 – $15 = $9

Decision: The company should emphasize Product S because its contribution margin at capacity is greater by $64,000.

Explanation:

When a constraint exists, such as the number of labor hours available, we must conduct our profit analysis in terms of the constraint. Since only 8,000 labor hours are available, our profit will be greatest if we produce those products which offer the highest contribution margin per labor hour. To compute the contribution margin per labor hour for each product, multiply the contribution margin per unit of each product times the number of units of each product that can be produced per hour. The product with the highest contribution margin per hour will provide the highest profit.

B.   Make or Buy

	Make	Buy and leave facilities idle	Buy and use facilities for other products
		Alternatives	
Direct materials	$ 6,000	–	
Direct labor	3,000	–	
Variable overhead	2,000	–	
Fixed overhead	5,000	$ 3,000	$ 3,000
Purchase price from outsider	–	13,000	13,000
Total cost of obtaining sponges	16,000	16,000	16,000
Profit contribution from other products	–	–	(2,000)
Net cost of obtaining 4,000 sponges	$16,000	$16,000	$14,000

Decision: The company should buy the sponges and use the facilities for other products.

Explanation

The important point to remember is that relevant information differs among alternative courses of action. Continuing to make the sponges will cost the same $16,000 that it currently costs. The current cost to produce is relevant because it will change if the sponges are purchased. If the sponges are purchased, the relevant information is the purchase price and the amount of fixed overhead that *will continue*. The problem tells us that $2,000 of fixed overhead will be saved. Since total fixed overhead is $5,000, $3,000 ($5,000 – $2,000) of fixed overhead will continue, and the sponges will cost $16,000. If the facilities are used to earn an additional $2,000 profit, the net cost of the sponges is $14,000 ($16,000 – $2,000). For this alternative, the additional relevant information is the profit from the other product that could be produced.

Demonstration Problem #2 Solved and Explained

Requirement 1 (payback period)

When the annual net cash flows are constant, the payback period is equal to the amount of the investment divided by the annual net cash flows.

$$\$40,000 \div \$12,000 = 3.3 \text{ years}$$

Requirement 2 (accounting rate of return)

The accounting rate of return is average annual operating income from the investment divided by the average amount invested. Average annual operating income is equal to net cash inflows from operations (0) minus annual depreciation (D). Average amount invested is the sum of the investment (I) plus residual value (RV) divided by 2.

$$R = (O - D) \div [(I + RV) \div 2] = (\$12,000 - \$8,000^*) \div [(\$40,000 + \$8,000) \div 2] = 0.167 = 16.7\%$$

$$* D = (\$40,000 - \$8,000) \div 4 \text{ years} = \$8,000$$

Requirement 3 (net present value analysis)

The steps to determine the net present value of a project are:

Present value of net equal annual cash inflows ($12,000 x 3.037)	$36,444
Present value of residual value ($8,000 x 0.636)	5,088
Present value of the equipment	41,532
Investment	40,000
Net present value	$ 1,532

Explanations:

Since the annual cash flow is the same amount, $12,000, it is an annuity. Multiply the annual amount, $12,000, by the present value of an annuity for 4 years. The present value of the cash inflows is $12,000 x 3.037, or $36,444.

The residual value of $8,000 is discounted to its present value ($8,000 x 0.636 = $5,088).

The present value of the equipment is $41,532 ($36,444 + $5,088).

The investment is $40,000.

The net present value of the investment is the present value of the equipment minus the investment.

NPV of Equipment = $41,532 – $40,000 = $1,532

Requirement 4 (decision)

The payback period is less than the useful life of the equipment. The accounting rate of return is higher than the 12% required return. Both methods indicate favorable potential for the investment. The net present value is positive, which indicates that the rate of return exceeds the 12% required return. Since the net present value considers both profitability and the time value of money, and is positive in this instance, the equipment should be purchased.